TRUTH AND THE END OF INQUIRY

Truth and the End of Inquiry

A Peircean Account of Truth

EXPANDED PAPERBACK EDITION

C. J. MISAK

CLARENDON PRESS · OXFORD

*This book has been printed digitally and produced in a standard specification
in order to ensure its continuing availability*

OXFORD
UNIVERSITY PRESS

Great Clarendon Street, Oxford OX2 6DP

Oxford University Press is a department of the University of Oxford.
It furthers the University's objective of excellence in research, scholarship,
and education by publishing worldwide in

Oxford New York

Auckland   Cape Town   Dar es Salaam   Hong Kong   Karachi
Kuala Lumpur   Madrid   Melbourne   Mexico City   Nairobi
New Delhi   Shanghai   Taipei   Toronto
With offices in
Argentina   Austria   Brazil   Chile   Czech Republic   France Greece
Guatemala   Hungary   Italy   Japan   South Korea   Poland   Portugal
Singapore   Switzerland   Thailand   Turkey   Ukraine   Vietnam

Oxford is a registered trade mark of Oxford University Press
in the UK and in certain other countries
Published in the United States
by Oxford University Press Inc., New York

ISBN 0-19-927059-7

For my parents

Preface to the Paperback Edition

I have tried not to succumb to the inevitable temptations which attend the revisiting of one's doctoral thesis. I have not tried to restate the arguments in the way I now think best. Nor have I tried to add all that I have learnt about the subject matter in the intervening years. Rather, in an effort to preserve the integrity of the book, I have made only two additions—additions which I think deepen our understanding of Peirce's account of truth.

One of these additions is an improvement on the programmatic comments about ethics I made in the first edition (see p. 29). I suggested there that Peirce's view of truth might be especially friendly to moral judgements. But at the time I thought that Peirce himself had placed obstacles in the way of such an extension of his account of truth and later (in *Truth, Politics, Morality: Pragmatism and Deliberation*, Routledge, 2000) I attempted to articulate a pragmatist account of how moral judgements might be seen as candidates for truth, while continuing to maintain that this extension of Peirce's theory of truth had to be made in the face of his objections. I have come to see, however, that Peirce was not only amenable to such a project, but had some rather sophisticated contributions to make to it. Chapter 5 tries to make amends.

The other addition is really an amplification of something I argued in Chapter 1 of *Truth and the End of Inquiry* and can be made more briefly here in the preface. Much has been written about Peirce's view of truth in the last decade and a half. The most significant contributions, in my view, are Chris Hookway's *Truth, Rationality and Pragmatism: Themes from Peirce* (OUP: 2000) and David Wiggins's 'Reflections on Inquiry and Truth Arising From Peirce's Method for the Fixation of Belief' (*The Cambridge Companion to Peirce*, CUP: 2004).

Amongst many other things, both stress a point I was at pains to emphasize in Chapter 1: it is a mistake to take Peirce to be offering a definition of truth. He is engaged, rather, in a distinctively pragmatic enterprise—that of exploring truth's role in assertion, belief, and inquiry.

The idea that we should turn our backs on the attempt to define truth has become popular amongst those who write about truth today. But unlike some of those contemporary philosophers who are wary of definition, Peirce does not hold that truth is indefinable or primitive. He tries to get us to see the difference between two respectable tasks. The first is the provision of an analytic definition of a concept, which might be useful to someone who has never encountered the concept before. The second is the provision of a pragmatic elucidation of a concept—an account of the role the concept plays in practical endeavours. His interest lies in the second of these tasks.

It continues to be important to hammer away at this point. For it is still commonplace for philosophers to mischaracterize Peirce's account of truth as a definition and then scoff at what a poor definition it is. Even those who end up adopting something very close to Peirce's account of truth (for instance, Crispin Wright (1992) and Huw Price (2003)) make this mistake.

Wiggins makes the corrective point very nicely: when a concept is 'already fundamental to human thought and long since possessed of an autonomous interest', it is pointless to try to define it (2002: 316). Rather, we ought to attempt to get leverage on the concept, or a fix on it, by exploring its connections with practice. As Peirce put it: 'We must not begin by talking of pure ideas,—vagabond thoughts that tramp the public roads without any human habitation,—but must begin with men and their conversation' (*CP* 8. 112). In order to really grasp a concept, we must connect it to that with which we have everyday 'dealings' (*CP* 5. 416).

It is easy to see that the concept of truth is one of those concepts, already fundamental to human thought, in which we have a long-standing autonomous interest. We take ourselves to be aiming at truth. We want to know what methods are likely to get us true belief and whether it is worth our time and energy to inquire into certain kinds of questions—whether a discourse such as moral discourse aims at truth or whether it is a radically subjective matter, not at all suited for truth-value.

The concept of truth, that is, is central to the human practices of belief, assertion, and inquiry. Peirce argues that we
must look to these practices in order to come to a full understanding of the concept of truth (*CP 5.* 416). Once we see
that the concepts of belief, assertion, inquiry, and truth live
in the same conceptual neighbourhood, we can learn something about the concept of truth by exploring the connections
between it and its neighbours. As Donald Davidson puts it,
we can illuminate truth by making clear the connections
between it and the 'human attitudes and acts that give it
body'—no 'definition of the concept of truth, nor any quasi-
definitional clause, axiom schema, or other brief substitute
for a definition' will do (Davidson 1996: 276).

The upshot of Peirce's exploration of these connections is
that we should think of a true belief as a belief that would
forever be assertible; a belief which would never lead to
disappointment; a belief which would be 'indefeasible' or not
defeated, were inquiry pursued as far as it could fruitfully go
(*CP 5.* 569, 6. 485). It should be clear that this is not to say
that truth has now been *identified* as that which satisfies our
aims in assertion and inquiry. For, again, Peirce is not in the
business of telling us what the essence of truth is; he is not in
the business of giving us an analytical equivalence between
truth and something else. As Wiggins says: 'To elucidate
truth in its relations with the notion of inquiry, for instance,
as the pragmatist does, need not . . . represent any concession
at all to the idea that truth is *itself* an "epistemic notion".'[1]

Hookway also admonishes us to focus on what Peirce
himself thought he was up to. Peirce's account of truth is a
direct product of the pragmatic maxim, which requires us to
ask what we would expect to be the case if *H* were true. We
are to ask ourselves, that is, what we are committed to when
we assert that something is true. What we expect, what we
commit ourselves to, roughly, is that experience would fall in
line with the belief; that the belief would survive the rigours
of inquiry and deliberation. This, of course, is another way

---

[1] Wiggins 2002: 318. Sellars saw the point as well. He noted that the pragmatist will not want to claim that truth is defined by or 'means' something like successful prediction in the long run (1962: 29).

of saying that our understanding of truth can be improved upon by looking at the role of truth in inquiry and deliberation.

Hookway goes on to note something that other Peirce scholars (myself included) have missed. Peirce argued that what we commit ourselves to is experience falling in line with the belief *or with some successor of it*; and what we expect is that the proposition *in some form* will survive future inquiry.

This amendment solves a pressing problem for Peirce: it explains how meaning can be preserved over time. When we assert that a belief is true, the content of what we commit ourselves to can be indeterminate (Hookway 2000: 57). We hope that the belief will prove to be indefeasible, that there will be a convergence upon the belief. But that convergence will be on a refined version of the current belief. What would prove to be indefeasible in the long run is some approximation of our current belief. So the connection between truth and assertion is not that to assert something is to assert it as absolutely true. An inquirer can successfully assert a proposition that she thinks is almost certainly not strictly true.

The concept of mass, for instance, has undergone radical revision, but we can still think that both Newton and contemporary physicists are referring to the same thing. Newton was committed to having not his precise beliefs about mass survive the rigours of inquiry, but some successors of his beliefs. The same holds for the beliefs of contemporary physicists. In this way we can refer to individuals and to kinds even if we do not fully understand their character. Changes in our view of x can be seen as moves within a general or vague picture. Earlier views present a partial grasp of a complex reality. Indexical reference anchors our beliefs to the world; it explains how we can have beliefs and theories about x, despite the fact that we get much wrong.

Hookway also appeals to the distinctive nature of the pragmatic project in an effort to solve for Peirce the problems revolving around bivalence. Peirce's account of truth is an account for those beliefs *which we assert*. That is, the goals of the pragmatist account of truth only reach to saying what we expect of a sentence we are prepared to assert. The question of truth does not arise in those situations in which we ought to not believe or assert.

I flirted with this thought in Chapter 4, but Hookway both properly embraces it and makes good on it by drawing our attention to those texts in which Peirce argues that sometimes there need not be a fact of the matter about what judgement we would reach, even if there is a fact of the matter about the underlying reality. Truth and falsity are properties of representations, thoughts, or utterances and thus the issue of truth may be indeterminate and the underlying reality determinate.

In one kind of case, the very content of utterances is indeterminate. There may be no fact of the matter whether 'Icabod is bald' is true, although there is a fact of the matter concerning the precise number of hairs on his head. Vagueness, Peirce saw, can produce indeterminacy of truth-value. He argued that when we are dealing with a skeleton which is on the borderline between being a human anthropoid or ape, there will be no determinate truth-value attaching to either 'This is a human skeleton' or 'This is not a human skeleton' (MS 596).

In another kind of case, there may be controversy about how to best judge whether an utterance is true. When trying to answer the question 'How many leaves are on the tree in my front garden?' I might find myself needing first to ask whether the new growth just escaping from the bud counts as a leaf or whether gnarled and half-dead leaves count. There is a determinate reality with respect to the tree, but if these controversies are not easily resolved, there may not be a determinate truth-value to statements about the tree. I ought not to assert that there are x number of leaves on the tree.

In a third kind of case, if I am confident that no evidence or argument will turn up for a statement about the remote past, then I will not assert or deny the statement. Hence, 'there is nothing that asserting it commits me to. I could only turn out to be wrong if the fact turned out not to be lost after all. (Hookway 2000: 61.)

Hookway's general point is this: if I think that a sentence is vague, or irredeemably controversial because we have difficulty formulating the question, or such that there could be no evidence for or against it, then I do not assert it. And if I do not assert it, I do not commit myself to its being such that it will stand up to experience and inquiry.[2] Only if I assert something am I committed to the hope that opinion will converge upon it.

This is another way of making a point I made in Chapter 4: Peirce argued that bivalence is a regulative assumption of inquiries in which we are actually engaged. The fact that we can trace a second Peircean argument—that which rides on the fact that reality can be determinate and truth indeterminate—makes the case much stronger. The pragmatist can think that the principle of bivalence holds of those statements for which it seems that it must hold[3]—statements into which we are inquiring and statements which we are prepared to assert or deny. But it must not be supposed to be a principle which governs every statement.

I am not only indebted to Wiggins and Hookway for their published contributions to Peirce scholarship. Both helped me get right the arguments in the first edition of *Truth and the End of Inquiry* and also those of the second. David Dyzenhaus, Huw Price, and Tom Short also gave me helpful comments on a draft of what eventually became Chapter 5, as did audiences at the universities of Auckland, British Columbia, Cambridge, Canterbury, McMaster, Otago, Oxford, São Paulo, Sydney, Sheffield, St Andrews, SUNY

[2] Brian Ellis (1992), in a critical notice of *Truth and the End of Inquiry* makes a similar point. If we think of bivalence as merely a semantically escalated version of the law of excluded middle, the pragmatist can think that it holds when it ought to hold. 'It is either true or false that *H*' amounts to 'It is true that either *H* or not *H*'. *If we agree that H and not-H exhaust all possibilities* in a given case, we should agree that bivalence holds for *H*. But bivalence need not hold unrestrictively—we might not always think that all possibilities are exhausted by *H* and not-*H*.

[3] Reynolds (2000: 308) is right that I made a slip when I first made this point (see pp. 126, 155–6). I suggested that we must assume that if a hypothesis is true, then inquiry would eventually settle upon it. But that invokes a prior conception of truth—a way of picking out the true hypotheses which have not been settled upon. It assumes that there must be more to an account of truth than what the Peircean account provides. I should have remained content with the thought that the principle of bivalence can be assumed to hold for those statements for which it seems that it must hold.

Buffalo, and York (Toronto). Danielle Bromwich helped with the bibliography and compiled the index for the second edition. Finally, I am happy to thank Peter Momtchiloff, the philosophy editor at OUP, for encouraging the thought that I might return to *Truth and the End of Inquiry* and for patiently waiting for the results.

Preface to the Original Edition

This book is about truth and inquiry. In explains how, following C. S. Peirce, we might think it correct to say that a true hypothesis is one which would be believed at the end of inquiry.

Peirce, however, conceived of himself as an 'architectonic' philosopher and so in order to get a grip on what he thought about truth, one must make serious excursions into his pragmatism, theory of signs, fallibilism, critical commonsensism, logic, categories, and scholastic realism. Matters are further complicated by the fact that Peirce's thought was constantly evolving: not much in his system lies static, isolated, or unconnected. Thus the account of truth that I shall put forward as Peirce's is one that has to be both excavated and reconstructed from the architectonic maze of forty years of diffuse papers. The resulting account, however, is not the product of purely historical scholarship. Although my argument is one firmly based at all points on Peirce's work, it is an argument about what the best account of truth is; it is an argument about what account of truth we *should* extract from Peirce's work.

The core of my interpretation is the view of truth and inquiry which Peirce first developed in the 1870s. The culmination of this work was published in a series of papers in the *Popular Science Monthly*, called 'Illustrations of the Logic of Science'. They include the famous papers 'How to Make Our Ideas Clear' and 'The Fixation of Belief'. The central philosophical ideas which I retain from this period were never abandoned by Peirce. There are numerous passages in the 1900s where he refers to and ratifies them. Thus references in my work to the earlier period represent what I take to be constant in Peirce's position—the theses he maintained into the 1900s.

In the late 1880s and early 1900s Peirce amended many of his doctrines. Where these are significant improvements, I take on the amendments. And so it is to this later period that my interpretation best attaches. But in order to keep the enterprise on the rails, I have to suppress certain doctrines of

Peirce's—those which I think do not hold up to scrutiny. The two most significant doctrines from which I want to distance myself are his distinction between science and practice and his very late claims about the need to find an ultimate aim for humankind. I shall give notice in the footnotes when these theses are especially relevant, but, for the most part, I simply ignore them because in both cases, Peirce could have reasonably and consistently exercised the option to go in another direction.

Thus the position I attribute to Peirce will not coincide with any résumé or consolidation of it that Peirce himself offered at a particular point in his intellectual career. But it is a position constructed solely out of doctrines that Peirce did indeed hold, whether or not he put them together in just this way himself. To any objection that I end up picking out one strand in Peirce's rambling system and thereby misrepresent the whole, I reply that what I offer represents a stable, coherent, and plausible Peircean position.

Because many of Peirce's doctrines will be discussed in what follows, the reader unfamiliar with Peirce will find here an extensive, if selective, introduction to his thought. My aim is to give just enough background to provide everything required to grasp Peirce's account of truth without imparting so much that the reader is bogged down in scholarship. Much of the scholarly load is borne by the footnotes. Since all of the background material referred to will be more or less explicitly related to Peirce's conception of truth, many relationships (such as that between the categories and the theory of signs) will remain untouched. To draw these out would only distract attention from the issue in question. The overriding aim is not to explicate the entire body of Peircean doctrine, but to develop a sensible Peircean position about truth.

Wherever my interpretation of Peirce is novel, more complete textual evidence is given. For instance, I claim in Chapter 1 that Peirce formulates pragmatism in at least three different ways, none of them providing a coherent doctrine that will meet all of his requirements. I then suggest a way of achieving the result which Peirce, on my view, desires. The reader may wonder why I bother with Peirce's misguided efforts in this way. The answer is that, first, if I am going to improve on what Peirce said, then to be fair, I must look carefully at what he actually did say. And secondly, part of my aim is to draw attention to a structure in Peirce's writings on pragmatism that has thus far gone unnoticed.

Those who are less interested in whether I have got Peirce right and more interested in the pragmatic account of truth *per se* might want to focus on Chapter 4. For it is there that the broad outline of the pragmatic account of truth is articulated. For those who want the whole picture, the book proceeds as follows. In Chapter 1, I distinguish the pragmatic project from the project of providing a definition or a logical equivalence. Peirce does not want to offer a straightforward biconditional of the sort: *H* is true *if and only if*, if inquiry were pursued as far as it could fruitfully go, *H* would be believed. But it turns out that he is well on the way to getting himself such an equivalence. He argues that it is a consequence of '*H* is true' that, if inquiry were to be pursued, *H* would be believed. So he seems to hold the left-to-right conditional—the conditional which moves from truth to the deliverances of inquiry. And his pragmatic scruples prevent him from holding that there is more to a true hypothesis than what is provided by the right-to-left conditional: *if*, if inquiry were pursued as far as it could fruitfully go, *H* would be settled upon, *then H* is true.

In Chapter 2, I argue that, despite first appearances, the right-to-left conditional (the conditional which moves from inquiry to truth) is something that is reasonable to suppose. Once the notions of inquiry and belief are construed in the proper way, the beliefs which inquiry would finally produce deserve the title 'true'. This conception of inquiry is fleshed out in Chapter 3 with Peirce's supplementary doctrines of logic; there we see why Peirce thought that inquiry would deliver beliefs that we would want to call true.

In Chapter 4, I try to identify the senses in which objectivity is preserved in the Peircean account of truth. The left-to-right conditional (the conditional from truth to inquiry) is taken up and its status is shown to be that of a regulative assumption of inquiry. I then return to the conditional which says that if a belief would be permanently settled by inquiry, then it is true. I spell out what is unique and important in Peirce's account of truth and suggest that even those who are suspicious of pragmatism can none the less accept some of these points. But the pragmatic arguments are powerful and I conclude that the whole of the pragmatic account of truth should be accepted.

I should note at the outset that the view of truth offered here rests on the assumption that a satisfactory account of the objectivity of subjunctive conditionals can be offered. I do not undertake the onerous task of providing an account of the status of these conditionals. I take it for granted that some ordinary hypotheses of the sort 'if you were to do x, then y would result' are sensible and determinately correct or incorrect.

Reference Policy

Referring to passages of Peirce's work is a complex business. He never threw away any of his scribblings and there is a tremendous bulk of material. Only three of a projected twenty-two volumes of a chronological edition of his work are in print as I write. The older (soon to be superseded) collection is incomplete and loosely arranged by subject.

My reference policy is as follows: if the passage appears in the new *Chronological Edition*, volumes 1–3, I cite that source as 'CE n, m', where n, m is volume number, page number. If it is not in the first three volumes of the *Chronological Edition*, but in the older *Collected Papers*, I cite the *Collected Papers* as 'CP n. m', where n. m is volume number, paragraph number. If it is available in neither, then I cite the manuscript number in the microfilm edition of Peirce's papers, as MS n, where n is the manuscript number. Occasionally I refer to *The New Elements of Mathematics* as NE, n, m, where n is the volume number and m is the page number. Full details of these works can be found at the beginning of the bibliography.

Unless specified, all emphases in quotations are Peirce's. I do not correct his spelling.

Acknowledgements

This project began as a D.Phil. thesis at Balliol College Oxford under the guidance of two extremely conscientious and generous supervisors. Susan Haack sharpened draft after draft, pointing out important distinctions and countless holes in my arguments. And David Wiggins somehow always had a view of the forest when I was barking up the wrong tree. He patiently returned me many times to the important points and tried to make me see just what was important about them.

David Dyzenhaus, Chris Hookway, and Jim Tiles commented extensively on various drafts of the manuscript and encouraged me to make scores of improvements. Isaac Levi directed me through Peirce's work on inductive and statistical inference; as anyone familiar with Levi's work will see, Chapter 3 owes much to him. Bill Newton-Smith threw obstacle after obstacle in the way of Chapter 4, only some of which it has managed to overcome.

I have also received helpful comments from Ted Bond, Jonathan Cohen, Henry Laycock, John McGuire, Calvin Normore, Thomas Pogge, Madison Powers, Gad Prudovsky, Eldon Soifer, Mary Tiles, John Upper, and Kathy Wilkes.

Thanks are also due to John Upper for compiling the index, to the staff in Duke Humphrey's at the Bodleian Library for lugging the microfilm of Peirce's manuscripts back and forth for three years, and to the members of the philosophy department of Queen's University (Kingston), especially Alistair MacLeod, for providing the congenial atmosphere in which the manuscript was finally revised.

I owe a special debt to Michael Kubara of the University of Lethbridge, who sparked my interest in philosophy and in Peirce. But for his scathing criticism and warm friendship I would not have continued in philosophy. I am also grateful for the support I have received from MaryAnn Ayim, Ronnie DeSousa, Ann Diller, Barbara Houston, Kate Morgan, Peter Preuss, Steve Patten, Leslie Thielan-Wilson, Ron Yoshida, and John Woods.

Last, but far from least, I want to thank David Dyzenhaus for countless discussions in Port Meadow about my work and everything else.

Contents

Introduction

Pragmatism is in fashion in certain philosophical circles. But most 'analytic' philosophers are quick to heap scorn upon it. This poor reputation is due in part to the founder of pragmatism himself, for Peirce was an iconoclastic thinker given to awkward expression and cumbersome terminology. But the reputation is mostly due to those who call themselves pragmatists and go on to put forward a view that the founder of the doctrine would have found abhorrent. These new pragmatists follow Peirce in eschewing a 'transcendental' view of truth, but they go much further than Peirce in arguing that this rejection entails that there is no sensible notion of truth to be had at all.

Peirce wanted to reject views which hold that truth goes beyond inquiry. But he also wanted to retain the notion that there is a right answer to a given question. In order to maintain such a precarious position, much subtlety is required. Peirce's view does not lend itself to snappy summaries. Even when it is put in the best light, it needs extended explanation before it can be seen as plausible.

But once the view is properly understood, some philosophical positions firmly in the analytic tradition and some positions scorned by that tradition can be seen to have affinities to Peircean pragmatism. These include positions which emphasize the context of inquiry, admonish us to take our background beliefs seriously when we theorize about the growth of knowledge and the revision of belief, and take the notions of community, consensus, and convergence to be central in discussing rationality and truth. The Peircean spirit is alive in the works of Popper, Ramsey, Quine, Putnam, Habermas, and a host of others.

Pragmatists of all stripes, however, might have profited by paying more attention to Peirce himself. For I shall argue that he succeeds in establishing a position which avoids taking truth to be something that transcends all perspectives and avoids taking it to be something that is relative to different perspectives. That is, the Peircean position does not unlink truth from inquiry nor does it tie truth to particular inquiries. It is a secular account of truth but it is none the less an account of what it is for a hypothesis to have a determinate truth-value.

Despite the fact that I have seen many opportunities to label Peirce's position, in contrast or sympathy with others, 'realist', 'objectivist', 'relativist', 'anti-realist', 'idealist', or 'subjectivist', I try to resist these temptations. Each of these labels depends on our acquiescence in a contrast that is in danger of being discredited by the very existence of a position like Peirce's. Even if Peirce had no. other claim on the attention of present-day philosophy, this fact would be sufficient to warrant it.

1
Pragmatism

Introduction

Peirce founded pragmatism.[1] Its central insight is that there is a connection between knowing the meaning of a hypothesis and knowing what experiential consequences to expect if the hypothesis is true. It follows, Peirce thinks, that it reflects badly on the content of a hypothesis if no consequences can be derived from it. Not only pragmatists have found such an insight compelling. The logical empiricists insisted that all meaningful statements are verifiable and contemporary 'manifestationists' argue that understanding requires an ability to manifest knowledge of what can be expected.[2]

The most serious problem which any such approach has had to face is how to establish a criterion precise enough to be functional without being unreasonably harsh. If a criterion requires that hypotheses (or the understanding of hypotheses) be connected to sensory experience, it runs the risk of ruling that only hypotheses which are explicitly about observations are legitimate. But if it relaxes the constraint of connection with experience, it runs the risk of ruling that all hypotheses are legitimate. A criterion needs to be found for what constitutes the required ability to manifest knowledge of experiential consequences which is neither so loose that it is ineffectual nor so strict that it rules out areas of discourse which seem to be perfectly well understood.

---

[1] In the 1900s, Peirce renamed his doctrine 'pragmaticism' to distinguish his position from that of James, Schiller, etc. (See *CP* 2. 99, 1902; 5. 552, 1905; 5. 555, 1906; 5. 3, 1901; 6. 485, 1908; 8. 205, 1905.) He thought that this new name was 'ugly enough to be safe from kidnappers' (*CP* 5. 414, 1905), but since it never caught on and since Peirce himself did not always adhere to this usage, I will use the more pleasing 'pragmatism'.

[2] Dummett (1978), Wright (1987), Peacocke (1988), and Luntley (1988) put forward different versions of a manifestation criterion of understanding, or in Luntley's case, of knowledge. Some of these considerations will be discussed, in an extremely broad way, in this section. The reader will notice that I do not see the same route from a manifestation criterion to a non-realist account of truth as do some of these others.

Peirce struggled with this problem. But he did not succeed in striking a balance between an extreme empiricist criterion and a criterion so weak that it does no work at all. He said many conflicting things about pragmatism. At times the pragmatic maxim was as strict as anything found later in logical empiricism. But I shall argue that these strong construals are not true to his intentions. For Peirce did not want to disqualify certain important kinds of expression (those about metaphysics and unobservable entities, for instance) from the category of the legitimate. A criterion which identifies genuine hypotheses with hypotheses which are linked to sensory experience is, Peirce thought, too stringent. He tried twice to formulate an empiricist criterion which rendered certain non-empirical hypotheses legitimate. In both attempts, however, he was left with a criterion so weak that every hypothesis meets the standard. And he certainly wanted something stronger than that.

Peirce, however, does provide the resources for a plausible, if not very precise, moderate empiricist criterion of legitimacy. Once it is articulated, we can employ it in the construction of an account of truth. For pragmatism generates Peirce's account of truth in a way that makes the status of that account unique. Peirce's construal of truth is not an analytic definition of truth, but a distinctively pragmatic elucidation of truth. It is an account of the relationship between truth and inquiry.

1. The Spirit of Pragmatism

The 'spirit' of pragmatism is captured in the following maxim: 'we must look to the upshot of our concepts in order rightly to apprehend them.' (*CP* 5. 4, 1901.) The pragmatic maxim is, roughly, that a person does not have a complete grasp of a predicate F if she is unable to say what would be the consequences of hypotheses of the sort 'a is F'.[3] Before I

---

[3] I take 'hypothesis', 'sentence', 'statement', 'proposition' and 'judgement' to be interchangeable. They are truth-bearers and the things to which meaning accrues. Peirce says that only propositions or judgements 'have truth or falsity'. (See *CP* 8. 115, 1900; 5. 569, 1901; MS 318, p.53, middle of manuscript, 1907; MS 328,

show how Peirce arrives at and clarifies this insight, it will be helpful to see what independent considerations sustain it.

If F is a dispositional predicate, it is quite obvious that if we are rightly to apprehend it, we must know what would be the consequences of '*a* is *F*'. For instance, if I thought that a consequence of the hypothesis 'this bottle is breakable' is (*ceteris paribus*) 'if you were to run a car over it, the bottle would turn pink', then (assuming I had an adequate grasp of 'car', 'bottle', 'pink', and 'running over') I would have a mistaken grasp of 'breakable'. If I believe that '*a* is breakable' has a certain consequence which it does not in fact have, then I have made a mistake in understanding. And if I am unaware of all of the consequences of '*a* is breakable', then my understanding of 'breakable' is incomplete, as opposed to mistaken. For instance, if I do not know just what the shattering patterns are of the material of a bottle when it breaks, then, to a certain extent, my understanding is imperfect.

So we can make this banal point about a dispositional predicate: one just does not get the notion 'breakable' right unless one knows that a consequence of 'this bottle is breakable' is that, if you were to run a car over it, it would shatter. We are motivated to formulate a pragmatic maxim: if a person knows the meaning of a predicate *F*, then she must be able to say something about what to expect if the hypothesis '*a* is *F*' is true (or false).

But it might be argued that this point holds only with respect to hypotheses predicating dispositional properties. And dispositional properties are unusual in that they, by their very nature, ascribe abilities, capacities, or tendencies to behave in certain ways under certain conditions. It would not be cogent to argue that because understanding a dispositional predicate requires one to know what would be the consequences of '*a* is *F*', understanding a non-dispositional predicate *G* requires one to know what would be the consequences of '*a* is *G*'.

p. 40, 1905.) But often he slips and talks of the truth of 'conceptions'. (See *CP* 5. 2, 1901.) I do not mean by 'consequences' deductive consequences so that a consequence of '*P*' is '*P* ∨ *Q*', where *Q* is any sentence one likes. Rather, I mean genuine expectations or predictions.

The point, however, can be generalized without relying on the notion of a disposition. For instance, one might focus on the thought that if no consequences can be derived[4] from a hypothesis, then it is compatible with every state of affairs. It would of course be logically incompatible with its negation and its negation's deductive consequences, but it would be compatible in another sense with any description of the way things are. For what makes a hypothesis incompatible with the way things are is that a consequence of the hypothesis does not hold. So we might say that, tautologies aside, hypotheses which have no consequences are illegitimate. For they assert nothing that can conflict with the way things are. It is hard to know what we would call them other than 'empty' or 'devoid of content'—Peirce calls them pragmatically meaningless.

Notice that this way of articulating the pragmatic insight is from the perspective of the adequacy of hypotheses rather than from the perspective of the adequacy of understanding. Peirce himself usually adopts the latter stance—he argues that in order to grasp the meaning of a hypothesis, one needs to know what to expect if it were true. But he sometimes adopts the former stance, arguing that a hypothesis from which no consequences can be derived is spurious. This shifting between grasp of meaning and the legitimacy of an expression is not pernicious. For the two notions are connected. The pragmatic insight can be put in terms of the adequacy of understanding and then it can be said that if a hypothesis has no consequences (if there isn't anything one could expect would be the case if it were true) then it lacks an important dimension. It lacks a property that we would have had to get right if we were to know the meaning of the hypothesis. Pragmatism labels such a hypothesis defective. Understanding requires that the consequences of a hypothesis be known and a hypothesis is legitimate only if it has consequences.

From the perspective of understanding, one might put forward the following (Wittgensteinian) generalized argument for the pragmatic insight. If a person is not in a position

---

[4] I do not mean 'logically derived', but something much looser.

to commit herself to anything about the way things would be different if the hypothesis were true (or false) then it is quite obscure what reason either we have or she has for thinking that she understands it. For if a hypothesis is about anything, her understanding it cannot *merely* be a matter of *thinking* that she knows what it means. If a hypothesis H purports to be about the world, then if it is true, there will be some consequences for the world. Thus if someone knows the meaning of H, she must be able to manifest knowledge of those consequences. It is not enough if she says that she knows the meaning of H because she can envision it or formulate it to herself. Understanding must be in part manifested by expecting experience to take a certain course.

Another way of putting the point is as follows. If I am to have a grip on the distinction between 'H seems right to me' and 'H is right', then there must be some consequences of H being right that are in principle ascertainable by someone other than myself.[5] That is, if I know what it would be for some hypothesis to seem right to me but to be wrong, there must be some consequence of the hypothesis which can manifest itself to someone other than myself. So if we assume that a legitimate hypothesis is one for which 'H seems right to me' is not a sufficient condition for 'H is right', then legitimate hypotheses need to have consequences.

These are the sorts of considerations that motivate one to formulate a generalized empiricist criterion, a criterion that captures the spirit of Peircean pragmatism. If a person does not have the ability to say what difference the truth or falsity of a hypothesis would make, then either she does not know the meaning of the hypothesis or the hypothesis is devoid of consequences and is thus illegitimate.

Peirce argues that if we focus on the consequences of 'H is true', 'the probability of H is n', 'x is real', etc., we will adopt the best philosophical conceptions of truth, probability,

---

[5] This consideration has been set against the possibility of anyone having a private language. If we are to maintain the distinction, then an utterly private language is not possible. For to say that H is a sentence in a private language is to say that there do not have to be any public consequences if H is true; H being true is something that is entirely a matter for the private linguist. But then 'H seems right to me' will always be a sufficient condition for 'H is right'. See Wittgenstein (1953) and Wright (1986).

reality, etc. And if a philosophical conception does not have consequences, it is illegitimate. Before we can see how his conception of truth arises from such pragmatic considerations, we must have a more precise idea of what sorts of consequences Peirce has in mind. Even if we grant to Peirce the thought that understanding involves knowing consequences, we require more details before we shall be in a position to say just what this pragmatic insight amounts to. Fortunately or not, Peirce does give us a tremendous amount of detail—he tries to show how pragmatism is a corollary of his theory of signs, account of belief, categories, 'scholastic realism', and logic. If my aim were to offer a complete account of Peirce's philosophy, I should now undertake the daunting task of working through all of these alleged relationships. But a brief outline of some of the connections is all that is needed to arrive at a coherent and textually sound account of pragmatism.

2. The Verificationist Formulation

The logical empiricists wanted to formulate a criterion that would determine which hypotheses are spurious and which are legitimate. Peirce shares this aim and, indeed, some of his statements of the pragmatic maxim seem to be prototypes of the verifiability criterion. Numerous versions of the verifiability criterion of meaningfulness were formulated by the logical empiricists, all of them declaring scientific statements legitimate and metaphysical statements illegitimate. One version stated that if a sentence is meaningful, there must be some experience that would verify or falsify it. A weaker version stated that there has to be some experience which would confirm or disconfirm a meaningful sentence. A weaker version still suggested that a sentence has to be a part of an 'empiricist language'. Sentences that failed to meet the standard were deemed to be 'pseudo-propositions'—literally meaningless and neither true nor false. Sentences about the Absolute, intrinsic good, or transcendental entities were thus said to be meaningless, as there is nothing we could possibly experience to verify them.

An exception was made for mathematical sentences and sentences of logic. The logical empiricists, as their name suggests, divided meaningful sentences into two classes: logical or formal ones and verifiable or empirical ones. Formal sentences are meaningful because they do not pretend to assert anything; they are mere tautologies. All other sentences are subject to the verifiability criterion. The radical conclusion was that the legitimate areas of discourse are science, mathematics, and logic. On some accounts, all of philosophy was rendered illegitimate; we were to *'reject all philosophical questions*, whether of Metaphysics, Ethics, or Epistemology' (Carnap 1934, pp. 21–2). On other accounts, only metaphysical statements were rendered illegitimate, and ethical and aesthetic statements were given a sort of 'non-cognitive' or 'emotive' meaning to allow them at least to express attitudes the utterer might have.

Peirce wants to formulate a pragmatic criterion which can serve as a standard for determining which expressions are 'metaphysical rubbish' or 'gibberish'.[6] In the 1878 paper 'How to Make Our Ideas Clear', he publicly unveils pragmatism and says that it is a method for clarifying our ideas so that they are not subject to metaphysical 'deceptions' (*CE* 3, 264). He sets out the pragmatic maxim as follows: 'Consider what effects, which might conceivably have practical bearings, we conceive the object of our conception to have. Then, our conception of these is the whole of our conception of the object.' (*CE* 3, 266.) In 1907 he altered the last line of this maxim 'in hopes of rendering it clearer, without substantially modifying it'. He says that your conception of these effects 'is the whole (meaning of) your conception of the object' (MS 322, p. 11, 1907).

Setting aside for the moment complexities which arise about the 'object of our conception', Peirce suggests in this paper that knowing the meaning of an expression is exhausted by knowing its 'practical' effects. And he characterizes practical effects here as 'effects, direct or indirect, upon our senses' (*CE* 3, 266). These effects can be described by conditionals of the sort 'if you were to do *A*, you would

---

[6] *CP* 8. 191, 1904; see also 5. 423, 1905; 5. 2, 1901.

observe *B*'.[7] He says 'we come down to what is tangible and practical, as the root of every real distinction of thought, no matter how subtle it may be; and there is no distinction of meaning so fine as to consist in anything but a possible difference of practice' (*CE* 3, 265). As an example of how this pragmatic maxim operates, Peirce examines the meaning of 'this diamond is hard'. He says that it means that if you try to scratch it, you will find that 'it will not be scratched by many other substances' (*CE* 3, 266).

Notice that the consequence in this example is formulated as an indicative conditional. Peirce sees that if he formulates consequences in this manner, it makes little sense to describe a diamond which is never scratched as being hard. He seems to be content with this conclusion in 'How to Make Our Ideas Clear'. But when he considers the matter later, he always insists on a subjunctive formulation. The consequences which concern pragmatism are those which would occur under certain conditions, not those which will actually occur. He says that, in 'How to Make Our Ideas Clear', he seemed to have 'wavered in his own mind' and is adamant that the 'will-be' in that paper be replaced with a 'would-be'.[8] He also chides himself for suggesting that habits, dispositions, or 'would-bes' are not real.[9] A realism about dispositions and subjunctive conditionals must, he thinks, be adopted: a disposition is more than the total of its realizations and a subjunctive conditional is determinately correct or incorrect.

Peirce's considered view about the untouched diamond is that 'it is a real fact that it *would* resist pressure' (*CP* 8. 208, 1905). For the behaviour of diamonds is governed by laws and, as we shall see in Chapter 2, Peirce argues that laws sustain subjunctive and counterfactual conditionals. The pragmatic meaning of 'this diamond is hard' is a set of subjunctive conditionals which include 'it is such that if you

---

[7] See *CE* 3, 266–7, 1878; MS 449, p. 52, 1903; *CP* 5. 9, 1907.

[8] See *CP* 5. 453, 1905; 5. 457, 1905; 8. 380n. 4, undated; 6. 485, 1906; MS 841, pp. 15, 16 of 'variants', 1908; MS 318, p. 11, 1907.

[9] See MS 675, 1911. Peirce distances himself from James's 'nominalist' version of pragmatism, which refuses to acknowledge 'would-bes'.

were to scratch it, it would resist'. And such conditionals are determinately correct or incorrect whether or not the antecedent is fulfilled.

So the consequences with which pragmatism is concerned are predictions; we can predict that if *H* is true, then if you were to do *A*, *B* would result. Notice that we cannot, as Peirce seems to suggest, derive such conditionals from 'concepts' or from 'objects of conceptions'. We can only derive them from sentences or hypotheses. It is significant that the examples in 'How to Make Our Ideas Clear' all involve whole sentences, not parts of them. Peirce says that he is seeking 'clear ideas' of hardness and weight, but the way he tries to attain that clarity is by asking 'what we mean by calling a thing hard' or what it means 'to say that a body is heavy' (*CE* 3, 266). If the hypothesis '*a* is hard' or '*b* is heavy' is true, then we expect certain practical conditionals to hold. He says: 'To analyse an idea, there is but one proper method. That method consists in considering what possible practical difference can be involved *in the truth or falsity of a proposition involving that idea.*' (MS 211, undated, my emphasis.) Thus, in the context of pragmatism, I will always talk about hypotheses rather than about parts of hypotheses. On Peirce's account, if a person grasps a predicate *F*, then she knows the consequences of hypotheses of the sort '*a* is *F*'.

In some of his statements of pragmatism, such as the one in 'How to Make Our Ideas Clear', Peirce maintains that these consequences must be observable ones. He suggests that understanding is exhausted by knowing the empirical consequences of the hypothesis in question and that the whole meaning of a hypothesis is the set of empirical consequences that can be derived from it.[10] In these moods Peirce holds that an expression for which you can make no predictions about what would be observable under certain conditions is meaningless. It is clear why Ayer says that Peirce's pragmatism 'allows no truck with metaphysics. Its standpoint is very closely akin to that which was later to be adopted by the logicial positivists. Peirce's pragmatic maxim is indeed

---

[10] See also MS 329, pp. 10 ff., 1904; *CP* 8. 191, 1904; 5. 2, 1901; 5. 434, 1905.

identical, for all practical purposes, with the physicalist interpretation of the verification principle.'[11]

3. Aspects of Linguistic Competence

While it may be true that, in his struggles to arrive at a pragmatic criterion of understanding and meaning, Peirce sometimes alighted on one very similar to the verifiability criterion, he is primarily concerned with a much broader account of what is involved in linguistic competence. I suggest that we ought to pay little attention to his claims that knowing the meaning of an expression is exhausted by knowing what its empirical consequences are. We ought to focus rather on the strand in his thought which claims that *a part* of what it is to know the meaning of an expression is to know what consequences can be derived from it.

Peirce frequently argues that there are three aspects of understanding, and the pragmatic aspect is but one. In order to grasp a term an interpreter must have a threefold competence. She must be able to

(1) pick out what objects the term refers to; that is, know Mill's 'denotation', Hamilton's 'extension' or 'breadth';

(2) give a definition of the term; that is, know Mill's 'connotation', Hamilton's 'intention' or 'depth', Arnauld's 'comprehension';

(3) know what to expect if hypotheses containing the term are true; that is, know the consequences of hypotheses containing the term.

Whereas his predecessors[12] located two sources of meaning (denotation and connotation), Peirce thinks that his contribution was to locate an important third source. He

---

[11] Ayer (1968), p. 55. See also Weiner (1958), pp. 113 and 181, Putnam (1975), p. 272, and Quine (1981).

[12] Hookway (1985) goes a long way towards showing how Peirce's theory of signs can be understood from a Fregean perspective, as opposed to the perspective of Mill, Hamilton, etc. But Peirce would not have been happy with this treatment, for it does not show, as he wanted to show, how pragmatism is a corollary of his theory of signs.

takes his three aspects of understanding to spell out completely what someone must be able to do if she grasps a concept or knows the meaning of an expression. And each aspect of understanding corresponds with a feature of the meaning of a sign. Pragmatic meaning is the feature of hypotheses that the third aspect of understanding is about: it is the set of consequences or predictions which can be derived from the hypothesis.

Oddly enough, one of Peirce's clearest statements of this 'aspects of meaning' or 'aspects of understanding' thesis can be found in 'How to Make Our Ideas Clear', where he seemed to be advocating something like the verifiability criterion. He argues that we can have three 'grades of clearness' or grades of 'apprehensions of the meanings of words'. 'The books', he says, 'are right in making familiarity with a notion the first step toward clearness of apprehension, and the defining of it the second.' (*CE* 3, 260.) But a 'far higher grade' (*CE* 3, 261) is knowing what to expect if hypotheses containing the term are true.

In a straightforward way, Peirce's claim that the third aspect is the most important simply rephrases the considerations which motivated his pragmatism. For those considerations suggest that the pragmatic maxim is a criterion for meaning identity. A purported difference which makes no practical difference is spurious; if two hypotheses have the same set of subjunctive conditional consequences, then they express the same content.[13] It is pointless to suggest that they differ in denotation or connotation. For instance, if one scientist discovers a type of sub-atomic particle and names it '*a*' and another discovers a particle and names it '*b*', and if *a* and *b* turn out to have identical ramifications in experiment and theory, then pragmatism has it that there is no non-terminological distinction between the hypotheses 'there goes an *a*' and 'there goes a *b*'.

But Peirce also suggests that the three aspects of understanding are ordered in strength because of the nature of interpretation. He thinks that the first level of interpretation is an ability to pick out objects to which a term refers.

---

[13] See *CE* 2, 483, 1871; *CE* 3, 108, 1873; *CP* 5. 2, 1901; 5. 196, 1903.

Understanding is increased when the interpreter is able to give a definition of the term and it is complete when the interpreter can use the term in accurate predictions.[14] I suppose that one could argue that the first aspect of competence presupposes the second: if you know, in general, how to apply a sign, you must know what qualities or attributes the sign connotes. There can be no accurate application without a rationale. And the second aspect presupposes the third: there can be no knowledge of connotation without there being some received interpretation. A received interpretation is a matter of the sign having the same sorts of effects on competent interpreters; it is a matter of interpreters making the same predictions of a hypothesis. The fact that a certain hypothesis has more or less uniform effects on interpreters is what makes it the case that terms in the hypothesis have this or that connotation and denotation.

But the three aspects of understanding cannot be separated and graded as easily as Peirce would sometimes have us believe. For instance, one of the ways in which one demonstrates a grasp of the connotation or sense of a term is by being able to determine what objects fall under the concept. One does not have to be able to provide a definition. And we shall notice in 1.7 that the 'lowest' aspect of understanding—specifying the extension—is by far the most ambitious aspect with respect to the predicate 'is true'.

Perhaps Peirce sensed these difficulties, for sometimes he denies that the aspects of meaning are sequential: 'Please observe, by the way, that I speak of three distinct Grades of clearness, which I also call Kinds, but never Stages, as if one were done with before the next began . . . ' (MS 649, p. 3, 1910). Given the difficulties and given Peirce's disclaimer about ranking the aspects of meaning on the basis of how interpretation progresses, I suggest that we focus on just two of his claims for the importance of the pragmatic aspect of meaning. First, it is a criterion of meaning identity. Secondly, it is an aspect of meaning or linguistic competence that has been, to philosophy's detriment, neglected.

[14] See *CP* 8. 218, 1910.

It is difficult to see why Peirce said, in 'How to Make Our Ideas Clear', that the whole meaning of an expression is exhausted by its practical consequences, when he so clearly suggests that there is more to meaning than that. In the 1900s, he frequently expresses regret that the 1878 formulation of the pragmatic maxim bypassed the 'aspects of meaning' account and was concerned solely with action and sensory experience.[15] For instance, in a manuscript called 'On Definition or The Analysis of Meaning', Peirce says that in 'How to Make Our Ideas Clear'

I believe I made my own opinion quite clear to any attentive Reader, that the pragmaticistic grade of clearness could no more supersede the Definitiary or Analytic grade than this latter grade could supersede the first. That is to say, if the Maxim of Pragmaticism be acknowledged, although Definition can no longer be regarded as the supreme mode of clear Apprehension; yet it retains all the *absolute* importance it ever had, still remaining indispensible to all Exact Reasoning.[16]

Moreover, the distinction between the three aspects was maintained by Peirce well before 1878. It shows up, for instance, in the 1867 'On a New List of Categories',[17] where Peirce argues that a sign has a 'triple reference': to the common characters of its objects, to its objects, and to an interpretant.[18] The first two of these 'referents' turn out to be connotation and denotation and they remain constant throughout Peirce's work. The third aspect (the interpretant) undergoes significant revision from this early formulation; we will see that it becomes an account of the consequences of an interpreter's accepting a hypothesis.[19]

Thus, throughout his career, Peirce distinguishes three

[15] See *CP* 5. 3, 1901; 5. 402n. 3, 1906; 5. 198, 1903; MS 284, 1905; MS 313, p. 29, 1903; CE 2, 45, 1867.

[16] MS 647, p. 2, 1910. For more talk of grades of meaning, see MS 449, p. 52, 1903; MS 649, p. 3, 1910; MS 290, p. 34, 1905; *CP* 5. 434, 1905; 6. 481, 1906; 3. 456, 1896; 5. 475, 1907; 4. 536, 1905.

[17] See *CE* 2, 49–59. Peirce later said that this was 'perhaps the least unsatisfactory' of any of his papers (*CP* 2. 340, 1885), and that it was 'his one contribution to philosophy' (*CP* 8. 213, 1905).

[18] He called the first referent the 'ground' and the second the 'correlate'.

[19] The original (1868) notion of interpretant is that of 'information' or 'the set of propositions of which the sign can be made subject or predicate'. The location of 'meaning' in the triadic sign relation changed with the change to the new theory of

aspects of meaning and understanding. Much of this work is done in the context of his theory of signs. He says: 'Pragmatism is . . . nothing more than a rule for ascertaining the meanings of words . . . Consequently, it must be founded exclusively upon our understandings of signs . . . '[20] In the next section, I will take a very selective look at Peirce's pioneering account of signs and meaning and try to disentangle the relevant points as far as possible from the cumbersome terminology. I shall not, however, be concerned with the adequacy of this account, especially since the contemporary project of arriving at a 'theory of meaning' is a different undertaking from Peirce's. His account of ascertaining the meanings of words is a method of clarifying our philosophical conceptions. It is that method I want to draw out and support, not his more technical theses about language, signs, and representation.[21] Just what this pragmatic method amounts to will become clearer below, as I show how Peirce tried, both within his theory of signs and with his notion of experience, to make pragmatism embrace more than just empirical or observable consequences.

4. The First Weak Formulation: Interpretants

Peirce's theory of signs has interpretation at its centre. He argues that the sign–referent relation is not able, on its own, to uphold a complete account of representation. Representation is triadic: it involves a sign, an object, and an interpreter. Each aspect of this representation relation corresponds to one of the elements in Peirce's division of signs

interpretants. Initially Peirce followed Mill in identifying meaning with connotation. (See CE 2, 49, 1867; CP 1. 339, undated; 4. 56, 1893.) He later identified the third aspect of meaning with the interpretant.

[20] MS 322, p. 12, 1907; see also CP 5. 475, 1907; 8. 119, 1900; 8. 191, 1904; letter to Ladd-Franklin in Ladd-Franklin (1916). Peirce says that in 'How to Make Our Ideas Clear' he 'did not there show how I had myself derived [the pragmatic maxim] from a logical and non-psychological study of the essential nature of signs' (MS 137, fragment marked p. 19, 63 pages from end of manuscript, 1904).

[21] For good discussions of Peirce's theory of signs, see Short (1982), Altshuler (1978), and Fitzgerald (1966).

into icons, indices, and symbols.[22] And in each of these an aspect of linguistic competence is prominent. Icons are signs that exhibit their objects by virtue of similarity or resemblance.[23] A portrait is an icon of the person it portrays and a map is an icon of a certain geographical area. Peirce argues that the meaning of iconic signs lies mostly in their connotation; what makes a painting or a map an icon is that its qualities or attributes resemble the qualities or attributes of its object.

Indices are signs that indicate their objects in a causal manner; an index 'signifies its object solely by virtue of being really connected with it'.[24] A symptom is an index of a disease and smoke is an index of fire. The essential quality of an index is its ability to compel attention.[25] A pointing finger, a knock on the door, or a demonstrative pronoun, such as 'there' or 'that', draws attention to its object by getting the interpreter to focus on the object. So an index, by being object-directed in this way, has its denotation or extension as its 'most prominent feature' (*CP* 8. 119, 1902). An index picks out or indicates its object; it points to 'that, that, and that' as its extension.

A symbol is a word, hypothesis, or argument that depends on a conventional or habitual rule; a symbol is a sign 'because it is used and understood as such'.[26] Symbols have 'principle' or pragmatic meaning; they have 'intellectual purport'.

In his review of Royce's *The World and The Individual*, Peirce contrasts pragmatic meaning with 'internal' meaning (which he associates with icons and connotation) and with 'external' meaning (which he associates with indices and denotation). He suggests that the pragmatic meaning of symbols has to do with a 'purpose' (*CP* 8. 119, 1900). A symbol has pragmatic meaning because if the utterer knows

---

[22] See *CE* 2, 56, 1867, 'On a New List of Categories'. Peirce had three primary divisions of signs (the icon/index/symbol division is one) which eventually allowed for a final 66 divisions.

[23] See *CP* 3. 362, 1885; 2. 299, 1893; 4. 447, 1903.

[24] *CP* 3. 360, 1885; see also 5. 73, 1903; 2. 92, 1902; 4. 447, 1903.

[25] See *CP* 1. 369, 1885; 2. 285, 1893; 2. 287, 1893.

[26] *CP* 2. 307, 1901; see also 1. 369, 1885.

how interpreters habitually interpret a sign, she can use the sign to cause a specific effect in the interpreter. And Peirce calls this effect the 'interpretant' of the sign. If, for instance, I write 'dog', I intend the sign to cause a certain effect in the interpreter (perhaps I want the interpreter to think of a dog) whereas if I write 'odg', I do not, as 'odg' is not a conventional sign. Or if I assert 'That bridge has a loose plank', I might want the interpreter to be careful when crossing the bridge.[27] Peirce characterizes an assertion as the attempt to produce a disposition in an interpreter; it is 'the deliberate exercise, in uttering the proposition, of a force tending to determine a belief in it in the mind of an interpreter' (*NE* iv. 249). But notice that this construal of pragmatic meaning is substantially different from Peirce's verificationist construal. In the verificationist construal, pragmatism is concerned with the observable consequences which can be derived from the truth of a hypothesis. But within Peirce's theory of signs, pragmatism seems to be about the consequences that the acceptance of a hypothesis has on the interpreter's behaviour or thought. That is, 'practical consequences' seem no longer to be 'effects, direct or indirect, upon our senses'; they are rather consequences for action *or* thought.[28] In 1905 we find him offering this version of the pragmatic maxim: 'The entire intellectual purport of any symbol consists in the total of all general modes of rational conduct which, conditionally upon all the possible different circumstances and desires, would ensue upon the acceptance of the symbol'.[29] 'Rational conduct', although Peirce thinks

---

[27] The distinction between icons, indices and symbols can be upheld despite the fact that agents also intend to produce effects in interpreters when they employ iconic and indexical signs. We must notice that convention (the feature characteristic of symbols) is necessary in both portraits (icons) and pointing fingers (indices). But convention is not the most prominent aspect; what is most characteristic of icons and indices is resemblance and causal connections. But when icons and indices function as signs, they must be signs *to an interpreter* who has learned how to recognize the underlying relations of similarity and causation and who intends to use them to produce effects in other interpreters. Thus the distinction between the three kinds of signs is merely a matter of one aspect of meaning being most prominent in each.

[28] See *CP* 5. 13 n.1, 1902; 8. 191, 1904.

[29] *CP* 5. 438, 1905; see also 5. 9, 1905. Chris Hookway pointed out to me that this formulation and the 1878 one are similar in the following respect. The predictions derivable from *H* being true will be of this sort: in circumstances *C*, if

that it will eventually manifest itself in a modification of the interpreter's disposition to behave, includes the conduct of one's thought. Practical effects do not have to be observable; they do not have to involve one's senses. This characterization of pragmatism as involving the effects the acceptance of a hypothesis would have on an interpreter's train of thought coincides with a development in the early 1900s in Peirce's theory of signs. That development is a complex theory of interpretants and Peirce locates pragmatic meaning within this theory.

He distinguishes three types of interpretants.[30] The 'immediate' interpretant is the fitness of a sign to be understood in a certain way; the 'dynamical' interpretant is the actual effect a sign has on an interpreter, and the 'final' interpretant is the effect which eventually would be decided to be the correct interpretation. (See *CP* 8. 184, undated.) Pragmatic meaning, he says, lies in a kind of dynamical interpretant: the 'ultimate logical interpretant'.[31] A sign, Peirce argues, sparks a subsequent sign, or a logical interpretant, in the mind of the interpreter, and since the logical interpretant is itself a sign, an infinite chain of interpretation, development, or thought, is begun. Peirce stops the regress by introducing the notion of an 'ultimate logical interpretant' or a 'habit-change'. We will see in the next chapter that he takes a belief to be a habit or disposition to behave. And so this new habit is a belief or a modification of the interpreter's tendencies towards action. (See *CP 5*. 476, 1907.) The pragmatic meaning of an

---

you were to do *A*, then *E* would result. And the 1905 formulation will result in these sorts of predictions: if I were to accept *H*, then in circumstances *C*, I would do *A* if my strongest desire was for *E*. Alternatively, if I were to accept *H*, then I would predict that, in circumstances *C*, if I were to do *A*, then *E* would result. But the difference which I want to point to between the 1878 and the 1905 statements of pragmatism is that the earlier formulation stipulated that *E* be experienceable: the 1905 formulation does not.

[30] See *CP* 8. 315, 1909; 5. 475, 1907; 4. 536, 1905; 8. 184, undated; MS 318, 1907.

[31] See *CP* 5. 476, 1907; 5. 491, 1907; 5. 494, 1907; MS 322, 1907. There are three types of dynamical interpretant: emotional, energetic, and logical. The first is the feeling of recognition produced in the mind of the interpreter because of the sign. For example, consider 'cta' as opposed to 'cat' and 'mat the the on is cat' as opposed to 'the cat is on the mat'. The energetic interpretant is an actual effort, internal or external, on the part of the interpreter. Peirce says that it is usually a mental effort; a train of thought or a silent soliloquy, but it may also be physical.

expression, according to Peirce's theory of interpretants, is the action (which includes the action of subsequent thought and which ends in a disposition to behave) that arises after an interpreter accepts it.

Quite accurately, Peirce says that his doctrine of kinds of interpretants and their associations with meaning are not 'quite free from mist' (*CP* 4. 536, 1905). He sometimes associates pragmatic meaning not with the dynamical interpretant, but with the final interpretant.[32] That is, he associates pragmatic meaning not with the actual effects of a sign, but with the effects that would be produced if the sign were 'properly understood'. And he sometimes associates pragmatic meaning with the 'intended interpretant', or the intended effect on the interpreter.[33] That is, pragmatic meaning is the effect that the utterer of an assertion wants to have on the interpreter. Pragmatism, he says, 'is not exclusively an opinion about the Dynamic Interpretant' (*CP* 8. 315, 1909).

I suggest that one reason for such indecision on Peirce's part is that he saw that if practical consequences are construed as actual consequences for trains of thought, the pragmatic maxim becomes uninteresting. If all that is required of pragmatically meaningful hypotheses is that they should, if believed, make some difference to how the believer thinks or acts, then everything will make the grade. Suppose that Russell's hypothesis is the sort that pragmatism is set against: 'the world and everything in it, including memories and fossils, was created five minutes ago'. Defenders of the hypothesis may argue against its opponents, they may use the hypothesis as a premise in arguments, or they may found a lively religion, paying homage to the powerful god who recently created the world. These must surely count as effects on the trains of thought and behaviour of interpreters. This version of the pragmatic criterion is too weak to do any work at all.

Peirce occasionally sees this difficulty but fails to solve it. He says:

But what is to prevent his [the pragmatist's] opponent from replying that there is a practical difference which consists in his

[32] See *CP* 8. 185, no date; 8. 315, 1909; MS 137, fragment marked p. 19, 64 pages from end of manuscript, 1904.
[33] See *CP* 5. 175, 1903; 1. 343, 1903.

recognizing one as his conception and not the other? That is, one is expressible in a way in which the other is not expressible. Pragmatism is completely volatilized if you admit that sort of practicality. (*CP 5*. 33, 1903, Harvard Lectures on Pragmatism.)

Peirce's suggestion that a practical consequence cannot be a 'mere difference in the meanings of words' is of little help. If a difference in the train of thought or behaviour of an interpreter counts as 'practical', Peirce has not arrived at a principled way to identify spurious hypotheses. His attempt to avoid extreme empiricism by allowing consequences on trains of thought to count as practical consequences does not succeed.

5. The Second Weak Formulation: Experience

Peirce's second route to a pragmatic maxim which does not over-emphasize sensory experience involves his extremely generous construal of experience. We have seen that pragmatism requires legitimate hypotheses to have practical considerations, considerations which have it 'that certain lines of conduct will entail certain kinds of inevitable experiences' (*CP 5*. 9, 1907). But what sort of hypothesis meets the pragmatic criterion depends on how the notion of experience is characterized. The way in which Peirce characterizes it allows hypotheses about metaphysics (and morality and highly theoretical matters) to have experiential consequences.

For Peirce, experience is a very broad notion—it is anything that is forced upon one. Perception, for instance, goes far beyond what our ears, eyes, nose, and skin report. He says

anything is, for the purposes of logic, to be classed under the species of perception wherein a positive qualitative content is forced upon one's acknowledgement without any reason or pretension to reason. There will be a wider genus of things *partaking* of the character of perception, if there be any matter of cognition which exerts a force upon us ... (*CP 7*. 623, 1903.)

A sensation or observation does not have to be caused by one's senses, for it 'is merely an idea arising in the mind, and not produced by previous ideas'.[34] Peirce takes anything that is compelling, surprising, brute, or impinging to be an experience, regardless of what causes us to feel compelled and regardless of whether we can identify the source of the compulsion. He says that 'By *brutally* I mean without appealing to our voluntary reasoning.' (MS 339, 'The Logic Notebook', 15 Oct. 1908.) Something impinges upon us if its 'immediate efficacy nowise consists in conformity to rule or reason' (*CP* 6. 454, 1908). And: 'The course of life has developed certain compulsions of thought which we speak of collectively as Experience.' (*CP* 8. 101, 1900.)

Peirce argues that there are two kinds of experience— 'ideal' and 'real'. The latter is sensory experience and the former is experience in which 'operations upon diagrams, whether external or imaginary, take the place of the experiments upon real things that one performs in chemical and physical research' (*CP* 4. 530, 1905, see also 1. 240, 1902, 3. 516, 1896). This sort of thought experiment or diagrammatic experiment is, he argues, at the core of mathematical and deductive inquiry. Such inquiry

involves an element of observation; namely, [it] consists in constructing an icon or diagram the relation of whose parts shall present a complete analogy with those of the parts of the object of reasoning, of experimenting upon this image in the imagination, and of observing the result so as to discover unnoticed and hidden relations among the parts.[35]

The mathematician operates or experiments on a diagram. For instance, he draws subsidiary lines in geometry or makes transformations in algebraic formulae and then observes the results. Peirce insists that 'his hypotheses are creatures of his own imagination; but he discovers in them relations which surprise him sometimes'.[36] Since surprise is the force of experience, such reasoning is an experiment. This sort of experiment 'is truly observation, yet certainly in a very

---

[34] *CE* 3, 41, 1872; see also *CE* 3, 35, 1872; *CP* 6. 492, 1896. I will examine Peirce's account of perception in Ch. 2.
[35] *CP* 3. 363, 1885; see also 4. 233, 1902; 5. 474, 1907; 2. 605, 1901; 1. 322, 1903; 5. 162, 1903; MS 328, p. 46, 1905. Susan Haack drew my attention to these sorts of passages.
[36] *CP* 5. 567, 1901; see also 5. 166, 1903.

peculiar sense; and no other kind of observation would at all answer the purpose of mathematics' (*CP* 1. 240, 1902).

Inference, on Peirce's account, can also be a sort of experience. It too can be compelling. For instance, Peirce suggests that in valid deductive reasoning, we are compelled to accept the conclusion—the facts stated in the premises could not be, if the fact stated in the conclusion were not.[37]

Traditionally, those who adopt an empiricist criterion of significance argue that mathematical and logical statements are empirically empty but significant on other grounds. They have a special status which exempts them from the empiricist test for significance. But unlike Hume and the logical empiricists, Peirce suggests that we ought to expose mathematical and logical statements to the empiricist criterion. Experiments performed on diagrams will provide the observable data. On Peirce's account, these observations do not verify or falsify the statements: rather, the fact that the statements have such consequences makes them legitimate or pragmatically significant.

Peirce sometimes puts his point about the breadth of experience by saying that everyone inhabits two worlds, the inner (or the ideal) and the outer (or the real). We react with the outer world through the clash between it and our senses, and we react with the inner world—the world of mathematics, logic, and reasoning—by performing thought experiments. Inquiry, Peirce says, has 'two branches; one is inquiry into Outward Fact by experimentation and observation, and is called *Inductive Investigation*; the other is inquiry into Inner Truth by inward experimentation and observation and is called *Mathematical* or *Deductive* Reasoning'.[38]

The distinction, however, between the inner and the outer worlds, or between 'external and internal facts', is not hard and fast. External facts are simply those which are 'ordinarily regarded as external while others are regarded as internal'

---

[37] See *CP* 2. 96, 1902; 6. 568, 1905; 6. 497, 1906; MS 453, 1903; MS 939, 1905. Peirce says that there is a difference between what he is suggesting and a psychologism which holds that validity is a matter of what people find compelling. We will see in Ch. 3 that he does not take validity to be a matter of 'compulsion of thought' (*CP* 3. 432, 1896).

[38] MS 408, p. 150, 1893–5; see also *CP* 3. 527, 1896.

(*CE* 2, 205, 1868). The distinction, Peirce says, between the two different sorts of experience is that the inner world exerts a comparatively slight compulsion upon us, whereas the outer world is full of irresistible compulsions. But none the less, internal experience is also 'unreasonably compulsory':[39] 'the inner world has its surprises for us, sometimes' (*CP* 7. 438, 1893). He intends to leave the difference between the two sorts of experience vague: 'We naturally make all our distinctions too absolute. We are accustomed to speak of an external universe and an inner world of thought. But they are merely vicinities with no real boundary between them.' (*CP* 7. 438, 1893.)

It is hard to know what to make of these suggestive remarks. Perhaps the contrast between the two sorts of experience is best made by Peirce's distinction between practical and theoretical belief. In the 1902 manuscript 'Reason's Rules',[40] he says that a practical belief such as 'anthracite is a convenient fuel' will manifest itself in a disposition to behave on the part of the believer. She would sometimes use anthracite were she in need of a fuel. And we should add that 'sensible' or empirical consequences can be derived from the hypothesis. For instance, if (*ceteris paribus*) you were to light anthracite, it would burn. On the other hand, a 'purely theoretical' belief has to do not with 'habits of deliberate action' or with sensible consequences, but with 'expectations'. As examples of theoretical hypotheses Peirce offers: 'there is an imaginary circle which is twice cut by every real circle' and 'the diagonal of a square is incommensurable with its side'. Of the latter, he says that, although it is 'difficult to see what experiential difference there can be between commensurable and incommensurable magnitudes', there are nevertheless expectations: 'a belief about the commensurability of the diagonal relates to what is expectable for a person dealing with fractions; although it means nothing at all in regard to what could be expected in physical measurements'.[41]

Now pragmatism holds that if a hypothesis results in expectations, then it is not 'metaphysical jargon' (MS 596,

[39] *CP* 7. 659, 1903; see also 5. 45, 1903; MS L75, Carnegie Application, 1902.
[40] MS 596, pp. 22 ff. See *CP* 5. 538–45 for a part of this manuscript.
[41] MS 596, p. 32; see also *CP* 5. 541, 1902.

p. 25). For an expectation is a prediction that could be overturned by recalcitrant experience. If a theoretical hypothesis involves an expectation, then the unexpected can surprise the believer. The only difference between a practical and a theoretical belief, says Peirce, is that the former involves sensation that is 'muscular' and the latter involves sensation that is not muscular.[42] Purely theoretical beliefs result in expectations that can be tested only in non-empirical ways—they are tested in diagrammatic experiments, reasoning, and theory.

The thought that practical or experiential consequences include consequences in theoretical contexts is tolerably clear. But as it stands it is not clear enough to provide us with a principled way of determining which sorts of internal experiences or experiences in theory pass the pragmatic criterion and which do not. Does the hypothesis 'the world and everything in it was created five minutes ago' have consequences for the theories of its believers? Does 'spiritual illumination from on high' count as internal experience?[43]

We do not yet have an adequate criterion for pragmatic legitimacy. The verificationist version is too strong and is anyway repudiated by Peirce. And Peirce's weaker versions, which try to provide a criterion that is concerned with both empirical and non-empirical consequences, are too weak. They admit hypotheses which should be inadmissible. It seems that any hypothesis can make a non-empirical practical difference: a difference in some interpreter's train of thought, in 'internal experience', or in theoretical contexts. In the next section, I will look at the various sorts of hypotheses that Peirce thinks are pragmatically legitimate, and propose a way of sorting them that allows the pragmatic maxim to do everything it was designed to do.

6. A Moderate Formulation

Peirce maintained, especially in his later writings, that the pragmatic maxim was best seen not as a true statement, but

---

[42] MS 596, p. 30/CP 5. 540.
[43] Peirce says that it does not count, but does not give a principled reason for ruling it out. See CP 8. 43, 1885.

as a *method*—a method of 'ascertaining the meanings of hard words and of abstract concepts'.[44] An examination of the different sorts of hypotheses to which Peirce applied this method can, I suggest, lead us to a principled way of determining what it takes for a hypothesis to meet the pragmatic criterion. For Peirce's indecision about what sorts of consequences count as practical reflects an important feature of language: different sorts of hypotheses have different sorts of content. They thus require different sorts of practical consequences.[45]

When Peirce applies the pragmatic maxim to hypotheses in science, he takes 'practical consequence' in a full-bodied empiricist spirit. Within science, the pragmatic maxim serves to determine 'the admissibility of hypotheses to rank as hypotheses'.[46] Scientific hypotheses must have consequences for sensory experience; the scientist must be able to say that if *H* is true, then 'if you were to do *A*, *B* would be observed'. Otherwise, the hypothesis cannot be tested inductively and it is of no use in scientific inquiry. The mistake made by the logical empiricists was to reduce the meaningful to this class of statements, to statements about the observable or the scientific. A moderate formulation of the pragmatic maxim would hold that the only sort of statement for which observable consequences must be derived are statements which purport to be about the physical world.[47]

The other kinds of hypothesis that the logical empiricists vindicated were mathematical or logical ones. Peirce too thinks that these hypotheses are legitimate. But whereas the logical empiricists had a split criterion of meaningfulness (one for formal hypotheses and another for all other sorts), Peirce, we have seen, proposes to expose formal hypotheses to his empiricist criterion. On his account, hypotheses about mathematics and logic face the empiricist test—and they

---

[44] MS 318, p. 8, 1907; see also *CP* 5. 6, 1907; 5. 206, 1903; 5. 464, 1906; 6. 490, 1910; 8. 191, 1904; 8. 259, 1904.

[45] See *CP* 3. 516, 1896, for a remark which points in this direction.

[46] *CP* 5. 196, 1903; see also 2. 511, 1883.

[47] Notice here the similarity with Popper's demarcation of scientific statements from non-scientific ones. See Popper (1959) and (1963).

pass.[48] They have practical consequences or effects on experience. These experiential consequences are had in thought experiments or experiments on diagrams, but this, Peirce insists, does not detract from their legitimacy.

A moderate pragmatist can adopt this thought. For there is a principled reason for the discrimination between the sorts of consequences relevant to mathematical hypotheses and those relevant to scientific hypotheses. For, whatever else they might be, mathematical objects are not objects that exist in the physical world; they are in some sense ideal objects. But if mathematical hypotheses do not purport to be about the external world, then it would be unreasonable to require that they have consequences for the external world. Mathematical hypotheses might have application in the physical world, but they need not. They need not be testable in a scientific experiment.

Here we can see the makings of our principle. Let us say, as a first approximation, that the pragmatic criterion holds that if a hypothesis purports to be about the physical world, then it must have empirical content. In order to be pragmatically legitimate, it must have empirical consequences of the sort envisioned by the logical empiricists[49] and the Peirce of 'How to Make Our Ideas Clear'.

The hypothesis '*the world and everything in it* was created five minutes ago' fails to meet this standard. The italicized part clearly purports to refer to the world. Yet there is no observable difference whatsoever between the consequences of this hypothesis and the consequences of the one we standardly believe.[50] The only difference is a difference in interpreters' trains of thought and behaviour. In other words, Russell's hypothesis has no observable consequences, for we

[48] See MS 318, pp. 28, 29 (towards end of MS), 1907. He says, for instance, that mathematical notions, such as irrational quantity and geometrical equality, are 'highly abstract and abstruse and yet [their] meanings should be quite unquestionable'. He then shows how we ought to expect certain things if they are true.

[49] The consequences, however, will be expressed by subjunctive conditionals on the pragmatist's account.

[50] It should become clear in Ch. 3 that a defect of Russell's hypothesis is that it has not been abducted to; it has not been invoked as an explanation of phenomena. The hypothesis we standardly believe has been arrived at because it is the best explanation of what we have observed (fossils, history books, etc.), so, on Peirce's account, it already has something going for it.

can say nothing about what would be different if the hypothesis were true or false. It purports to have a kind of content but it does not have the practical consequences which ought to accompany content of that sort.

The hypothesis 'The diagonal of a square is incommensurable with its side', on the other hand, does not purport to be about the external world; it purports to be about what we might call the ideal world.[51] So it needs to have consequences in diagrammatic or theoretical contexts, which it does.

Thus, on this formulation of the pragmatic maxim, there is a nice way of showing that mathematical and logical hypotheses are legitimate. Because they do not purport to be about the external world, they do not require exactly the same sorts of consequences that scientific hypotheses require. They must have consequences for ideal experimental set-ups, as opposed to external experimental set-ups.

This is not to say that there is a sharp demarcation between scientific and mathematical statements. Mathematics has obvious applications in empirical science; the results of inward experience have bearing on outward experience. But although mathematical hypotheses might have straightforward consequences for outward experience, they need not. The content of the two domains is distinct and thus the practical consequences *required* for hypotheses in each domain differ. What must not be lost sight of is that, on this reading of the pragmatic maxim, mathematical and logical statements are not merely formal. They have content, for they have practical consequences. However, they require a different *sort* of practical consequence than do empirical statements.

Notice that it will be quite easy for a logical or mathematical hypothesis to qualify itself. The pragmatic criterion is merely a criterion of significance (not of truth, of warranted assertability, or even of plausibility). On this criterion, if a mathematical or logical statement has consequences for theory, it is significant. It should be of no surprise that most mathematical and logical statements will pass the test.[52] The

---

[51] See CP 5. 565, 1901, for a passage suggesting this. Chris Hookway got me to see this point.

[52] Thus you will not find here an argument which tries to rule out the principle of bivalence or double negation elimination on grounds of lack of significance.

sort of statements that the pragmatic criterion will be set against will be highly unusual ones such as Russell's hypothesis or a theoretical statement which is supposedly different from another but which has exactly the same deductive consequences as that other. The work done by the pragmatic criterion will, for the most part, be in areas of inquiry which purport to be about the world. Most importantly, it will do work in metaphysics.

Empirical and mathematical hypotheses are not the only ones in which we might be interested. We might, for instance, be uneasy with the logical empiricists' disqualification of hypotheses about metaphysics and morals. These areas of inquiry are different from mathematical inquiry at least in that they are dispute-ridden, whereas there is tremendous agreement amongst mathematicians. I shall take up the thorny issue of the status of metaphysics and postpone the status of morals for another project. But notice that, given Peirce's broad construal of experience, there is at least room in his account for hypotheses in moral inquiry to try to qualify themselves. Hypotheses about what is right and wrong might have consequences for a kind of experience, that encountered in thought experiments.[53]

Peirce claims that in metaphysics 'one finds those questions that at first seem to offer no handle for reason's clutch, but which readily yield to logical analysis' (*CP* 6. 463, 1908). Metaphysics, 'in its present condition' is 'a puny, rickety, and scrofulous science' (*CP* 6. 6, 1903). But it need not be so, for many metaphysical hypotheses are meaningful and important: 'instead of merely jeering at metaphysics . . . the pragmatist extracts from it a precious essence'.[54] A position

---

[53] Although his usual opinion is that the inquirer ought to go on instinct in moral matters, Peirce sometimes says: 'But what else, when one considers it, can our "truth" ever amount to, other than the way in which people would come to think if research were carried sufficiently far? That would seem to be all that our truth ever can be. So good morals is the kind of human behavior that would come to be approved if studies of right behavior were carried sufficiently far.' (MS 673, p. 12, 1911; see also *CP* 5. 566, 1901.) Inquirers, in trying to settle their beliefs, will find some arguments, thought experiments, analogies, and examples compelling. Since we hope that all inquirers will tend to feel the force of this experience, we hope that belief will tend to converge. This will be the issue taken up in my forthcoming *Pragmatists, Truth, and Morality*.

[54] *CP* 5. 423, 1905; see also *CE* 2, 128, 1867; *CP* 2. 661, 1910; 5. 422, 1905; 5. 453, 1905; 5. 597, 1903; 5. 423, 1905; *CE* 2, 45, 1867. Peirce includes the

which regards 'metaphysics as moonshine' is, he thinks, pernicious. (See MS 313, p. 25, 1903.) A decent empiricist criterion of meaningfulness will legitimize 'higher matters [such] as honor, aspirations, and love' (*CP* 6. 493, 1896), as well as 'Pure Being, Quality, Relation, Agency, Freedom, and the like' (MS 313, p. 25, 1903).

So whereas the logical empiricists wanted to establish that all metaphysics (and perhaps epistemology and ethics as well) is gibberish, Peirce only wants to establish that some of it is. There is bad metaphysics and there is good 'scientific' metaphysics. It is the business of the pragmatic maxim to identify which is which: 'once accepted [the maxim] speedily sweeps all metaphysical rubbish out of one's house. Each abstraction is either pronounced to be gibberish or is provided with a plain, practical definition'.[55]

Peirce plausibly suggests that metaphysical hypotheses are like scientific ones in that they purport to be about the world. Thus they should have empirical consequences:

Mathematical reasoning has for its object to ascertain what would be true in a hypothetical world which the mathematician has created for himself,—not altogether arbitrarily, it is true, but nevertheless, so that it can contain no element which he has not himself deliberately introduced into it . . . The metaphysician, on the other hand, is engaged in the investigation of matters of fact . . . [56]

He notes that metaphysics, unlike science, is said to be inscrutable 'because its objects are not open to observation'. But he blames the 'backward state' of the discipline not on its non-observational nature, but on the fact that 'its leading professors have been theologians'. For metaphysics is indeed an 'observational science' (*CP* 6. 5, 1898). It 'really rests on observations, whether consciously or not; and the only

following as being the sort of questions which press for 'industrious and bold investigation': whether there be any real indefiniteness, possibility, indeterminacy, strictly individual existence, distinction between the external and internal worlds, etc. See MS 283, p. 29, 1905; *CP* 6. 6, 1903.

[55] *CP* 8. 191, 1904. Notice that Peirce was not strict about using the term 'definition' to apply to the second grade of linguistic competence. For the 'plain, practical' unpacking of the term in question will be a pragmatic unpacking.

[56] *CP* 8. 100, 1900, review of Royce's *The World and The Individual*, see also 3. 428, 1896.

reason that this is not universally recognized is that it rests upon kinds of phenomena with which every man's experience is so saturated that he usually pays no particular attention to them' (*CP* 6. 2, 1898). Legitimate metaphysics rests on empirical observation of a 'banal' sort.[57] He contrasts this sort of observation with the kind found in science, which 'essentially involves special, new experience. A scientific man is simply one who has been trained to conduct observations of some special kind, with which his distinctive business begins and ends.' (*CP* 5. 568, 1905) The scientist's phenomena are 'remote from everyday life', as they require special instruments, precautions, and skill. The phenomena observed by metaphysicians, on the other hand, are 'harder to see, simply because they surround us on every hand; we are immersed in them and have no background against which to view them' (*CP* 6. 562, 1905, see also 1. 134, 1901). Commonplaces, Peirce argues, are underrated; they are universal experiences and deserve more attention. Observing commonplaces is 'observation in a peculiar, yet perfectly legitimate, sense'.

So it seems that Peirce thinks that metaphysics purports to be about the world, but about it in a general way, so that the relevant kind of experience is experience that is universal or common to all. A metaphysical hypothesis, in order to be pragmatically legitimate, must have ordinary observational consequences, for 'there is no conception so lofty and elevated that it cannot be fully defined in terms of the conceptions of our homely, instinctive everyday life' (MS 313, p. 29, 1903). Unfortunately, Peirce does not give us any details as to what this ordinary observation and experience is.[58] A clear enough example will be given in the next section. But since the absence of discussion of the issue by Peirce is conspicuous, it is worth taking a quick look at how he tries to grapple with those details in 'A Neglected Argument for the

---

[57] See *CP* 1. 184, 1903; 1. 242, 1902. Peirce, however, seems to have been suspicious of 'familiar experience' in the 1870s. See *CE* 3, 41, 1872.

[58] Perhaps he means it to be the business of phenomenology: the 'observational science' which requires 'the faculty of seeing what stares one in the face' (*CP* 5. 42, 1903). Phenomenology studies experience of whatever 'comes before the mind'. See *CP* 1. 238–55, 1902.

Reality of God'. In the three drafts of this paper,[59] he sets himself the task of showing that the hypothesis asserting the reality of God has consequences which can be tested by induction. But each of the drafts breaks off just as he tries to carry out this task.

He says that one sort of consequence which cannot be derived from the hypothesis 'God is real' is what God's conduct would be.[60] This, he claims, is 'counteracted' by the fact that the hypothesis has a 'commanding influence over the whole conduct of life in its believers'.[61] But we have seen that such a consequence is not enough to render a hypothesis pragmatically legitimate. For the hypothesis 'the world was created five minutes ago', a hypothesis which is surely pragmatically empty, could have a similar influence on its believers. What we need to be able to derive are predictions about common empirical experience: if the hypothesis about God's existence were true, then we would expect things to be a certain way.

Peirce sees that more than a 'commanding influence' is required, for he does offer some vague predictions for empirical experience. He suggests that if 'God is real' were true, then we would expect there to be a tendency towards 'growth' and 'habit-taking' and we would expect that things would be harmonious in the world.[62] He concludes that the hypothesis 'God is real' is pragmatically legitimate. He also thinks that the hypothesis is a good explanation of the phenomenon of growth—growth of motion into displacement, and the growth of force into motion'.[63]

There is much to disagree with here. It is not at all clear what we would expect if the hypothesis 'God is real' were true, nor is it clear that we would expect what Peirce suggests. He seems to have been aware of the sogginess of his

[59] MS 842 is a 1905 draft, MS 841 is the 1908 published version (*Hibbert Journal*, 7, repr. in *CP* 6. 452 ff.), MS 843 is an undated interwoven rough draft of 841 and 842.
[60] MS 842, p. 15; MS 843, p. 70, second page from the end of the manuscript; *CP* 6. 489.
[61] *CP* 6. 490; MS 842, p. 16; MS 843, unmarked page, 105 pages from the end of the manuscript.
[62] See *CP* 6. 465; MS 842, p. 127.
[63] This, in effect, is his 'neglected argument'. We will see in Ch. 3 that this sort of inference to the best explanation is what Peirce called abduction.

argument, for each time he begins to talk about 'tracing out a few consequences of the hypothesis', he quickly changes the subject.[64] But Peirce was a stubborn theist and at the end of the 1910 'Additament' to the paper, he simply says: 'the doctrine of the *Ens necessarium* has a pragmaticist meaning, although I will not here attempt to sum up the whole of its meaning. So far as it has such meaning, it is verifiable.'[65]

Peirce's lack of success in showing how the metaphysical hypothesis 'God is real' is pragmatically legitimate is not, however, indicative of the poverty of pragmatism. Pragmatism says that if the statement 'God is real' is pragmatically legitimate, then we would expect there to be certain experiential consequences in the world. The fact that it is extremely difficult in this case to specify these consequences simply means that the hypothesis is in a precarious position. The theistic pragmatist will try to articulate expectations of the cosmological sort that Peirce envisions and there will be controversy over whether the articulation is convincing. But the pragmatist should expect difficulty in determining just what, if any, predictions fall out of highly abstract metaphysical hypotheses. The fact that Peirce's pragmatic criterion does not provide us with an effective procedure for determining the spurious from the non-spurious should not cause concern. To search for such a procedure is far too ambitious.

The moderate version of pragmatism does deliver the following substantial things. It gives us a straightforward criterion for demarcating scientific from non-scientific hypotheses. It gives us an account of the sorts of experiential consequences of mathematical and logical hypotheses. And it leaves room for metaphysical and moral hypotheses to try to qualify themselves. But, perhaps most importantly, it provides a general recommendation or methodological principle

---

[64] See, for instance, MS 842, p. 127.

[65] MS 844, last page, see also CP 6. 491, 1910. Peirce ends MS 843 with this remarkable statement (p. 71): 'But there is an important class of exceptions to the rule that nothing is deducible from the Infinite . . . we can distinguish in some respects between effects on our conduct and cognition produced by a Real God and those produced by a fictive one, among which effects is that produced by searching out and by finding the hypothesis itself.'

for the formulation of metaphysical hypotheses. That principle is that philosophers should aim to formulate their
hypotheses so that they have consequences. Wherever we
can, we ought to formulate hypotheses the truth or falsity of
which would have experiential effects. Along with this
recommendation comes a standard for evaluation and
criticism. A philosophical hypothesis is *flawed* if there is no
way its truth might make any difference in the world.

Peirce adds that we will find that the application of the
pragmatic maxim has 'wholesome effects' (*CP* 8. 210, 1905).
For if we set out the consequences of a hypothesis, we can see
how it can be useful in one practice or another. If the
consequences of H are empirical, then H may be useful in
science. If the consequences are in diagrammatic experience,
then H may be useful in purely theoretical contexts. And if
the consequences are in ordinary experience, then H may be
useful for some practice that we all engage in, such as
everyday inquiry. Thus formulating philosophical hypotheses
according to the pragmatic maxim should result in a useful
philosophy, for a 'pragmatic interpretation' of a metaphysical notion will tell us what sort of things to expect. The
pragmatic maxim holds that we ought to unpack a concept in
such a way that 'fruitful reasoning can be made to turn upon
it, and that it can be applied to the resolution of difficult
practical problems' (*CP* 3. 457, 1897).

For instance, Peirce explictly applies the pragmatic method
to the notion of a relation.[66] To specify the denotation, he
briefly connects the term with 'familiar experience' and to
specify the connotation, he defines a host of other terms and
shows how they interlock with the notion of relation. The
pragmatic grade of clearness is elucidated by developing a
system of graphs or diagrams for relations. Peirce draws an
analogy between relations and unsaturated bonds of chemical atoms. Relations are of the form '————loves————'; they
have unsaturated or incomplete parts. He develops a complex
method of graphing relations and experiments to show how
the various n-place relations are related to each other. And he
argues that a full and complete understanding of these graphs
can shed light on some problems of algebra. That is, if you

[66] See *CP* 3. 456, 1896, 'The Logic of Relatives'.

construe relations in the manner in which he suggests, there will be substantial (and beneficial) effects on reasoning. We will find that we can solve many problems which seemed intractable.[67]

So pragmatism admonishes us to accord the proper status to the consequences of a hypothesis. Its consequences are a part of what the hypothesis means and if we know something about the consequences, then we know something important about the hypothesis. The pragmatist will criticize hypotheses if they have no consequences and are thus useless for the kind of inquiry which we are engaged in (scientific, mathematical, moral, etc.). The philosopher who wants to put forward a metaphysical position must look to those practices and see what philosophical notions would be relevant for them: 'We must not begin by talking of pure ideas,—vagabond thoughts that tramp the public roads without any human habitation,—but must begin with men and their conversation'. (*CP* 8. 112, 1900.) With this rough-and-ready pragmatic method in hand, we can turn now to the notion of truth and see what, if anything, follows for it.

7. Definition, Pragmatism, and Truth

If we are to take seriously the insights which we have garnered from pragmatism, we must cultivate a sensitivity to the difference between providing a definition of a term and the less formal business of spelling out the implications of hypotheses containing the term, i.e. of providing a pragmatic elucidation of the term. For, unlike many philosophers, Peirce does not take his project to be one of definition.

He thinks that if one engages in the project of definition, the danger is that one word will be 'defined by other words, and they by still others, without any real conception ever being reached' (*CP* 5. 423, 1905, see also MS 329, 1904). This, he says, is the flaw of much of metaphysics. The pragmatic maxim, on the other hand, gets to the 'real

[67] Similarly, when Peirce wants to find out 'what does the word *probable* mean?', he says: 'Pursuing that method [the pragmatic method], we must begin by asking, what is the use of calculating probabilities?' (MS 211, undated, p. 5).

conception' by articulating the consequences of hypotheses containing the term. Thus he thinks that the pragmatic project overshadows any other.

Now the notion of what it is to give a definition is a matter of controversy. We can avoid getting embroiled in the debate and safely enough contrast a pragmatic elucidation with what might be called an 'analytic' definition. Such a definition specifies necessary and sufficient conditions for 'x is an F', where F is the term to be defined, x is a variable, and the conditions do not make essential reference to F. Thus the definition of 'brother' is formulated by a biconditional: x is a brother *if and only if* x is male and x is a sibling. Being a brother is logically equivalent to being a male sibling.

Peirce says that the problem with providing such definitions is that we might end up merely asserting the 'two words are synonymous'. And in that case, our position will be 'not a doctrine of philosophy, but only a proposition in English lexicography' (MS 330, p. 6, undated, see also CP 5. 533, 1905). He warns of this danger apropos the notion of truth. We may fail to say anything philosophically interesting if we busy ourselves with tinkering with the definition of 'true'.

There is a further danger in trying to arrive at a formal equivalence between 'H is true' and some other predicate. For the other predicate may not be pragmatically significant. In that case, our definition, Peirce, says, is a 'nominal' or 'formal' or trivial one.[68] It is this sort of definition that he is especially set against.

Peirce suggests we can avoid these empty definitions (merely analytic and/or pragmatically spurious ones) by starting with the project of specifying consequences, rather than the project of definition. Rather than begin with the specification of necessary and sufficient conditions for 'H is true', we ought to specify the consequences of 'H is true'. In doing so, we might find ourselves with some necessary conditions—but they will be substantial ones. Pragmatism will thus offer, at least in the first instance, something other than a biconditional definition of 'H is true'. A pragmatic

---

[68] Peirce refers to Kant's usage. See Kant (1781), A58. Perhaps he also had Locke in mind.

characterization of truth, Peirce thinks, will be better than 'a mere dispute about a definition', which might very well be a 'profitless discussion' (*CP* 8. 100, 1900).

So if we are to acknowledge the distinctively pragmatic character of Peirce's account of truth we must studiously avoid taking his thoughts on truth to be in direct competition with accounts of truth which focus on one of the first two aspects of understanding. An account of how to identify or pick out true hypotheses or a logical equivalence of '*H* is true' with a pragmatically empty predicate would not be in direct competition with the Peircean account. Peirce wants to absorb these two projects, for recall that he holds that definition retains all of its importance. But Peirce regards the most important thing to be said about truth to be a specification of what we can expect of a true hypothesis. Yet, since the pragmatic aspect of understanding is only one of three, we ought not to expect the properties of truth that the pragmatist determines to be an exhaustive list. A pragmatic elucidation will articulate the most salient properties, but there will be others as well.

Of course, at one level, the accounts will be in competition, for Peirce offers what he thinks is a superior way of thinking of philosophical notions such as truth. Pragmatism is opposed to positions which explicitly or implicitly maintain that the necessary and sufficient conditions for '*H* is true' are the most important things the philosopher can say about truth.

These points require careful elaboration, for they have implications for the status of Peirce's account of truth. The most illuminating way to see what Peirce is getting at here is to look at why he thinks that 'correspondence' or 'transcendental' theories of truth are inadequate.

The correspondence theory offers a definition of truth of the following sort: *H* is true if and only if *H* stands in a certain relation to a 'fact' or 'state of affairs'. Many theories parade under the correspondence banner and Peirce is happy to let one of them stand as a 'nominal' or 'formal' definition.[69] He says,

[69] Peirce does not say who he has in mind when he speaks of the correspondence theory of truth. Prior (1967) tells us that 'the origins of the word "correspondence"

So what is truth? Kant is sometimes accused of saying that it is correspondence of a predicate with its object. The great analyst was guilty of no such puerility. He calls it a nominal definition, that is to say, a suitable explanation to give to a person who has never before seen the word 'Wahrheit'. (MS 283, p. 39, 'assorted pages', 1905.)

But Peirce thinks that these definitions fail to meet the pragmatic standard; they cannot be made the centre-piece of a substantial account of truth. He makes this point about the most contentious version of the correspondence theory, the version that says that a true hypothesis is one which is in agreement with an unknowable 'thing-in-itself'. He says,

You only puzzle yourself by talking of this metaphysical 'truth' and metaphysical 'falsity' that you know nothing about. All you have any dealings with are your doubts and beliefs . . . If your terms 'truth' and 'falsity' are taken in such senses as to be definable in terms of doubt and belief and the course of experience . . . well and good: in that case, you are only talking about doubt and belief. But if by truth and falsity you mean something not definable in terms of doubt and belief in any way, then you are talking of entities of whose existence you can know nothing, and which Ockham's razor would clean shave off. Your problems would be greatly simplified, if, instead of saying that you want to know the 'Truth', you were simply to say that you want to attain a state of belief unassailable by doubt. (CP 5. 416, 1905.)

His point is that if one offered an account of '*H* is true' in terms of its consequences for doubt, belief, and experience, one would be offering a pragmatic elucidation of truth. And that, if it were a correct specification of the consequences, would be a satisfactory account of truth. But a definition of truth which makes no reference to belief, doubt, and experience is a nominal or trivial definition of truth. It is pragmatically empty and hence philosophically unsatisfactory. It is only useful to those who have never encountered the notion.

Peirce sometimes states this objection to the correspondence definition of truth by labelling it a 'transcendental'

used to denote the relation between thought and reality in which the truth of thought consists, appear to be medieval'. Peirce was extremely well versed in medieval philosophy and so he may have got his conception of the correspondence theory of truth there.

account of truth (*CP* 5. 572, 1901.) Such accounts regard truth 'as the subject of metaphysics exclusively'—spurious metaphysics, not pragmatically legitimate metaphysics. That is, on the correspondence definition, truth transcends the commonplace notions of belief, doubt, experience, and inquiry. Another kind of transcendental definition 'identifies' truth with 'the real characters of things'. Another says that truth is 'indistinguishable from reality, or real existence'; another says that it is 'conformity of things to their essential principles'. Peirce does not elaborate on these positions, but it seems that they have two distinguishing features. First, the identifications of truth with 'real characters' or correspondence to 'reality' or 'essential principles' seem to be propositions in 'English lexicography' rather than philosophical doctrines which get to the 'real conception'. For the definitions identify truth with something which itself needs definition. For instance, Peirce says Kant's definition of truth as 'the conformity of a representation to its object'

is nearly correct, so far as it is intelligible. Only, what is that 'object' which serves to define truth? Why it is the *reality*: it is of such a nature as to be independent of representations of it, so that . . . there is some character which that thing possesses, whether that sign . . . represents the thing as possessing that character or not. Very good: now only tell me what it means to say that an object possesses a character, and I shall be satisfied . . . the only meaning which we can attach to the phrase that a thing 'has a character' is that something is *true* of it . . . [We are] thrown out at that very conception of truth at which we entered . . . how futile it was to imagine that we were to clear up the idea of *truth* by the more occult idea of *reality*! (*CP* 1. 578, 1902.)

Secondly, it seems that 'real characters', 'reality', and 'essential principles' are the subjects of metaphysical inquiries which go beyond experience. The consequences of '*H* is true' are not considered in the transcendental definitions of truth. A transcendental account of truth unlinks truth from experience and inquiry.

Peirce suggests that the notion of an unknowable thing-in-itself[70] has no consequences for ordinary experience. We can

---

[70] Peirce's account of and objections to the correspondence theory vary. But he always argues that the notion of an unknowable thing-in-itself is a pragmatically

say nothing about it: 'The *Ding an sich* . . . can neither be indicated nor found. Consequently, no proposition can refer to it, and nothing true or false can be predicated of it. Therefore, all references to it must be thrown out as meaningless surplusage.' (*CP* 5. 525, 1905). The correspondence theorist cannot say that the world as it is in itself has properties *a* and *b*. So if truth is defined as correspondence with that world, no expectations can be derived from '*H* is true'. If we do not know what correspondence with the world would be like, we cannot know what to expect of hypotheses which so correspond. A theory of truth that centres around something unknowable utilizes 'ghost-like hypotheses about things-in-themselves which anybody can set up but nobody can refute' (*CP* 7. 370, 1902). Since an account of truth purports to be about the world, it must have consequences for experience—not experiences in special experimental set-ups, but experiences which we can all have. The correspondence theory does not have such consequences and thus it is spurious.

Peirce holds that because truth is the aim of inquiry, there is all the more reason to insist that our conception of truth be pragmatically legitimate, for the adoption of such a conception will have a 'wholesome effect' on inquiry. But if we look at the experience of inquirers which seems most relevant to truth—the evidence they have for and against hypotheses—the correspondence theory seems unable to say anything about it. For on that account, there is an unbridgeable gap between what we can have evidence for and the inaccessible reality: truth transcends our evidence. We could have the best possible evidence for a hypothesis and yet that hypothesis might fail to be true.

So Peirce thinks that because the correspondence theory does not tell us what we can expect of a true hypothesis, it will not be useful in inquiry. It is not capable of guiding us in our actions and deliberations.[71] If truth is the aim of inquiry,

spurious notion. See *CE* 3, 56, 1872; *CP* 6. 492, 1896; 6. 95, 1903; 5. 553, 1905; 5. 452, 1905. Some correspondence theorists make no use of the notion of a thing-in-itself. See Austin (1950).

[71] A more sustained argument for these claims is given in Chapter 4.

then on the correspondence construal, inquirers are left completely in the dark as to how they should conduct their investigations. The aim is not, Peirce says, 'readily comprehensible' (*CP* 1. 578, 1902). How could anyone aim for a sort of truth that transcends experience? How could an inquirer develop a means for achieving that aim?

In anticipation of certain kinds of naturalized epistemologies, Peirce's claim is that truth is not to be discussed in lofty transcendental terms, but rather, in the more humdrum terms of inquiry, belief, doubt, and experience.[72] For talk of something that transcends these notions is bound to be mysterious. Peirce thinks that the correspondence theorist makes 'truth' 'a useless word' (*CP* 5. 553, 1906). And 'having no use for this meaning of the word "truth", we had better use the word in another sense presently to be described' (*CP* 5. 553, 1906).

The inquirer, Peirce insists, must think of truth in the following way: 'that to which the representation should conform, is itself something in the nature of a representation, or sign—something noumenal, intelligible, conceivable, and utterly unlike a thing-in-itself'. Peirce focuses on what he thinks the transcendentalist has lost sight of—the link between truth and inquiry. Peirce's account deals with the common experience that constitutes inquiry: the ordinary notions of doubt, belief, experience, and perceptual disappointment. Thus it offers a conception of truth that can be a guide for inquiry. On Peirce's view, truth transcends experience and inquiry here and now, but it does not transcend experience and inquiry altogether: 'A true proposition is a proposition belief in which would never lead to . . . disappointment . . . ' (*CP* 5. 569, 1901).

[72] Peirce's epistemology, however, is not naturalized in other senses of the term. It is not the naturalized epistemology of Goldman (1979) and Armstrong (1973) which has it that knowledge should be analysed as a causal relation between a belief and the world. Nor is it Churchland's (1979) which has it that knowledge is a product of physiological systems that have, through natural selection, proved viable. Nor is Peirce a naturalist in the sense that he holds that the natural sciences, or theories about the nature of spatio-temporal things, will have the last word. Inquiry will, he thinks, have the last word, but inquiry goes beyond the observable and the spatio-temporal. Nor does Peirce adopt the Quinean position that epistemology is simply a branch of the natural sciences—something like neurophysiology or psychology.

This is an account of what we can expect from a true belief. An expectation is expressed by a subjunctive conditional: if *H* is true, then we would expect that if you were to do *x*, *y* would result. Peirce suggests that we would expect the following if *H* is true: if we were to inquire into *H*, we would find that *H* would encounter no recalcitrant experience.[73] We can predict that if we were diligently to inquire about *H*, *H* would not, in the end, be overturned by experience. An alternative way of making the point is to say that we would expect the following: if inquiry with respect to *H* were to be pursued as far as it could fruitfully go (i.e. far enough so that the hypothesis would no longer be improved upon), *H* would be believed (it would not be doubted).[74] For if *H* would be believed after such a prolonged inquiry, then *H* would not have been overturned by experience; it would not have been put into doubt. A true belief is a permanently settled belief. Notice that a true hypothesis may be believed, then doubted, then believed again. A true hypothesis or a permanently settled belief is simply one that *would be*, at the hypothetical end of inquiry, settled.

So a pragmatic elucidation of truth is neither a definition nor a criterion of truth. It is a specification of what one can expect of a true hypothesis. That is, a pragmatic elucidation aspires to do in a different way what an analytic definition does. An analytic definition will, in a sense, tell us what to expect of a true hypothesis, for '*H* is true' will be locked into a set of entailment relations with some other property, such as '*H* corresponds to the world'. So we can expect that if *H* is true, it corresponds to the world. But the pragmatist is interested in a different kind of expectation. The expectation must be pragmatically significant—it must really lead us to expect something of the course of experience.

Thus Peirce is not simply putting forward an equivalence of the form: '*H* is true if and only if it would be believed at the end of a prolonged inquiry'. This biconditional may epitomize Peirce's account of truth. But it is a misunderstanding of the doctrine which this formula represents to treat the

---

[73] At least, it would encounter little or negligible recalcitrant experience.
[74] See *CP* 2. 775, 1901; 3. 432, 1896; 5. 430, 1905; 5. 494, 1907; 8. 41, 1885; 2. 29, 1902, for statements of Peirce's account of truth.

epitome as an analytic definition of truth. The difference, however subtle, is substantial. For one thing, because Peirce does not begin with the equivalence, the two conditionals are in principle detachable. One can be held without the other. And one can have a different status than the other. We must take a careful look at each of the conditionals in the purported Peircean biconditional. One is the left-to-right conditional, which I shall refer to as the T–I conditional (truth to inquiry). It is: '*if H* is true *then* if inquiry relevant to *H* were pursued as far as it could fruitfully go, *H* would be believed'. We have seen that what Peirce is after is a specification of what we would expect of '*H* is true' and the T–I conditional is his suggestion.

One thing to notice is that the consequent of the T–I conditional is a prediction or expectation which is articulated by a subjunctive conditional. T–I is not part of an equivalence which is entirely in the indicative mood. A definition of truth such as the correspondence definition sets up a formal equivalence in the indicative mood—it says that '*H* is true if and only if it corresponds to reality'. Although part of T–I is in the indicative mood ('If *H* *is* true'), the right-hand side is in the subjunctive mood ('then, *were* inquiry to be pursued as far as it could fruitfully go, *H would* be believed').

But the most important difference between T–I and the transcendentalist's claim 'if *H* is true, then it gets *x* right' (where *x* is 'the world', 'essential principles', etc.) is that T–I has an unusual status. We shall see in Chapters 2 and 4 that it is not an assertion, but a hope. It is not put forward as a true statement but as a regulative assumption of inquiry.

Notice that the right-to-left conditional, hereafter I–T (inquiry to truth), certainly does not follow from a specification of the consequences of '*H* is true'. It does not follow that: *if*, if inquiry were to be pursued, then *H* would be believed, *then H* is true. Independent argument, if it is desired, is needed. We shall see, again in Chapters 2 and 4, that Peirce does provide independent argument. First, he argues that *the inquirer* ought to think that truth is the property of those beliefs which would never be overturned by experience. And then he suggests that one's pragmatic scruples ought to lead one to think that the best philosophical account of truth is the account that is useful in inquiry and deliberation.

We shall see that he also puts forward the following argument. If *H* would be overturned by experience, then we would doubt it, but as long as it survives potentially falsifying tests, we believe it. If *H* would pass all such tests in an indefinitely pursued inquiry, then, he argues, *that is all we could ask of it*. Truth is the property of hypotheses that would be believed if inquiry were pursued as far as it could fruitfully go. To suggest that there is more to truth than that is to abandon the pragmatic methodology in favour of transcendental metaphysics.

In both arguments, it is pragmatism that warns us not to add anything spurious to our conception of truth. If we want our conception of truth to be pragmatically legitimate, we must see that there is nothing in the notion of truth over and above what can be squeezed out of the notion of inquiry. Whatever the transcendentalist adds will be a piece of 'metaphysical surplusage'.

These arguments will be elaborated in Chapter 4. The point here is that Peirce does assert the I–T conditional; he argues that truth is the property of permanently settled belief. So in one well-understood sense, he does offer a 'definition' of truth. Truth is that feature belonging to all beliefs that are as good as they can be; beliefs that would be permanently settled upon or 'indefeasible' (*CP* 6. 485, 1908). The sense in which Peirce's account of truth is not a definition is that it is not a logical equivalence between truth and permanently settled belief. It would be against the spirit of his position to take him to be providing such a definition, for we have seen that he objects to that conception of philosophy—such definitions are often just a shuffle of words and pragmatically empty. And it is against the letter of his position as well. For whatever Peirce thinks about the virtues and vices of providing such equivalences, he does not in fact offer one. One of the conditionals in the purported biconditional is put forward as a hope or a regulative assumption of inquiry.

But there is much to do before this account of the relationship between truth and inquiry can begin to cohere with the inquirer's commonsense conception of truth. Each of Peirce's two conditionals seems, at first glance, to clash with what we think truth is like. To understand Peirce's claims, it is necessary to place them in the context of his doctrine of inquiry. It needs to be asked what is so special about inquiry that it has this relation to truth. How is it that inquiry can give us what we want? How is it that inquiry can give us permanently doubt-resistant beliefs? And how can we accept that a belief's permanent resistance to doubt is enough?

2

Inquiry: The Fixation of Belief

Introduction

Peirce's task is to elucidate the notion of truth by spelling out its relation to inquiry. He begins, however, with a claim that is on the surface extremely unappealing—it seems that no inquirer should adopt it. He insists that 'the sole aim of inquiry' is to settle belief and that a belief that would be permanently settled upon is true. An objection is immediately sparked, which Peirce himself took very seriously. It seems to follow that if a totalitarian state or religion were successful in settling a belief permanently, then that belief would be true by virtue of its being settled upon. Similarly, if there were a pill that would forever freeze our beliefs, then it seems that Peirce must say that those beliefs would be true and that choosing to settle your beliefs in this way would be a good methodology.[1]

That is, Peirce's conditional I–T (*if*, if inquiry relevant to H were to be pursued as far as it could fruitfully go, then H would be believed, *then* H is true) is exposed to a family of objections. Inquiry may be pursued and belief may be settled in ways that would not, we want to say, guarantee the truth of what is believed. Although Peirce's explicit response to these difficulties is not satisfactory, we can find in his work the outlines of an interesting and convincing response. I shall argue that the adoption of specious methods such as the ones mentioned above is inconsistent with the fulfilment of the antecedent of the I–T conditional. Those methods do not settle the propositional attitude we call belief and they are not genuine methods of inquiry. Thus Peirce's position is that the aim of inquiry is to settle belief permanently, but not just any method can do this. If a method of genuine inquiry does

---

[1] Frankfurt (1958) puts forward this sort of objection to Peirce's account of truth.

permanently fix genuine belief, then it fixes something worthy of our aim. Once it is interpreted correctly, Peirce's account of inquiry and its aim is uncontentious. We shall see that it has a sane empiricism at its core: inquirers, whatever else they might aim for, aim to get beliefs that fit with experience, broadly construed. When we replace a belief (or a bit of our web of belief) which has come into doubt, the new belief is probably a better one. It stands up better than the old one. So we accept it, act on it, and think that it is true. But we know very well that it eventually might be overthrown and shown to be false. Peirce adds the more contentious claim that what we aim for is permanently settled beliefs. When we have beliefs that would forever withstand the tests of experience and argument, what is the point of refusing to confer upon them the title 'true'? The pragmatist says that there is no point at all—only a spurious desire for transcendental metaphysics.

1. The Theory of Inquiry

The notion of inquiry occupies a central place in Peirce's thought: 'From the moment when I could think at all, until now, about forty years, I have been diligently and incessantly occupied with the study of methods [of] inquiry, both those which have been and are pursued and those which ought to be pursued.' (*CP* 1. 3, 1897.) Because he made numerous and significant contributions to science and mathematics,[2] he was well placed to undertake this study. His scientific training surely must have played a part in his insistence that the following motto 'deserves to be inscribed upon every wall of the city of philosophy: Do not block the path of inquiry.'[3]

Peirce characterizes inquiry as the struggle to rid ourselves of doubt and achieve a state of belief. An inquirer has a body of settled belief; a set of beliefs which are, in fact, not doubted. Beliefs in this body, however, are susceptible to

---

[2] See Fisch (1982), Lenzen (1964), and *CP* 1. 175, 1897.

[3] *CP* 1. 135, 1899, see also 7. 480, 1898. The conception of inquiry which I sketch was first put forward by Peirce in the 1870s and, as my citations will indicate, approved in the 1900s. See *CP* 5. 563, 1906.

doubt, if it is prompted by some 'positive reason', such as a surprising experience.[4] We have seen that Peirce takes experience to be that which impinges upon us—experience, he says, teaches us 'by practical jokes, mostly cruel' (*CP* 5. 51, 1903). When experience conflicts with an inquirer's belief (or with some part of her interconnected corpus of belief), she is immediately thrown into doubt.[5] And doubt 'essentially involves a struggle to escape' (*CP* 5. 372 n. 2, 1893). Inquiry is that struggle to regain belief.

Peirce does not take these points merely to be observations about human psychology; he thinks that psychology should be kept out of logic and the theory of inquiry. He adopts Alexander Bain's conception of belief—belief is a habit or disposition to act in a particular way in appropriate circumstances.[6] Doubt and belief, although they do have psychological aspects, such as making the inquirer feel comfortable or uncomfortable, are best thought of in terms of habits. A 'belief-habit' manifests itself in an expectation: if we believe *H*, then we habitually expect the consequences or the predictions we derive from *H* to come about when the appropriate occasion arises. Thus inquirers are thrown into doubt when a recalcitrant experience upsets or disrupts the smooth working of a belief or expectation. (See *CP* 5. 569, 1901.) As soon as the inquirer is thrown into doubt, inquiry

---

[4] See *CP* 5. 51, 1903; 5. 512, 1905; 5. 57, 1903. Peirce insists that recalcitrant experience is the primary motivation for doubt, but he often mentions other things that can cause doubt, such as the contrary opinions of others, curiosity, and 'feigned hesitancy' (imagining that you doubt something and noticing the consequences). See *CP* 4. 77, 1893; 5. 373 n. 3, 1877; 7. 58, 1902. These other motivations, however, can be seen to be connected to experience. We are motivated by the fact that there are potential experiences which we can imagine, or which others say that they have had, such that if we had them, they would put a belief into doubt.

[5] Davidson (1983) and Popper (1959) would argue that the thought that beliefs cohere or conflict with experience is problematic. For the causal and logical relations between beliefs and experience are not at all clear. It seems that the only things that beliefs can cohere or conflict with are other beliefs. But Peirce, it seems, does not owe us an account of the logical relationship between belief and experience. His position is not that experiences *justify* beliefs—beliefs simply do resign in the face of experience which we take them to be in conflict with. For his account of the causal relationship, see section 5 of this chapter.

[6] See *CE* 3, 247, 1877, 'The Fixation of Belief'; *CE* 3, 263, 1878, 'How to Make Our Ideas Clear'; 5. 12, 1907; 8. 270, 1902; 5. 542, 1902; 8. 294, 1904; and Bain (1859), pp. 568 ff. For a good discussion of Peirce and Bain, see Haack (1982) and Fisch (1954). For more recent accounts of belief as a disposition, see Braithwaite (1932) and (1946), Ryle (1949), and Levi and Morgenbesser (1964).

is ignited and continues until a belief or habit of expectation is re-established. So Peirce characterizes the path of inquiry as follows: belief —surprise—doubt—inquiry—belief. On this conception of inquiry, only pragmatically legitimate hypotheses can be the subject of an inquiry. Our beliefs must manifest themselves in a set of expectations or predictions. If they do not, then we cannot inquire whether expectations are upheld or knocked down by experience, broadly construed. [7] So only with respect to pragmatically significant hypotheses will there be the possibility of surprise initiating an inquiry.

There are three stances an inquirer may have with respect to a hypothesis: believe it, believe its negation, or consider the matter open to inquiry. Only in the third stance are we left without a habit of expectation and thus it is agnosticism which is the undesirable state. That is, doubting whether H is not equivalent to believing $-H$, rather, it is not knowing what to believe about H.[8] What is wrong with this state is not that it is psychologically uncomfortable, but that it leads to paralysis of action. An inquirer has some end in view, and two different and inconsistent lines of action present themselves, bringing action to a halt: 'he waits at the fork for an indication, and kicks his heels . . . A true doubt is accordingly a doubt which really interferes with the smooth working of the belief-habit.' (*CP* 5. 510, 1905.) Doubt arises because of not knowing how to act. And action can include action in diagrammatic and thought experiments.

[7] It is tempting to say (as I sometimes do) that recalcitrant experience falsifies a hypothesis, and at times Peirce does suggest this. (See *CP* 5. 569, 1901.) But what recalcitrant experience does is put the inquirer into doubt. If H is in our body of settled belief and we are surprised by the shock of an experience of something incompatible with H (or incompatible with H's deductive consequences, or even something we think is incompatible with either), then we will doubt H.

[8] Peirce also distinguishes the following: (*a*) having no opinion as to whether H and (*b*) being in a state of doubt as to whether H. 'There is something further removed from belief than doubt, that is to say not to conceive the proposition at all . . . pure unconscious ignorance alone . . . is the true contrary of belief' (*CE* 3, 21, 1872). 'Doubt is not the same as ignorance, nor as the consciousness of being ignorant; for if one does not care to know, one cannot be said to be in doubt.' (*MS* 828, p. 1, 1910.) Peirce is not concerned with this attitude of 'calm ignorance' (see *MS* 334, p. marked 'C', undated). Also, if we speak strictly, it is not 'not believing' that is undesirable, but 'believing, then not believing'. That is, Peircean doubt is the interruption of a habit rather than simply not having a habit.

Peirce's 'critical commonsensism' is a position about how we ought to regard those beliefs which are settled upon. It holds that there are many things which inquirers do not doubt and that inquiry must start with a background of beliefs which are not doubted.[9] A body of settled belief is presupposed for the operation of inquiry in that there has to be something settled for surprise to stir up. We should not pretend to doubt hypotheses which we find compelling.

The doctrine of critical commonsensism arose as a response to Peirce's conception of Descartes's project—a systematic attempt to bring into doubt all hypotheses about which error is conceivable. Peirce argued that such doubts would be 'paper' or 'tin' doubts (MS 329, p. 12, 1904). They are not genuine and they cannot motivate inquiry. The mere possibility of being mistaken with respect to what one believes is never a reason to revise those beliefs. Any of our beliefs might be false, but it would be absurd to doubt them all because of this. If we did, we would not possess a body of stable belief by which to judge new evidence and hypotheses, and hence we would block the path of inquiry. We can doubt one belief and inquire, but we cannot doubt all of our beliefs and inquire. Peirce's point against Descartes is that if we were to set the requirements on knowledge as high as Descartes does, we would have nothing left to go on. He says,

there is but one state of mind from which you can 'set out', namely, the very state of mind in which you actually find yourself at the time you do 'set out'—a state in which you are laden with an immense mass of cognition already formed, of which you cannot divest yourself if you would . . . Do you call it doubting to write down on a piece of paper that you doubt? If so, doubt has nothing to do with any serious business . . . there is much that you do not doubt, in the

---

[9] Peirce sometimes says that there is a list of (relatively fixed) beliefs which are not doubted for all inquirers. See *CP* 5. 498, 1905. But he also says that critical commonsensism 'is the doctrine that there are quite indubitable beliefs. In the form in which I have held the doctrine, ever since I have trusted to my own wings in philosophy, it does not necessarily imply that there is any fixed collection of beliefs that are the same for all men . . . '. (MS 290, p. 3, 1905, 'Issues of Pragmaticism'.) Critical commonsensism is a consistent feature of Peirce's philosophy. See *CE* 2, 212, 1868; 5. 439, 1905. This picture of inquiry, knowledge, and truth has recently attracted advocates, although many do not realize the Peircean origins of the position. See, for instance, Shapere (1979), Forrest (1985), Shimony (1987), Levi (1983). See Misak (1987) for a discussion of Peirce and Levi.

least. Now that which you do not at all doubt, you must and do regard as infallible, absolute truth. (*CP* 5. 416, 1905.)

Our body of background beliefs, by virtue of being our beliefs, exerts some force on us. It takes an even stronger force—that of external or internal experience—to upset them. Peirce says:

He [the inquirer] is under a compulsion to believe just what he does believe . . . as time goes on, the man's belief usually changes in a manner which he cannot resist . . . the force which changes a man's belief [is] . . . in all cases, called a *gain of experience*. This will be to take the word experience in a much wider sense than usual, so as to include effects of reflection, forgetfulness, passion, etc. (MS 1342; undated, see also *CP* 1. 129, 1905.)

Another feature of critical commonsensism is that, just as we should not doubt that 2+2=4 or that the earth is round, we should not doubt our philosophical convictions. The standard for acceptance or belief should be set at the same level for philosophical inquiries as it is for other sorts. He says:

I am neither addressing absolute sceptics, nor men in any state of fictitious doubt whatever. I require the reader to be candid; and if he becomes convinced of a conclusion, to admit it . . . If you, the reader, actually find that my arguments have a convincing force with you, it is a mere pretence to call them illogical. (*CE* 2, 243, 1869; see also MS 329, p. 9, 1904.)

Peirce is not concerned with sceptical questions about foundations for certainty and his arguments are not addressed to those who are. For he is also a 'contrite fallibilist', holding that all our beliefs can be doubted; that is, that none of them are certain. Our body of fallible background beliefs is not, and cannot be, doubted, and hence the sceptical abyss that has us doubting each of our beliefs is not a matter of serious concern. The fact that there can be no proof that any belief is absolutely true is something to be taken for granted and should not cause anxiety.

So Peirce would invoke his critical commonsensism to respond to certain philosophers who will deny his claim that if a hypothesis never would be overthrown by inquiry then it is true. Such a philosopher will think that some mere possibility is a serious one.[10] She may think that there might be someone or something who fixes it so that experience can be entirely supportive of a false hypothesis. The newest version of this old story is that we might be brains in a vat, with some evil and clever neuroscientist making us 'see' trees and houses where there really aren't any there. Or perhaps the possibility which is being taken seriously is that our theories survive the test of experience by mere fluke—a highly unlikely arrangement of the universe 'fools' us into thinking that our beliefs are by and large correct because they fit with experience.

But critical commonsensism is set against taking such possibilities for more than what they are—paper doubts. The philosopher concerned with bare possibilities and with the sort of scepticism that arises from taking them seriously will find no solace in Peirce's philosophy.

There is an apparent tension between fallibilism and critical commonsensism: how can it be that all our beliefs are fallible, or subject to doubt, but nevertheless some of our beliefs must not be doubted if inquiry is to be possible? The tension arises because Peirce is not always careful with the term 'infallible' and because he makes numerous conflicting remarks over the span of his career. But the tension can be resolved.[11]

In the context of his critical commonsensism, he uses 'infallible' to make the point that we do not doubt what we believe. But by 'infallibilism' he means the position which is opposed to his own fallibilism; the position that our beliefs (or at least some of them) are incorrigible, or not the sort of things that are ever in need of revision. And Peirce insists that an inquirer must 'be at all times ready to dump his whole cartload of beliefs, the moment experience is set against them' (*CP* 1. 55, 1896). He cannot have 'any such immovable beliefs to which he regards himself as religiously bound to be loyal' (*CP* 6. 3, 1898). Such an attitude would block the path of inquiry because our minds would be closed, and hence we would never be motivated enough to inquire.[12]

---

[10]   The terminology here is Levi's (1983, 1984*b*). See also Misak (1987).

[11]   Levi (1983) disagrees.

[12]   Peirce intends these last remarks to apply to scientific inquirers, as opposed to those engaged in practical or 'vital' matters. He argues that hypotheses in science

One of Peirce's reasons for endorsing fallibilism is the fact that our faculties sometimes fail us, and we cannot be sure when these failures occur.[13] He asks if you would repeatedly make this sort of bet: your life[14] against a penny on the truth of some statement which you do not, in fact, doubt. We can see how we would be hesitant to make these bets with respect to most empirical statements, and Peirce extends this hesitancy to statements about perceptions and mathematics. Even the greatest mathematicians, he notes, are susceptible to make the simplest mistakes in arithmetic—all it takes is a little lapse of attention. And so no rational person would make these kinds of bets on the truth of statements which she does not, in fact, doubt: 'You certainly ought not to do so; for you could not go on making very many millions of such bets before you would lose!' (*CP* 1. 150, 1897.)

Peirce's reconciliation of fallibilism with critical common-sensism is made in terms of his notion of truth. He thinks that many of our beliefs are indeed those which would be included in the final opinion,[15] but since we cannot know for any given belief whether or not *it* would be in that opinion, we cannot know that it is true. That is, we do not know if the antecedent of this subjunctive conditional is fulfilled: 'if inquiry were pursued as far as it could fruitfully go, then *H* would be believed'. Inquiry may or may not have been pursued far enough with respect to *H*, and so we cannot have certainty with respect to any belief. The final opinion does not glow in the dark.

But the uncertainty or fallibility that in principle accompanies every one of our beliefs does not entail that we

ought not to be believed or accepted; they merely must be held provisionally. I suggest that we close the gap that Peirce saw between science and practice and regard his remarks in the following light. He thought that scientists, to avoid being 'cocksure' and blocking the path of inquiry, must be always aware of the provisional or fallible status of their beliefs. The practical inquirer, on the other hand, needs something to go upon immediately, and so must emphasize the indubitability of her beliefs. The actor in practical affairs must emphasize the critical commonsensist aspect of inquiry and the scientist must first and foremost be a fallibilist.

[13] For other reasons, see *CP* 4. 105, 1893; 1. 55, 1896; 1. 136, 1899; 1. 145, 1897; 6. 13, 1891; 1. 132, 1893; 1. 402, 1890. The argument I give in the text is the only one Peirce offers for the fallibility of mathematical statements; they are fallible only because of the possibility of the failure of the agent. See MS 335, undated.

[14] Peirce's version has a very wealthy man betting his fortune against a penny. See MS 329, p. 13, 1904, for a claim that a man *would* bet his life on such propositions.

[15] See *CE* 2, 239, 1868; *CP* 5. 172, 1903; 5. 494, 1907; 8. 43, 1885.

doubt our settled beliefs. 'Practically speaking', he says, many things are 'substantially certain' (*CP* 1. 152, 1897); we do not doubt them. While 'it is possible that twice two is not four . . . it would be difficult to imagine a greater folly than to attach any serious importance to such a doubt' (*CP* 7. 108, 1910). But substantial certainty is different from the 'absolute certainty' which would result from knowing that we have permanently settled belief. Peirce notes that we may have this settled opinion about many questions, but we must not infer from this that we 'perfectly know when we know'. Again, we cannot know that any given hypothesis is permanently settled upon or true—we cannot have absolute certainty. Nevertheless, in every state of intellectual development and information, there are things that seem to us sure, 'so that even though we tell ourselves that we are not sure, we cannot clearly see how we fail of being so' (*CP* 4. 64, 1893). Practically, we must treat some hypotheses as certain.[16]

Later, Peirce puts the distinction in terms of the hypothetical final community. 'Absolute truth' would be the settled belief of the final community of inquirers, and 'indubitable propositions' are the settled opinions of inquirers here and now. No individual can be absolutely certain with respect to any hypothesis, as she does not have the verdict of the final community. Since we cannot know whether a hypothesis would withstand further inquiry, human knowledge is fallible. All we can have is rational belief; the best belief given the available evidence. We cannot know if we have the truth with respect to any question, for the truth would be the best belief given the available evidence, were it all to be available. And we cannot always know if we are missing significant evidence. Yet the inquirer must regard her settled beliefs as infallible, in the sense that she does not doubt them for the purposes of inquiry; science has 'established truths' to be used as premises in further deliberation.[17] In this sense, we do not doubt what we believe, but in another sense, each of our beliefs can, or could be, doubted.

On Peirce's account, then, there are two kinds of certainty; a practical or substantial one which we can have (indubit-

---

16 *CP* 1. 633, 1898; see also 2. 75, 1902; 2. 192, 1902.
17 See *CP* 1. 635, 1898; 5. 589, 1898.

ability), and an absolute or abstract one which we cannot (infallibility). He sums up his position:

> It is quite true that [what] one cannot doubt today one may be able to doubt tomorrow and the day after may be compelled to deny . . . but nevertheless, if one deliberately finds himself unable to doubt a proposition, then as long as he is in this condition he should regard it as absolutely certain except so far as this certainty is modified by his general sense of human fallibility. (MS 329, p. 12, 1904.)

2. Peirce's Argument against Specious Methods

An important feature of Peirce's theory of inquiry is that the 'sole object of inquiry' is the settlement of belief:

> We may fancy that this is not enough for us, and that we seek, not merely an opinion, but a true opinion. But put this fancy to the test, and it proves groundless; for as soon as a firm belief is reached we are entirely satisfied, whether the belief be true or false. (CE 3, 248, 1877; see also CE 3, 24, 1872; CE 2, 354, 1869; CP 6. 498, 1906.)

On the surface, this is an embarrassing view. Peirce seems to think that any permanently settled upon belief would be true, no matter how it came to be settled. He says:

> it is a consensus of common confession which constitutes reality. What he [the inquirer] wants, therefore, is to see questions put to rest. And if a general belief, which is perfectly stable and immovable, can in any way be produced, though it be by the fagot and the rack, to talk of any error in such belief is utterly absurd. (CE 2, 471, 1871.)

Peirce realizes that these claims will seem wild.[18] No acceptable account of truth can hold that beliefs permanently settled by torture are true by virtue of their settledness. Surely we aim for more than stubborn or immovable belief. And if we were to get a stubborn belief by adopting a specious method, then those beliefs would not be true simply by virtue

---

[18] It should be clear that the apparent wildness is not due to the assertion that settlement here and now is a criterion of truth. On Peirce's view, neither the strongest intensity in a belief nor total consensus here and now guarantees truth. To the objection 'What! Do you mean to say that . . . what a man does not doubt is *ipso facto* true?' Peirce gives this critical commonsensist response: 'No, but . . . *he* has to regard what he does not doubt as absolutely true.' (CP 4. 416, 1905.)

of being stubborn. What if a totalitarian state, a religion, or the faggot and rack were successful in settling belief permanently—would this belief be true?

Peirce answers 'yes', but argues that such methods are in fact *unable* to settle belief permanently. His argument, which can be found in the 1877 'The Fixation of Belief',[19] is that the only method that is able to result in true beliefs is the method that, prima facie, we want to affirm—the method of science and reasoning. That is, true beliefs are not 'merely' going to be permanently settled upon. They would in fact be settled in a way which we all think is admirable.

This is not the first answer that comes to mind to the question 'Why don't beliefs permanently fixed by torture or propaganda deserve to be called true?'. The first answer we think of is that some methods are intrinsically bad ones for producing what we call 'rational belief'. We want to invoke some prior conception of rationality, and rule out beliefs produced by the specious methods with that notion. Similarly, the first answer that comes to mind to the question 'What is wrong with an inquirer who chooses a specious method of inquiry?' is that such a person would not be rational or would not be a sincere seeker of the truth.

But Peirce does not want to appeal to such normative notions; he must keep his account of truth naturalized. Methods of inquiry should be judged in terms of how well they promote the aim of inquiry; the only normativity Peirce is willing to countenance in evaluating methods of inquiry is that the means ought to promote the end. He says 'Any kind of goodness is the adaptation of its subject to its end . . . I do not know that we shall find a more succinct statement of the principle of pragmatism than this.' (MS 313, p. 11, 1903.) The point is that Peirce refuses to construe the aim or end of inquiry as the acquisition of right, correct, or rational beliefs.[20] And since he holds that the aim of inquiry is the

---

[19] See CE 3, 242. Peirce intended the 'Fixation of Belief' to comprise chapters of his later works: 'Search for a Method' (1893), 'How to Reason' (1894) (see MS 399, 1893), and 'Studies in Meaning or Essays Toward the Interpretation of Our Thoughts: My Pragmatism' (1909) (see MS 620, 1909). The paper was drafted many times, and in my reconstruction, I rely on those drafts as well. The earlier drafts can be found in CE 3. A later 1893 draft can be found at MS 407.

[20] When he says that the aim of inquiry is the truth, he means truth as he conceives it: permanently settled belief.

settlement of belief, he is right to insist that he can appeal only to efficiency in that regard to judge methods of inquiry. He notes that the method of 'tenacity'—holding on to your present beliefs come what may—is 'utterly irrational; that is to say it is foolish from the point of view of those who do reason. But to assume that point of view is to beg the question.' (*CE* 3, 15, 1872.)

So the problem which faces Peirce is that if a specious method of inquiry fixed beliefs in such a way that they were permanently resistant to doubt, there seems to be, on his account, no reason for criticizing it. Peirce considers four methods of fixing belief and suggests that it is hard *really* to end the irritation of doubt. We would want to call three of the four specious.[21]

The first is the method of tenacity, or holding on to your beliefs come what may. It will not work, Peirce says, because doubt will be sparked when one notices that the opinions of others differ from one's own. Secondly, beliefs produced by an authority (for example, a state or religion) will similarly be subject to doubt when one notices that those in other states or religions believe different things. Beliefs produced by the third, a priori method—adopting beliefs which are agreeable to reason—will eventually be doubted when it is seen that what the experts take as being agreeable to reason shifts like a pendulum and is really a matter of intellectual taste. None of these methods will produce permanently settled belief because they have a self-destructive design; the beliefs settled by them eventually would be assailed by doubt.[22]

The agent of destruction which Peirce sees in each of the specious methods seems to be a purported fact about our psychological make-up: if an inquirer believes H, and notices that other inquirers believe $-H$, that first inquirer will doubt H. This impulse, Peirce says, is 'too strong in man to be suppressed, without danger of destroying the human species' (*CE* 3, 250, 1877). If this psychological hypothesis expresses a universal fact about us, then the unsatisfactory methods will indeed prove unreliable in the long run. They will not produce permanently settled belief and we should refrain from using them.

---

[21] The fourth is the scientific method.
[22] See also *CP* 2. 160, 1902; *CE* 3, 17, 1872.

Peirce goes some way to making the psychological hypothesis plausible by suggesting that, because inquirers are members of a community,[23] they utilize the results of other members. An inquirer sees that others say that they have had experiences which he might have had and which, if he had them, would have thrown him into doubt. Peirce says: 'the inquirer more or less vaguely identifies himself in sentiment with a Community of which he is a member . . . and he speaks of the resultant cognitive compulsions of the course of life of that community as Our Experience' (*CP* 8. 118, 1900). We are so accustomed to utilizing these second-hand experiences that we think that 'one man's experience is nothing, if it stands alone. If he sees what others cannot, we call it hallucination.' (*CP* 5. 402 n. 2, 1893; see also *CE* 3, 25, 1872.)

But this argument does not suffice to rule out the specious methods.[24] Not only is the psychological hypothesis false, but even if it were true, it would not be effective. For judgements of the competence of others are always made relative to a body of background beliefs. Communities which have their beliefs settled by a religious authority, or by a charismatic guru, or by astrology, may adopt the principle 'doubt what competent others doubt', but those who do not believe what the pope, the guru, or the astrological charts dictate will be judged incompetent. If the community is homogeneous enough, the psychological principle will never be put into action so as to topple the method of authority. Some methods seem well equipped to insulate themselves from the effects of contrary opinions.

Peirce needs, in order to preserve both the naturalism and the plausibility of his account of truth, a way of ruling out specious methods without begging the question. He needs to tell us why the products of specious methods would not be true and what is wrong with using them. I suggest that he provides the materials for such an argument.

---

[23] Peirce thought that the community at least included all human inquirers. Sometimes he says that the community 'may be wider than man': *CE* 2, 271, 1869; see also *CE* 3, 274, 1878; *CP* 8. 43, 1885; 6. 501, 1906; MS 596, 1900.

[24] Notice also that the fact that there is controversy in science would seem to make the method of science succumb to Peirce's psychological hypothesis as well. The 'results' of science are not unanimously believed among scientists.

3. Belief and Inquiry

The problem with Peirce's construal of the aim of inquiry (as the settlement of belief) is that it seems to suggest that an inquiry is anything that makes a hypothesis stick in an inquirer's head and a belief is anything that sticks. And since he holds that hypotheses that would be believed at the end of inquiry would be true, what is true seems to depend on what methods are efficient in making hypotheses stick. But if we take the notion of fixing belief seriously, then it becomes clear that the specious methods are not methods of fixing belief. They might fix some other mental state, but only the method of science and reasoning can fix genuine belief.

Some methods, such as torture, clearly aim not at making people believe a certain hypothesis, but rather at making them decide to assent to it or say that they believe it. Other methods, such as brainwashing and authority, do, at first glance, seem to aim at getting people to believe, as opposed to merely saying that they believe. But the emphasis is on achieving a certain predetermined state in people. It is not an attempt to get people to decide where the weight of evidence lies. And genuine belief, I suggest, must be sensitive to evidence or experience, broadly construed. [25]

We have seen that Peirce holds that the very notion of belief is such that an inquirer stops believing (i.e. she doubts) in the face of a surprising experience that upsets an expectation produced by the belief. Beliefs automatically resign in the face of recalcitrant experience. We can expand on Peirce's point and argue that the psychological reality of belief, as opposed to some other mental state such as choosing arbitrarily what to 'believe', saying that one believes, or lying about what one believes, is such that belief must be sensitive to experience. It must be sensitive to empirical experience and to experience in diagrammatic, argumentative, and theoretical contexts. In short, it must respond to evidence. If an inquirer says that she is going to believe *H*, irrespective of what the evidence is or may turn out to be, she is mistaken in thinking that her propositional

---

[25] See Wiggins (1987), pp. 341–4, for this point. Both he and Susan Haack have emphasized it in discussion.

attitude is one of belief. There is a distinction between deciding that the evidence favours *H* and thereby believing *H*, and deciding to believe *H*, irrespective of evidence. It is not at all clear that, given what belief is, the latter is possible.[26] Notice that an inquirer can decide to believe the results of a certain process or routine and that this can be a way of fixing genuine belief.[27] For instance, she can decide to believe what her senses and certain experts tell her. But in such cases, she is not deciding to believe a hypothesis irrespective of the evidence, for the decision is a prior decision to believe hypotheses that are the results of certain routines. And the decision will be taken because the inquirer thinks that these routines are sensitive to the evidence. That is, when an inquirer decides to adopt such a strategy, she will have reasons for the adoption. Experts, her senses, or perhaps the astrological charts or the guru have proved, she thinks, reliable in the past; she thinks that these authorities have access to evidence, argument, or insight that lend weight to their judgements. The distinction between thinking that the evidence favours *H* and 'deciding to believe' *H* is maintained. For in deciding to trust the astrologer, the inquirer (perhaps mistakenly) is deciding to go with a method which she thinks will result in hypotheses which would fit with and respond to the evidence. She is not making a decision to believe a hypothesis irrespective of the evidence. If, on the other hand, I tried to get myself to believe something by flipping a coin, I would find myself unable to do so. I might, through psychological trickery, deceive myself into thinking I had the appropriate mental state. But it would not be belief.

So, given that a belief, in order to be a belief, must be sensitive to evidence for and against it, the aim of inquiry, on Peirce's account, is to get beliefs which are not merely fixed, but which are fixed in such a way that they fit with and respond to the evidence. The aim is not to fix a hypothesis in the mind of an inquirer so that the hypothesis is not doubted. Rather, the aim is to fix genuine beliefs which would not

---

[26] The oddity of the phrase 'deciding to believe *H*' is the oddity of what is in question. See Williams (1973) for a discussion of whether we can decide to believe something.

[27] For the notion of a routine expansion strategy, see Levi (1983) and (1984*b*).

encounter recalcitrant experience. If an inquirer adopts a routine which is sensitive to the evidence and which has a high degree of success, then she is promoting the aim of inquiry. She will acquire beliefs for which there is no recalcitrant experience. If the inquirer adopts a routine which does not respond to experience or which has a low degree of success, then she is frustrating the aim of inquiry. One would expect her to see that the routine is a bad one and that the specious methods are not good ways to fix belief.

In 'The Fixation of Belief' Peirce comes close to making this point about the very notion of belief:

> Now, there are some people, among whom I suppose my reader is to be found, who, when they see that any belief of theirs is determined by any circumstance extraneous to the facts, will from that moment not merely admit in words that that belief is doubtful, but will experience a real doubt of it, so that it ceases to be a belief. (*CE* 3, 253.)

Beliefs are such that they resign (i) in the face of recalcitrant experience and (ii) in the face of the acknowledgement that they were fixed by a method which did not take experience into account. If they do not resign in these circumstances, they are not genuine beliefs.

In 1911, Peirce puts the point in terms of the sanity of the believer. He corrects a 'great' error he made in 'The Fixation of Belief'[28] which 'betrays an illogical obstinacy' on his part. He said there that belief is such that we do not wish to transform it into 'a belief in anything else'. But in 1911 he notes that it is possible that there are 'persons who would reverse their belief if they could'; persons who would like to believe what is contrary to the evidence. If there are no such persons, then, Peirce says, that settles the matter. But

> If there are, it proves that an unwillingness to reverse one's belief is not an essential character of the belief, and should not have been stated as such. I should now content myself with the following statement: Belief, once attained removes all the discontent inherent in doubt; and moreover the believer well knows that there is no different belief that could long maintain itself in his mind, while he

---

[28] He corrects two 'great errors', the other being the suggestion that habits are not real.

remains sane, unless, indeed, he should discover that the real state of facts was quite contrary to his belief. It follows that no thoroughly sane man will desire that the matter of his belief should be changed unless by some such discovery. (MS 675, sheets marked '8', 1911, 'A Sketch of Logical Critics'.)

Similarly:

it is one of the essentials of belief, without which it would not *be* belief, that it brings peace of mind, or at least relief from the struggle of doubt; so that a man could hardly be considered sane who should wish that though the facts should remain lamentable, he should believe them to be such as he would wish them to be. (MS 673, p. 11, 1911.)

So Peirce argues in 1911 that no sane inquirer would adopt a belief that was contrary to or paid no attention to the evidence for and against it. Given his naturalism, however, the appeal to sanity is out of place.[29] He should stay with his original thought that being responsive to evidence is one of the 'essentials of belief, without which it would not *be* belief'. Given what belief is and that it is knocked down by recalcitrant experience, no one who is interested in fixing her beliefs will change her beliefs unless by the discovery that (i) experience is set against them or (ii) they were caused by a method which paid no attention to experience.

Peirce again hints at such an argument when he suggests that we do not have to take certain sorts of inquirers seriously: 'A person who arbitrarily chooses propositions which he will adopt can use the word truth only to emphasize the expression of his determination to hold on to his choice.' (CE 3, 272, 1878, 'How to Make Our Ideas Clear'.) We can add that such a person is restricted to using the word 'belief' in the same faulty way. Those who adopt the a priori method are in this camp (as are those who adopt the methods of tenacity, authority, torture, and the belief-freezing pill). Peirce says that they are more concerned with 'inquiring what belief is most in harmony with their system' (CE 3, 273, 1878) than with inquiring what belief would fit with experience or what belief is true. They aim for beliefs which are 'agreeable to reason', but Peirce says that this 'does not

---

[29] Unless an account of sanity could be produced along naturalized, say biological, lines.

mean that which agrees with experience, but that which we find ourselves inclined to believe' (*CE* 3, 252, 1877, 'The Fixation of Belief'). Inquirers who adopt the a priori method aim for the internal consistency of their beliefs and thus their conception of truth, Peirce says, must be that truth is coherence with their other beliefs. The internal consistency of their beliefs is more important than consistency of beliefs with experience. Their method does not aim to fix experience-sensitive belief. It does not aim to fix real belief; accordingly, their conception of truth is a strange one.

Other methods of inquiry go hand in hand with other conceptions of the aim of inquiry and truth. For Peter Abelard, who adopted the method of tenacity, Peirce says, 'the truth is simply his particular stronghold'. And 'When the method of authority prevailed, the truth meant little more than the Catholic faith . . . the idea of loyalty replaced that of truth-seeking . . . ' (*CE* 3, 272, 1878, 'How to Make Our Ideas Clear').

Peirce's suggestion is that, whatever else these methods of inquiry are (effective means of social control perhaps) they do not fit with our conception of the aim of inquiry. He argues that the method of science and reasoning, the method which we pre-theoretically want to affirm, coheres perfectly with his account of truth.[30] This method, he says, is based on the thought that 'things are not just as we choose to think them'. Thus those who adopt the scientific method think of truth as that which will impinge upon us, as 'the opinion which is fated to be ultimately agreed to by all who investigate' (*CE* 3, 273). There is a natural affinity between the method we take for granted as being the best and the account of truth which says that a true belief is one which would not be overturned by experience. If we start with a minimal conception of inquiry as the fixation of belief, we rule out the specious methods of inquiry and we arrive at a substantial account of truth.

Notice that a corollary of the point about the very nature of belief is a point about the very nature of inquiry. If we assume that the aim of a particular activity defines the activity, then, once we take belief seriously, we are committed to a certain conception of inquiry. Not just anything

[30] Skagested (1987), p. 79, makes this point.

goes as a method of inquiry—only a method that aims to fix genuine experience-sensitive belief is a method of inquiry. And this point also fits with our pre-theoretical conception of inquiry. Inquiry is investigation[31]—we always investigate the truth or falsity of some hypothesis. Peirce says that inquiry is an 'activity animated by the desire to know something' (MS 828, p. 1, 1910). We want to find out or discover whether or not H and thus we do not know what the 'answer' is before we start to inquire. Of course inquirers will often start an inquiry with a promising hypothesis to test. They may even believe that it is true. But they are not yet fully committed to it—their subsequent inquiries can overturn their favourite hypothesis.

But notice that only some of the methods Peirce mentions are methods of investigation or methods of finding things out. The others are methods of getting others to believe a certain hypothesis or methods which involve deciding to adhere to a certain hypothesis. They are methods of instilling a *predetermined* belief. It appears that only the method of observation and reasoning is a genuine method of inquiry. It is the only method that inquires about a hypothesis without knowing the results of the process beforehand. The methods that strike us as most unsatisfactory (tenacity, authority, torture, the belief-freezing pill) can be ruled out without invoking a prior conception of rationality; they are not legitimate methods of investigation.

Peirce flirted with this argument as well. He says that inquiry involves seeking permanently stable belief or the truth, 'whatever it may be, not knowing beforehand that it is the truth'.[32] He notices that the unsatisfactory methods of inquiry 'produce a particular, already believed, belief', whereas the scientific method 'tends to unsettle opinions at first, to change them and to confirm a certain opinion which depends only on the nature of investigation itself' (CE 3, 17, 1872; see also CE 3, 19, 1872).

Now one might ask whether I have not merely redefined belief and inquiry in a way designed to disguise some

---

[31] Susan Haack emphasized this point in discussion. In some drafts of 'The Fixation of Belief', Peirce uses 'investigation' to mean 'inquiry conducted according to the scientific method'. I use it in the ordinary sense, which has it meaning the same as 'inquiry'.

[32] MS 597, p. 2, variant pp. of 'Reason's Rules', 1902.

normative principles. The redefinitions build (good) scientific methods into the notions of belief and inquiry. I have indeed done something of this sort, but it is not pernicious. The normative principles are not being covertly disguised here; they are being explicitly recognized as being a part of what we take belief and inquiry to be. The normativity which is still left out in the cold is of the following sort: true beliefs are beliefs which have the virtue of corresponding with reality, with 'essential principles' or with 'real characters'. The naturalism which I attribute to Peirce is not a naturalism which eschews the normative. It is merely a naturalism which insists that truth is the product of inquiry, not something which outruns inquiry. But inquiry is laden with norms.

So Peirce holds that the aim of inquiry is merely to settle belief, but it appears that some methods (such as flipping a coin) do not count as inquiry and their results do not count as belief. A 'belief' that was permanently settled upon by such a method of 'inquiry' would not be true. An acceptable inquiry—an inquiry that is capable of producing true belief—must not start with the answer in hand and must be constrained by experience. The conditional that was put in question by objections about specious methods is: *if*, if inquiry were pursued as far as it could fruitfully go, *H* would be believed, *then H* is true. If a hypothesis is settled upon by the specious methods, the antecedent of that conditional, namely, 'if inquiry were pursued, *H* would be believed', is not fulfilled. Inquiry is not pursued (it isn't an inquiry at all) and *H* is not believed (some other propositional attitude is taken to *H*). And Peirce is not an extensionalist who thinks that conditionals with false antecedents are *ipso facto* true; we cannot conclude that *H* is true.

Suppose our challenger tries to improve her case by asking us to imagine that the set of 'beliefs' that, say, the hypothetical pill freezes is an empirically adequate set. Or she might ask us to imagine that we find a black box that turns out to be a perfect predictor—for every question we ask it, it gives us a correct prediction. An inquirer who chose such a method would be choosing a method that fixed beliefs not only permanently, but in such a way that they would always fit with experience. On Peirce's account, has the aim of inquiry been achieved? Should we quit inquiring?

Peirce would answer 'no'. First, he does not take sensory prediction to be the sole aim of inquiry. We also want to know how to predict in theoretical or diagrammatic contexts; we want theoretical knowledge which will explain why our predictions are fulfilled.

Secondly, the 'beliefs' produced by the pill or the black box would not be truly *sensitive* to experience—they would simply happen to cohere with experience. These methods are not genuine methods of fixing belief because they do not fix belief which responds to experience. If a belief is responsive to experience, and no experience ever proves recalcitrant, then belief is not artificially fixed. It is fixed in the best way possible—by being a belief which perfectly gets along with the world. But if inquirers seal themselves off from inquiry by adopting the method of the pill or the black box, then inquiry has prematurely ceased. It no longer responds to evidence.

Recall that Peirce takes the most important philosophical maxim to be: do not block the path of inquiry. If we are not to impede inquiry, then experience, criticism, and points of view must be considered. If they are not, then inquiry ceases. The methods of tenacity, authority, the pill, and the black box are not methods of inquiry because, under them, inquiry is not conducted. The 'greatest lesson logic has to teach', Peirce says, 'is to allow inquiry to have full swing' (MS 426, very end, 1902).

Notice that the constraints which I have suggested we impose on inquiry, while having normative characters and consequences, do not beg the question in favour of the scientific method. All we ask of a method of inquiry is that:

(1) it fixes real belief (it is responsive to argument and evidence);

(2) it is a method of inquiry (it does not start with the answer in hand);

(3) it continues (it remains responsive to argument and evidence).

4. The End of Inquiry

I have suggested that if we took a 'belief'-freezing pill, then, as inquirers, we would be as good as dead. If all of our beliefs were frozen, or if we were frozen, or if the world were to end tomorrow, then we would no longer be engaging in an experience-responsive inquiry. Peirce argues that the fact that inquiry might cease does not alter what would have been determined to fit perfectly with experience and argument had inquiry continued. And this point blocks a number of objections to his account.

Some philosophers think that Peirce runs into serious difficulties because inquiry will most likely have a premature end. Royce,[33] for instance, suggests that Peirce's theory is unsatisfactory because there is no guarantee that the final opinion will ever be reached. If a true belief is one which would be believed at the end of a sufficiently prolonged inquiry, then if inquiry does not get the chance to be extended, it seems that there are no true beliefs. If the final settled opinion will not in fact ever materialize, what sense does it make to say that many of our beliefs are true (would be in the final opinion)? Russell (1939) suggests that Peirce's account of truth implies that the beliefs of the last people on earth will be the true ones and he notes that those people may well be entirely occupied with the most basic of necessities.

The first thing to notice by way of Peirce's response is that he admits that there 'cannot be a scintilla of evidence to show that at some time all living beings shall not be annihilated at once . . . ' (*CE* 2, 271, 1869; see also *CP* 8. 43, 1885; 5. 494, 1907). Before Peirce became settled in his realism about subjunctive conditionals, he sometimes suggested that his position required the thought that inquiry will continue forever. But we have seen that his considered view is that subjunctive conditionals can be determinately correct or incorrect. The problem with the above objections is that they do not take this feature of Peirce's position seriously. They assume that Peirce is claiming that a necessary condition of a hypothesis being true is that it *will be* believed at the end of

---

[33] Royce (1899) does not mention Peirce by name, but Peirce took him to be arguing against a theory very much like his. See *CP* 8. 100 ff., 1900.

inquiry. If that necessary condition fails to come about, then the hypothesis in question cannot be true. And if the necessary condition is not fulfilled for any hypotheses (i.e. if inquiry has a premature end), then no hypotheses are true. It would follow, as Royce and Russell suggest, that Peirce is offering a definition of truth and that it is not a very good one.

In his review of Royce's *The World and The Individual*, Peirce answers Royce's objection by first invoking a regulative hope: an assumption, such that, without making it, the participants in a practice could make no sense of that practice. (See *CP* 8. 113, 1900.) We must, Peirce says, hope or assume that the community will continue indefinitely and we must hope that there would be, if inquiry were pursued far enough, a final settled answer to 'the particular questions with which our inquiries are busied' (*CP* 6. 610, 1891). He says, 'a reasonable disputant disputes because he hopes, or at least, goes upon the assumption that the dispute will come to something; that is to say, that both parties will at length find themselves forced to a common belief which will be definitive and final. For otherwise, why dispute?'[34] Inquiry is the asking of questions, and a presupposition of inquiry is that the questioner hopes for an answer. This hope is 'single and supreme, and *all* is at stake upon it . . . the only assumption upon which [we] can act rationally is the hope of success' (*CE* 2, 272, 1869). We have, Peirce says, some ground for this hope because all sorts of questions that seemed at one time to be completely resistant to resolution have been resolved.[35]

So Peirce argues that the 'would be' in his construal of truth is 'readily resolved' into a hope for a 'will be' (*CP* 8. 113, 1900). We 'bank upon' the fact that there will be a final upshot to any given question (*CP* 4. 79, 1893). But since we can see that our hope is tenuous, we construe truth in terms of what *would be* the upshot of inquiry.

Peirce then invokes his realism about subjunctives (*CP* 8. 113, 1900). He insists, especially in the 1900s, that truth is the property of beliefs which would be 'the result of

[34] *CP* 2. 29, 1902; see also *CP* 8. 153, 1900; 2. 113, 1901; 5. 609, 1901; *CE* 3, 285, 1878; MS 425, *c*.1900; MS 408, pp. 146–7, *c*.1893.
[35] See *CE* 3, 274, 1878; *CP* 2. 229, 1902.

investigation carried *sufficiently far*'—far enough so that the hypothesis would no longer be improved upon.[36] We aim for beliefs which would be settled 'if they were sufficiently ventilated' (MS 698, undated). Because subjunctive conditionals can be determinately correct or incorrect, hypotheses are determinately true or false whether or not inquiry continues. For, just as a diamond that sits on the ocean floor destined never to be touched is hard, a belief which would have been in the final opinion, despite the final opinion never coming to pass, is true. A belief which would be the best belief that inquiry would come to is true, whether or not inquiry gets the chance to come to it. The consequences remain, whether or not the diamond is ever scratched or whether or not we find out if the belief is unscathed by experience. After chiding himself for construing the diamond example in 'How to Make Our Ideas Clear' with an indicative conditional, Peirce affirms the objectivity of subjunctive conditionals:

Pragmatism makes the ultimate intellectual purport of what you please to consist in conceived conditional resolutions . . . and therefore the conditional propositions, with their hypothetical antecedents . . . must be capable of being true, that is, of expressing whatever there be which is such as the proposition expresses, independently of being thought to be so . . . [37]

Again, Peirce holds that: *if*, if inquiry were pursued sufficiently far, then *H* would be believed, *then H* is true. If the antecedent of the subjunctive conditional is unfulfilled, the truth-value of the whole conditional, Peirce argues, is unaltered. For the following subjunctive conditional is an objective matter: if inquiry were to be pursued sufficiently far, *H* would be believed, whatever we may think at present.

So Peirce's response to Royce is that the fact that the final opinion may never materialize does not alter the truth-value of conditionals asserting that if the final opinion were to materialize, then *H* would be in it. And his response to Russell would be that the beliefs of the last people on earth need not coincide with the hypotheses which would be

[36] *CP* 5. 453, 1905; see also MS 841, p. 15 of 'variant pages', 1908.
[37] *CP* 5. 453, 1905; see also 5. 528, 1905. We will see in Ch. 4 how this last line is consistent with his other claims about truth.

believed if inquiry were to be pursued as far as it could fruitfully go.[38]

This response does a good deal of work in Peirce's position. For it is also the appropriate response to the following objection. Imagine that a revered historian of the period, for a joke, slips into her well-received biography of Churchill the false claim that Churchill counted his sneezes, and that he sneezed exactly seventy-seven times in 1940.[39] This hypothesis is not likely to excite anyone to further inquiry, and even if it did, there would not, we think, be any evidence forthcoming. It may, however, be permanently settled, since the sole evidence supports it. But it is false. Again, the antecedent of Peirce's conditional is not fulfilled— inquiry has not been pushed sufficiently far. A question might be permanently settled, but if it is settled just because no one continues to inquire into it, say, to find that the historian had an odd sense of humour or that Churchill was uninterested in counting sneezes, then it does not enjoy the kind of settlement that is called truth.

We must turn now to Peirce's argument in favour of the scientific method. In this argument lies yet another considera- tion against the specious methods. For Peirce argues that we have no choice but to adopt the method of experience.

5. The Categories and the Force of Experience

Peirce argues that philosophy must not ignore the 'Outward Clash . . . this direct consciousness of hitting and of getting hit enters into all cognition and serves to make it mean something real.' (*CP* 8. 41, 1885.) He stresses that 'Inquiry must react against experience in order that the ship may be propelled through the ocean of thought.' (*CP* 8. 118, 1900.) In order fully to comprehend what he means by these

[38] A variation of the objection is as follows. What if a nuclear holocaust (or some such thing) were to leave inquirers defective—would the final product of their inquiries be true? Again, the Peircean must say that in such a case, inquiry, as we know it, would not have been pursued by inquirers, as we know them. The hypotheses would not be the best hypotheses that it is possible for beings of our kind to have.

[39] More discussion of Churchill's sneezes (See Smart 1986) will follow in Ch. 4.

remarks, we must understand some general points about his doctrine of categories. We must see how his account of experience and perception fits with his account of truth. This ubiquitous classificatory scheme—the categories of firstness, secondness, and thirdness—is designed to cover any object of thought. It is a classificatory scheme that takes each category to be an 'independent and distinct element of the triune Reality' (*CP 5*. 431, 1905). The doctrine is extremely complex, vague, and difficult to understand. But the points which I need to cull from it are relatively straightforward, and require only a superficial gloss of Peirce's categories.

Peirce had three methods for arriving at his list of categories. The first and earliest one is found in the 1867 'On a New List of Categories'. The project is a Kantian one—to find out what 'is' or 'has being' by 'reducing the manifold of sense impressions to unity' via an analysis of the proposition. The second is an argument from phenomenology,[40] which 'ascertains and studies the kinds of elements universally present in the phenomenon' or 'whatever is present at any time to the mind in any way' (*CP 1*. 186, 1903). Both of these methods aim to show that everything that we experience or identify—i.e. anything that 'is'—has an element of each of the three categories in it, and that we do not experience anything that goes beyond the three categories.

Both the Kantian and the phenomenological derivations of the categories rest on the Aristotelian/scholastic method of analysis, called abstraction or prescission.[41] This method separates or distinguishes different elements of a concept so that, although we cannot imagine a situation in which one of them is actually isolated, we can tell that the elements are distinct. We can 'suppose' one without the other, for we can, by attending to one feature and neglecting others, isolate features of phenomena which are not in fact separable. We

---

[40] Peirce sometimes called it 'phaneroscopy'—the description of the 'phaneron'. See *CP 1*. 284, 1904; 2. 197, 1902; 5. 37, 1903; 2. 20, 1902.

[41] See *CE 2*, 50, 1867; *CP 1*. 353, 1880. Peirce sometimes distinguishes two other types of abstraction or mental separation. 'Dissociation' is actually imagining one thing without the other. My pen consists of case and ink, but I can imagine the case without the ink and vice versa. 'Discrimination' is distinguishing between two things, but being unable to imagine them separated—not even in a possible world. Colour, for instance, is distinguishable from space, but we cannot suppose colour without space.

can, for instance, suppose space without colour, even though colourless space is not imaginable. Prescission, however, is not reciprocal, as it is a matter of discerning a logical priority of notions. Hence, although we can prescind space from colour, we cannot prescind colour from space—we cannot suppose colour without spatial extension. With respect to the categories, Peirce argues that we can abstract or prescind certain notions from experience and classify them as belonging to one or another of the categories. We can prescind firstness from secondness and we can prescind both from thirdness, but we cannot prescind in the other direction.

So the categories are designed to describe the general features of each of the classes of elements that come before the mind or are experienced. Each class is distinct, but its members cannot stand in isolation. Each of the categories is present in everything we experience, but there are many cases in which one or the other of the categories is emphasized or predominant: 'although they are so inextricably mixed together that no one can be isolated, yet it is manifest that their characters are quite disparate' (*CP* 1. 284, 1905).

Perhaps the easiest way to set out Peirce's doctrine of categories is to suppress the Kantian and Hegelian derivations, and concentrate on Peirce's third derivation via the logic of relations.[42] The categories are, on this method, represented by *n*-place relations. Peirce argued that all relations fall into one of three fundamental classes: monadic, dyadic, and triadic. Each is irreducible to the others, and all predicates with more than three places are reducible to triadic ones.[43] For instance, '*a* is red' is monadic, '*a* hit *b*' is dyadic and '*a* gives *b* to *c*' is triadic. (See *CP* 3. 456, 1896.) A four-place predicate such as '*a* put *b* between *c* and *d*' is reducible to two three-place ones: '*a* put *b* in spot *e*', 'spot *e* is between *c* and *d*'. 'Gives', on the other hand, is not reducible to '*a* put *b* down' and '*c* picked *b* up', as the latter set fails to express the intention of *a* that *c* have *b*.

The results of each of the three ways of inquiring into the

---

[42] This 'third' method is discussed by Peirce as being part of the 'second' (i.e. phenomenology). See *CP* 1. 288, *c*.1908. I separate them for convenience.

[43] See *CP* 7. 537, undated; 1. 370, 1885; 1. 293, 1884; 1. 345, 1903; 1. 298, 1905. For a reconstrual and defence of Peirce's 'reduction thesis', see Herzberger (1981).

ultimate categories merge. Here is a brief description of those results, one which does not undertake the intimidating task of sorting out the relationships between all of the things that supposedly manifest each category. The third category involves a medium or connecting link between two things; irreducibly triadic action is such that an event *A* produces an event *B* as a means to the production of an event *C* (see *CP* 5. 473, 1907). Thirdness is characteristically manifested in psychological concepts. For instance, Peirce argues that representation is such that an interpreting thought mediates between sign and object. Similarly, we cannot grasp what it is for *a* to give *b* to *c* without the notion of intention mediating between *a* putting *b* down and *c* picking up *b*. There must be an intention to give on *a*'s part and a realization of that intention on *b*'s part. Peirce also says that law, necessity, and generality manifest thirdness. A law, or a necessary connection, mediates between the action of one thing upon another, making it more than an accident that they behaved in the way in which they did.

Peirce's claim is that everything that is real can be represented by a monadic, dyadic, or triadic relation. But in effect, everything that we experience is a matter of thirdness—our access to the other two categories can only be by prescission. For he argues that everything that we experience is of the nature of a sign or representation. There is no experience independent of our representation of it.

We can cognitively isolate secondness as the duality of action and reaction without any mediating force. It is brute existence and hence is the modality of actuality.[44] It is found (by prescission) most clearly in the notions of struggle, action/reaction, cause/effect, and brute force. (See *CP* 1. 427, 1903.) The second category is one 'which the rough and tumble of life renders most familiarly prominent. We are continually bumping up against hard fact.' (*CP* 1. 324, 1903.) And 'We can make no effort where we experience no resistance, no reaction. The sense of effort is a two-sided sense, revealing at once a something within and another something without. There is binarity in the idea of brute force; it is its principal ingredient.' (*CP* 2. 84, 1902.) Things

[44] See *CP* 1. 175, 1897; 1. 325, undated.

which exist impinge upon us, and compel us to take note of them (*CP* 4. 541, 1905). And Peirce argues that one cannot deny this impinging force: 'Even the idealists, if their doctrines are rightly understood have not usually denied the existence of real external things.' (*CE* 3, 44, 1872.)

A first is a simple monadic element. Peirce says that it suggests spontaneity, and it is real 'regardless of anything else'. In virtue of its very nature, it is indescribable; it can only be grasped by prescission:

> It cannot be articulately thought: assert it, and it has already lost its characteristic innocence; for assertion always implies a denial of something else. Stop to think of it, and it has flown! . . . that is first, present, immediate, fresh, new, initiative, original, spontaneous, free, vivid, conscious, and evanescent. Only, remember that every description of it must be false to it. (*CP* 1. 357, 1890.)

These 'qualities of feeling' are mere possibilities: 'I do not mean the sense of actually experiencing these feelings . . . that is something that involves these qualities as an element of it. But I mean the qualities themselves which, in themselves, are mere may-bes, not necessarily realized.' (*CP* 1. 287, 1905.) So the first category is that of possibility.

One upshot of Peirce's doctrine of categories is that he thinks that reality comes in three grades. He is a 'realist' with respect to all of the categories—possibility, actuality, and generality are real. He says, 'the *will be's*, the actually *is's*, and the *have beens* are not the sum of the reals—they only cover actuality. There are besides *would be's* and *can be's* that are real.' (*CP* 8. 216, *c.*1910.) His 'scholastic realism' is opposed to nominalism, and insists that laws or thirds are real; they are not mere mental constructions. He takes nominalism—the doctrine that '*laws* and general *types* are figments of the mind' (*CP* 1. 16, 1903)—to be pernicious. He says, 'the property, the character, the predicate, *hardness*, is not invented by men, as the word is, but is really and truly in the hard things and is one in them all, as a description of habit, disposition, or behavior' (*CP* 1. 27 n. 1, 1909).

Peirce thinks that the fact that we can predict things ought to convince us of realism about generals.[45] Realism explains

---

[45] He says, 'my argument to show that law is reality and not figment . . . is that predictions are verified' (*CP* 8. 153, 1901; see also 1. 26, 1903; 6. 99, 1901).

prediction, for laws and dispositions have causal efficacy: 'if there is any *would be* at all, there is more or less causation; for that is all that I mean by causation' (*CP* 8. 225 n. 10, 1904). If a prediction has a tendency to be fulfilled, it must be the case that future events have a tendency to conform to a general rule. Peirce concludes that some laws or generals are real.[46] Laws and dispositions mediate between possibility (firstness) and actuality (secondness)—it is the law that makes the possible actual, for laws or general patterns cause their instances.

But Peirce does not think that possibilities and generals are existent; he does not adopt a modal realism. Universals or generals are not 'things'. The realm of existence is the second category, and so possibilities and generals are real but not existent.

Notice that Peirce's construal of experience seems to be such that experience is a matter of secondness.[47] He says:

Experience is that determination of belief and cognition generally which the course of life has forced upon a man. One may lie about it; but one cannot escape the fact that some things *are* forced upon his cognition. There is the element of brute force, existing whether you opine it exists or not. (*CP* 2. 138, 1902.)

But his doctrine of categories has it that whenever we think about or experience that which brutally reacts against us, we are involving ourselves in all three categories. It is only by cognitively neglecting the third element and attending to the others that we can suppose or prescind secondness or brute reaction. All three categories are essential elements in experience. So, although it is undeniable that existent things bump against us, this bumping is not a full characterization

---

[46] He does not argue that all general terms refer to real universals; merely that some do. See *CP* 6. 361, 1901. What universals are real will be determined at the end of inquiry. See Boler (1963) and Skagestad (1980) for a good discussion of scholastic realism.

[47] For the characterization of experience in terms of secondness and compulsion, see *CP* 8. 330, 1904; 5. 539, 1902; 6. 340, 1908; 1. 431, 1896; 5. 57, 1903; 2. 84, 1902; MS 304, 1903. Peirce at times distinguishes experience from perception—we perceive objects and perceive events. The two are connected in that we experience changes in and contrasts of perceptions. Experience encompasses perception, but experience 'includes much that is not, strictly speaking, an object of perception. It is the compulsion, the absolute constraint upon us to think otherwise than we have been thinking that constitutes experience.' (*CP* 1. 336, 1905.)

of what we experience. We cannot say anything of the bumping as it is in itself. For the articulation of any description will involve signs and thought—it will involve all three categories.

This point has a parallel in Peirce's account of perception. Perception gives us access to the world, but only of a limited sort. Perception is not a guide to the world as it is in itself. In Peirce's writings on perception, although his terminology changes and is thus misleading, one can always distinguish two, and sometimes three, tiers.[48] There is the 'percipuum' (the clash), the percept (what we are aware of), and the perceptual judgement. The first tier (which is at times absent from Peirce's account) is the actual clash between the world and our senses. But this clash, this brute reaction, is only comprehensible by an exercise of prescission. These 'first impressions of sense' are 'chimerical'; we cannot say anything of them (*CP* 2. 141, 1902; 5. 53, 1903).

The second tier involves the phenomena. It is what we call experience proper because it is the clash that we are aware of. Peirce calls this the percept and says that, because it is forced upon one, it is independent of one's will and 'absolutely dumb' (*CP* 7. 622, 1903). The most important tier is the third—the 'perceptual facts'. These are our descriptions of percepts and, unlike percepts, they can be true or false. For a perceptual judgement is a belief. A percept, on the other hand, is an 'image or moving picture or other exhibition' (*CP* 5. 115, 1903) and so it is not a candidate for a truth-value. Peirce's point is that what we experience is a matter of interpretation; a 'theory of interpretation' is required to form a perceptual judgement.[49] Peirce describes what he sees in his study and says

But hold: what I have written down is only an imperfect description of the percept that is forced upon me. I have endeavored to state it

---

[48] See *CP* 1. 145, 1897; 2. 141, 1902; 5. 54, 1903; 7. 643, 1903; 5. 116, 1903; 5. 568, 1901; 5. 416, 1905; 1. 253, 1902; 2. 84, 1902; 5. 581, 1898; 7. 643, 1903; 2. 784, 1901; *CE* 3, 44, 1872; *MS* 328, 1905. At *CP* 5. 416 he uses 'percept' to label what he elsewhere labels 'perceptual judgement' and at *CP* 5. 568 he uses 'percept' to label what he elsewhere labels 'first impressions of sense'. See Bernstein (1964) for a discussion of Peirce's theory of perception.

[49] *CP* 5. 183, 1903. This does not mean that perceptions are anything like actual 'inferences' or self-conscious judgements.

in words. In this there has been an endeavor, purpose—something not forced upon me but rather the product of reflection . . . I recognize that there is a percept or flow of percepts very different from anything I can describe or think. What precisely that is I cannot even tell myself . . . I am forced to content myself not with the fleeting percepts, but with the crude and possibly erroneous thoughts, or self-informations, of what the percepts were. (*CP* 2. 141, 1902.)

Any articulation of what we perceive involves thirdness; an alteration of whatever hold we had on what actually impinged upon us.

So Peirce argues that sensory observations are theory-laden descriptions of our memories of the action of the world on our senses, and hence they are subject to error. Everyday experience depends not only on judgement, but on memory, 'which is a Judas'.[50] He says: 'Practically, the knowledge with which I have to content myself, and have to call "the evidence of my senses" instead of being in truth the evidence of the senses, is only a sort of stenographic report of that evidence, possibly erroneous.' (*CP* 2. 141, 1902.) 'We all know, only too well, how terribly insistent perception may be; and yet, for all that, in its most insistent degrees, it may be utterly false—that is, may not fit into the general mass of experience, but be a wretched hallucination.' (*CP* 7. 647, 1903.)

The percept causes the perceptual judgement, but still, that judgement may conflict with further experience. And this conflict will throw the judgement into doubt. If a perceptual judgement conflicts with others, then, on Peirce's account, it was mistaken, for the only difference between a 'real perception' and a hallucination is that prediction based on the latter 'will be apt to be falsified'. (See *CP* 7. 644, 1903.) The only way we can correct or recompare perceptual judgements is to 'collect new perceptual facts relating to new percepts'. Since 'going back to the first impressions of sense' 'would be the most chimerical of undertakings' (*CP* 2. 141, 1902), we cannot have any harder evidence than that of additional perceptual judgements.

But what is the nature of the causal relation between the

[50] MS 299, p. 34, 'variants', 1905.

percept and the judgement? The perceptual judgement, Peirce argues, is an index of the percept.[51] Since a percept arises because of the clash between us and the world, the perceptual judgement is an index of the world. Peirce says: 'We can only *indicate* the real universe; if we are asked to describe it, we can only say that it includes whatever there may be that really is.' (*CP* 8. 208, 1905.)The external world cannot, Peirce says, be described as it 'really' is; it can only be denoted by indices (*CP* 4. 530, 1905). But all that indices do is ' provide positive assurance of reality and of the nearness of their objects', without giving 'any insight into the nature of those objects'.[52] An interpreter connects the index (the perception) and its object (the stimulus) by a belief in a causal law; i.e. a theory. Although the judgement is 'unlike' the reality, 'it must be accepted as true to that reality' (*CP* 5. 568, 1901). All that can be inferred about the world, on Peirce's account of experience and perception, is the following: 'The only thing that we can infer is that the observations have such a character that they are fated to lead to one conclusion.' (*CE* 3, 57, 1872; see also *CP* 2. 143, 1902.) We make theory-laden descriptions from our bumps with the world and perhaps the most we can say about that world is that 'it is'.

But, despite the fact that perceptions are not authoritative in the sense of being accurate and infallible descriptions, they are, on Peirce's account, authoritative in the sense that they force themselves upon us. A perceptual judgement is what we, at the time, do not doubt. We have no critical control over these judgements and are compelled to accept them: 'If one *sees*, one cannot avoid the percept; and if one *looks*, one cannot avoid the perceptual judgement. Once apprehended, it absolutely compels assent.' (*CP* 7. 627, 1903, see also 5. 181, 1903.) Peirce says that 'it is idle to discuss the "legitimacy" of that which cannot be controlled. Observations of fact, have therefore, to be accepted as they occur.' (*CP* 6. 522, *c*.1901.) Critical commonsensism holds that we must be content with our perceptual judgements, as we cannot aspire to any greater certainty: 'Now the "hardness" of fact lies in the insistency of the percept, its entirely irrational insistency, the element of Secondness in it. That is a

---

[51] See *CP* 7. 628, 1903.
[52] *CP* 4. 530, 1905, see also 8. 41, 1885.

very important factor of reality.' (*CP* 7. 659, 1903.) Since percepts are brute and forceful, we, for the most part, believe what our senses indicate we should believe.

Peirce's claim that perceptions are descriptions or judgements of the immediate action of the world on our senses is not, notice, the claim that perceptions are *mere* appearances, that they always fall short of the percept.[53] His fallibilism holds that we cannot be *certain* of the truth or even the reliability of our perceptual judgements. But that does not mean that they are not generally true and reliable. They are all that we have to go on.

6. The Scientific Method

Now that the relevant points about experience and perception have been made, we can examine Peirce's argument for why the scientific method is good for settling belief. Peirce characterizes the scientific method as the method that takes experience seriously. Science is not a systematized body of knowledge, but an activity.[54] The scientist is engaged in trying to discover the truth by 'comparing his idea with experimental results'.[55] He always remembers the fallible character of belief: 'He stands ready to abandon one or all as soon as experience opposes them.' (*CP* 1. 635, 1898.) The 'fundamental hypothesis' of the scientific method is:

There are Real things, whose characters are entirely independent of our opinions about them; those realities affect our sense according to regular laws, and, though our sensations are as different as our relations to the objects, yet, by taking advantage of the laws of perception, we can ascertain by reasoning how things really are, and any man, if he have sufficient experience and reason enough about it, will be led to the one true conclusion.[56]

---

[53] See McDowell (1982) for the distinction between these two arguments: (*a*) one cannot tell the difference between deceptive and non-deceptive experience, therefore experience is at best a defeasible ground for knowledge, and (*b*) experience is either a mere appearance or a fact making itself manifest.

[54] See MS 615, 1903; MS 1342, 1905.

[55] *CP* 1. 44, 1896; see also 2. 227, c.1897; 8. 118, 1900; 4. 28, 1893.

[56] *CE* 3, 254, 'The Fixation of Belief', 1877. We have seen that the line which says that 'we can ascertain by reasoning how things really are' should be recast as: 'we can get an indication of how things really are'.

The hypothesis is an elaboration of the point that experience impinges upon us—'things are not just as we choose to think them' (*CE* 2, 355, 1869). Because of this, we would be led, if inquiry were to be diligently pursued, to a final agreement, which, on Peirce's account, is the truth about the way things are.

Whether Peirce manages to describe accurately the details of the way that scientists conduct their business is not important at this stage of the argument. For surely it is true that the scientific method is the method that acknowledges the force of experience (see *CP* 2. 227, 1897); it is the method that goes out of its way to test hypotheses by experiment. And this uncontentious characterization of the scientific method is all that Peirce requires for his arguments in its favour to get off of the ground. He offers two reasons why the method of experience guards best against doubt and provides stable beliefs.

First, external experience is public in the sense that it affects, or might affect, anyone in roughly the same way, and so the conclusions of different inquirers will tend to be the similar.[57] Observations are such that, although no two of them are the same, they tend to result in one upshot. My observations of my bicycle, made at different angles, in different lights, and at different times, will tend to cohere with each other, and I will arrive at some beliefs about the nature of my bicycle. And the observations of my friends will tend to result in similar beliefs. Peirce argues that scientists, observing the same phenomenon, but using different instruments and methods of observation, tend to arrive at the same conclusion.

The reason why this feature of observation makes the scientific method a good means to achieving the aim of inquiry is that that aim is community-wide permanently settled belief. Although Peirce says that inquirers are 'entirely satisfied' by a 'firm belief', he insists that the aim of inquiry is to ascertain what beliefs would be *agreed upon* by the

---

[57] See *CE* 3, 48, 1872, and the whole of the 'Logic' of 1873, which is found at *CE* 3, 14–108. It might be suggested that those in very different cultures do not 'see' things as we do; there are incommensurable viewpoints. Peirce would disagree about the incommensurability. He thinks that there is one community of inquirers—the one which takes experience seriously.

community of inquirers were inquiry to be pursued indefinitely far. The 'Cartesian criterion'—'Whatever I am clearly convinced of is true'—makes single individuals judges of truth, which is 'most pernicious'.[58] The aim of inquiry is to get beliefs which the community acknowledges as being the best beliefs possible. Peirce argues that if the method of science is adopted, then individuals who aim to settle their own beliefs in their own inquiries would tend to be in agreement with others in the community; satisfying the one aim has the effect of satisfying the other. We ought to plod along, settling our own beliefs by making them coherent with experience and with our other beliefs, and we can expect that, in the long run, there would be a consensus within the community.

Thus Peirce argues that followers of the a priori method, who are concerned mostly with getting beliefs that cohere with their own system, are adopting an unsatisfactory method: 'In contenting themselves with fixing their own opinions by a method which would lead another man to a different result, they betray their feeble hold of the conception of what truth is.' (*CE* 3, 273, 1878.) True belief is more than belief which an individual finds that she cannot doubt. True belief is belief which the community of inquirers, at the hypothetical end of the day, would find that they cannot doubt.

The second way in which the method of experience leads to settled belief has to do not with the tendencies of belief (to cohere about observation), but with the causes of doubt. Recalcitrant experience is the thing which puts beliefs into doubt: 'It is important for the reader to satisfy himself that genuine doubt always has an external origin, usually from surprise . . . ' (*CP* 5. 443, 1905).[59] So if we arrive at our beliefs by testing them for consistency with experience, we will tend to arrive at beliefs for which there will be no doubt-inducing surprises. If we acquired beliefs by a method which disregarded experience, those beliefs would be more likely to

---

[58] See *CE* 2, 212, 1868; see also *CP* 5. 402 n. 2, 1893.

[59] The 'external' should not be taken too seriously here. Peirce was far from consistent in his terminology, despite his writings on 'The Ethics of Terminology'. His considered judgement is that both external and internal experience can surprise us.

conflict with experience and hence would be unsettled by doubt.

So the method of science is a good means to the end of inquiry. It will deliver a 'maximum of expectation' and a 'minimum of surprise' (MS 693, p. 166, undated). It is important to keep in mind that it is not mere agreement that is the aim of inquiry. Rather, the thought is as follows. Inquiry is more or less alright as it stands. Inquirers have standards for hypothesis formation and revision. The most important standard—one which inquirers are compelled to adopt—is empirical adequacy. But there are others, such as explanatory power, fecundity, simplicity, and the like. At the end of the day, the hypotheses that inquirers would agree upon would have these virtues (or other virtues which might be taken to supersede the current ones). And it is having these virtues—being the very best they could be—that makes settled hypotheses worthy of our aim. Although we might fix hypotheses by, say, scrupulous avoidance of anything that might disturb them, we ought to see that a far better way to settle genuine belief would be to anticipate anything that might disturb it and fix belief so that it could cope with those disturbances.

Notice that we are provided here with yet another argument against the specious methods. If the scientific method is the one that will best promote the aim of inquiry, we should reject other methods. Peirce's advice for settling belief is as follows: an inquirer should consider each method 'and then he should consider that, after all, he wishes his opinions to coincide with the fact, and that there is no reason why the results of these [first] three methods should do so' (*CE* 3, 256, 1877). Facts, we saw, will impinge upon us and if we want our beliefs to be in line with them, our inquiries ought to pay attention to experience. In 'The Fixation of Belief' Peirce says: 'It is certainly best for us that our beliefs should be such as may truly guide our actions so as to satisfy our desires; and this reflection will make us reject every belief which does not seem to have been formed so as to insure this result.' (*CE* 3, 247.)

Once you see that the method which is constrained by brute experience is the only one that would deliver stable beliefs, you ought to reject any method which is not so constrained. Hence an inquirer ought to reject a method like the 'divine' or 'spiritual' method, which is a matter of wanting very much and working very hard to believe something. It will not do, 'since the world in which [inquirers] are interested in has this peculiarity: that *things are not just as we choose to think them*. Consequently, the accord of those whose belief is determined by a direct effort of the will [the 'divine' method], is not the unanimity which these persons seek.' (*CE* 2, 355, 1869.)

It is important to remember that the constraint on belief imposed by experience is a negative one. The world affects our beliefs not by our finding out positive things about it, but rather, by providing recalcitrant or surprising experience which upsets an expectation produced by a belief. The role which the world plays is not one of providing something for our beliefs to correspond to, but rather, one of letting us know when we have a belief that conflicts with it: 'All that experiment can do is to tell us when we have surmised wrong. The right surmise is left for us to produce.' (*CP* 7. 87, 1901.) It is only by surprise that experience teaches us (see *CP* 5. 51, 1903). All that experience does is *constrain* belief. Belief that conflicts with experience resigns. Peirce says: 'To most questions [nature] curtly cries "No!". She never says "yes"; but at most "H'm, well!" ' (MS 329, p. 3, 1904). Inconsistency of belief with experience prompts doubt, but again nothing about the character of the world need be inferred. Peirce says:

As for this *experience*, under the influence of which beliefs are formed what is that? It is nothing but the forceful element in the course of life. Whatever it is . . . in our history that wears out our attempts to resist it, that is *experience* . . . The maxim that we ought to be 'guided' by experience means that we had better submit at once to that to which we must submit at last. 'Guided' is not the word; 'governed' should be said. (MS 408, p. 147, 1893–5.)

And:

The authority of experience consists in the fact that its power cannot be resisted . . . The maxim that we ought to be 'guided' by experience amounts to this, that what we have got to yield to at last we shall economically do well to be submissive to from the first. 'Guided' is too egotistical a word. (*CP* 7. 437, 1893.)

So Peirce's argument for the use of the scientific method relies entirely on the fact that experience is compulsive.[60] And we have seen that it is this sort of empiricism that takes the sting out of his remarks about the aim of inquiry. What inquirers aim for is settled belief, but this is equivalent to belief that responds to and coheres with experience, broadly construed. Peirce admits that his position is that the true is that which is forever cognitively 'satisfactory': 'But to say that an action or the result of an action is Satisfactory is simply to say that it is congruous to the aim of that action.' (*CP* 5. 560, 1906.) And the aim, he says, is to get beliefs which would always stand up to experience. This is why permanently settled belief is something worthy of our aim. Peirce's position is not one of 'cognitive hedonism'.

It is also the notion of compulsion which ensures that his account 'is not a Berkleyan conception of truth; but quite the contrary. It is the compulsion that makes the truth; and compulsion is essentially extrinsic'.[61] The forcefulness of experience not only makes us choose the scientific method, but it also rules out certain philosophical positions. Peirce says

the reality of the external world *means* nothing except that real experience of duality. Still, many [idealists] do deny [the reality of the external world] or think they do. Very well; an idealist of that stamp is lounging down Regent Street . . . when some drunken fellow . . . unexpectedly lets fly his fist and knocks him in the eye. What has become of his philosophical reflections now?[62]

We are not able to ignore experience, or the fist flying into our eye—we simply do not doubt some things. And since we

---

[60] This appeal to compulsion is frequently invoked by Peirce to temper his initially strong-sounding claims. For instance, he sometimes says that truth is what the community is 'destined' or 'fated' to believe at the end of inquiry. (See CE 3, 44, 45, and 81, 1872–3.) The 'strangeness of this fact', Peirce says, 'disappears entirely' when we realize that sensory observation is the result of our interaction with outward things. The 'fate' Peirce invokes comes to this harmless notion: if we diligently follow the scientific method, experience will point in one direction. Hence, that belief, in a sense, was 'destined' to be arrived at. He explicitly rejects a stronger notion of fate at CE 3, 44, 1872.

[61] MS 817, p. 4, undated; see also MS 283, p. 7 of 'assorted pages', 1905.

[62] CP 5. 539, 1902; see also 2. 64, 1902; 1. 431, 1896.

do not doubt the reports of our senses, when looking for a method that will convert our doubts to beliefs, we choose one that takes observation seriously. The critical commonsensist will adopt the method of observation. It is the only method that gives due weight to the fact that we live in a world which impinges upon us. Peirce's account of truth retains the intuitive idea that truth is that which one can discover *despite oneself*.

What all of this suggests is that choosing the scientific method is more than just a good strategy; we cannot help but generally adopt it. Since the scientific method has experience at its core, the element of compulsion involved in experience becomes transferred to a compulsion to adopt the scientific method. We shall see in the next chapter that Peirce thinks that that which is not subject to self-control cannot be the subject of criticism. Consequently, adopting the method of experience is something that is beyond criticism. There is no room for a normative theory of rationality to pronounce upon whether we ought not to accept the method.

But it does not follow that our beliefs are out of our control. Peirce says,

the conclusion forces itself upon us irresistibly in the first place, even if it be only regarded as probable . . . no sooner is the conclusion reached than we proceed to criticize it by comparing it with our Norms. For the conclusion forces itself upon us *irresistibly*; and yet reasoning, properly speaking, is *controlled* thought. The only sense in which it can be controlled is that, after the inference is drawn, it can be criticized, and if necessary rejected.[63]

An understanding of Peirce's theory of inquiry requires an understanding of his logic—the norms that are involved in the scientific method. We must see how inquirers, given that experience merely constrains belief, can gain positive knowledge.

[63] MS 453, p. 21, 'loose sheets', 1903; see also *CE* 3, 259, 1878; *CP* 7. 659, 1903; 5. 442, 1905.

3
Logic

Introduction

We have seen that the scientific method is bound to promote the aim of inquiry because it is the method which acknowledges experience. But there is more to the method than that, for brute experience alone is not enough to guide us in the fixation of belief. If all of our thoughts were immediately produced by observation then: 'investigation would be almost an involuntary process. We might will to investigate but we could not change the course which investigation should take.' (*CP* 7. 326, 1904.) The method of science, Peirce says, has two parts—observation and reasoning.[1] Experience forms the involuntary part of the scientific method and logic forms the voluntary part. We have control over inquiry because we engage in the self-controlled activity of reasoning. So although Peirce's empiricism has it that doubts are sparked by experience (broadly construed), he also argues that we need to make inferences regarding these experiences. The self-controlled activity of reasoning gives our inquiries room to manœuvre and our belief sets room to expand.

One of my aims in this chapter is to show how the thin characterizations of inquiry and the scientific method articulated in Chapter 2 are accompanied by a powerful system of norms that can transform 'learning from experience' into the most sophisticated sort of investigation. And this set of norms is not merely paper-clipped to Peirce's account of truth and inquiry. We have seen that he thinks that the aim of inquiry is to get beliefs which result in a 'maximum of expectation' and a 'minimum of surprise'. We want beliefs (expectations) which would encounter no recalcitrant experience (surprise). One of the three types of inference that

[1] *CE* 3, 40 ff., 1872; see also *CP* 8. 41, 1885; *CE* 3, 8 and 16, 1872; MS 749, p. 4, undated; MS 596, p. 7, 1902, 'Reason's Rules'.

Peirce distinguishes—abduction—gives us beliefs. The other two types—deduction and induction—make those beliefs secure. We shall see that Peirce takes each kind of inference to be a stage or task in the scientific method.

But another of my aims is to show how a common interpretation of Peirce's account of truth is wrong-headed. Many think that Peirce's view about truth falls out of an attempt to solve Hume's problem of induction: an attempt that is much like Reichenbach's. This interpretation has Peirce holding that science is self-correcting and must eventually converge upon the truth. But I shall argue that this is a mistaken reading of Peirce's account of the progress of science and the growth of knowledge. Once the correct account is provided, we will have a coherent picture of how Peirce conceived of inquiry, progress, and truth.

1. Normative Science and Reliable Methods

Peirce had outlines or drafts of a number of books about logic: 'Search for a Method' (1893), 'How to Reason' (1894), 'Reason's Rules' (1902), 'Reason's Conscience' (undated), and 'Minute Logic' (1902). He divided logic into three branches—the theory of signs, the classification of inference types, and the theory of method or the theory of how inquiries ought to be conducted.[2] The theory of method will be the concern of this chapter, for it is 'the theory of deliberate self-controlled search for truth'.[3]

We have seen that Peirce holds that: 'To believe the absolute truth would be to have such a belief that under no circumstances, such as would actually occur, should we find ourselves surprised.' (MS 693, p. 166, undated.) Since logic is 'the doctrine of truth, its nature and the manner in which it is to be discovered' (CE 3,14, 1872), it 'may be defined as the

---

[2] In this classification, he called them, respectively, 'Logical Syntax' or 'Speculative Grammar', 'Critic', and 'Methodeutic'. Peirce had a number of such classifications, but the study of method was always present: see MS 452, 1903; CP 1. 191, 1903; MS 746, undated.

[3] MS 283, 'assorted pages'. p. marked '31', 1905. Since I focus on the theory of method, I shall not discuss Peirce's technical work on deductive logic which does not fit nicely with the notion of deductive inference as a task in the scientific method.

Logic

science of the laws of the stable establishment of beliefs'.[4]
Thus the aim of reasoning, like the aim of inquiry in general,
is to fix beliefs that would perfectly cohere with experience:

> Facts are hard things which do not consist in my thinking so and so
> . . . It is those facts that I want to know, so that I may avoid
> disappointments and disasters. Since they are bound to press upon
> me at last, let me know them as soon as possible, and prepare for
> them. This . . . is my whole motive in reasoning. Plainly, then, I
> wish to reason in such a way that the facts shall not, and cannot,
> disappoint the promises of my reasoning . . . Consequently, I ought
> to plan out my reasoning so that I evidently shall avoid those
> surprises. (*CP* 2. 173, 1902; see also 2. 327, 1903; 2. 448, 1893;
> MS 313, p. 15, 1903.)

The rules of logic will be justified in so far as they lead to
stable beliefs. Although fallibilism tells us that doubts about
any of our beliefs may spring up in the future, we can fix our
beliefs in ways which will minimize the risk. Peirce provides
us with a sophisticated logic which will do this: a logic which
may get revised and improved upon but, none the less, one
which does a good job. If the rules are followed, beliefs
produced by our inferences 'will prove far more unshakeable
by any doubt' than if the rules are not followed. (*CP* 1. 606,
1903.)

So belief, on Peirce's account, is not correctly fixed in an
automatic sort of way; inquiry is not on autopilot. To neglect
logic is to adopt the 'wild oats' doctrine, which advises one to
give thought a free rein (*CP* 8. 240, 1904). This, Peirce says,
involves 'unspeakable waste'. If there is to be hope of
reaching a final opinion which is as good as it can be,
inquirers must use something like the method of abduction,
deduction, and induction. Peirce's theory of truth does not
license a 'logical fatalism' which has it that science is destined
to reach the truth and so it 'can therefore make no difference
whether she observes carefully or carelessly' (*CP* 7. 78,
undated).

The scientific method is the method of experience and
logic. Peirce is fond of saying that logic is a 'normative

---

[4] *CP* 3. 429, 1896; see also MS L75, 1902; MS 453, 1903; MS 1147, *c*.1910;
MS 698, p. 3, undated; *CP* 2. 782, 1901.

science' and this claim covers a variety of theses.[5] Sometimes he means the following: 'Logic is a normative science; that is to say, it is a science of what is requisite in order to attain a certain aim.' (MS 432, p. 1, 1902, see also MS 684, p. 7, 1913.) Logic is the science of reasoning, but it asks not what reasoning is, but what it ought to be in order to further the goal of inquiry.[6] Sometimes he says that logic is normative because it is critical.[7] Approval or disapproval of acts, he says, requires that we are able to control those acts; approval presupposes that the act was voluntary. Peirce says, 'Reasoning unconsciously can hardly be called reasoning at all. As long as I simply find myself seized with a belief, without being able to give any account of how I came by it, logic has nothing to say except to warn me of the extreme danger that I shall err.' (*CP* 7. 458, undated.) A mental process counts as reasoning only if the conclusion is deliberately approved:

an *inference* is essentially deliberate, and self-controlled. Any operation which cannot be controlled, any conclusion which is not abandoned . . . as soon as *criticism* has pronounced against it . . . is not of the nature of rational inference—is not reasoning. (*CP* 5. 108, 1903; see also 2. 182, 1902; 2. 204, 1901; 5. 55, 1903; 7. 444, 1893; 7. 457, undated; MS 692, 1901.)

There is an analogy, he suggests, with morals: 'logical thought is self-controlled thought, as moral conduct is self-controlled conduct' (MS 453, p. 18, 1903; see also *CP* 8. 191, 1904).

So logic is concerned with deliberate or self-controlled

---

[5] One is that a scientist must have the moral virtue of devotion to the pursuit of truth. (See MS 693a, p. 136, undated.) And in his later writings he insists that logic is normative in that it requires a study of our ultimate aim. It requires ethics (the study of ends) and aesthetics (the study of what is admirable in itself). (See *CP* 1. 611, 1903; 5. 36, 1903; 1. 579, 1902.) Although Peirce expresses doubts about his competency in these areas (see *CP* 2. 197, 1902; 5. 111, 1903; MS 310, p. 5, 1903), he suggests that a good aim is an aim that can be consistently pursued and that our ultimate aim is the development of 'reason' or 'creation'. (See *CP* 1. 615, 1903.) I find these passages neither clear nor helpful. Fortunately, Peirce sometimes explicitly says that science 'does not involve opening the question of ethics', but rather, it values finding 'truths' which will prevent surprise and support predictions (*CP* 7. 186, 1901; see also 7. 201, 1901).

[6] See *CP* 5. 39, 1903; 2. 7, 1902; 2. 52, 1902; 1. 281, 1902.

[7] *CP* 1. 606, 1903; see also 5. 108, 1903.

conduct—conduct which can be evaluated and improved upon: 'The conclusion was in the first instance irresistible. It came upon the mind before there was any time to control it. But it is no sooner there than the critical comparison is made between it and our logical ideal . . . ' (MS 453, p. 19, 1903.) The way in which we criticize reasoning is by comparing inferences with a logical ideal; we recognize them as belonging or not belonging to a class of sound reasonings. He says

> we all have in our minds certain *norms*, or general patterns of right reasoning, and we can compare the inference with one of those and ask ourselves whether it satisfies that rule . . . If we judge our norm of right reason to be satisfied, we get a feeling of approval, and the inference now not only appears as irresistible as it did before, but it will prove more unshakable by any doubt. (*CP* 1. 606, 1903.)

These norms, we shall see, are rules of inference which are more or less reliable. In this respect, Peirce's approach to inquiry is similar to F. P. Ramsey's. We will see that Peirce would have agreed with Ramsey that

> The human mind works essentially according to general rules or habits; a process of thought not proceeding according to some rule would simply be a random sequence of ideas; whenever we infer *A* from *B* we do so in virtue of some relation between them. We can therefore state the problem of the ideal as 'What habits in a general sense would it be best for the human mind to have?' (Ramsey 1926, p. 49.)

They both give the same answer: good habits or rules of behaviour are those which, for the most part, lead to reliable opinions. All inferences are governed by a rule or habit, and we ought to seek good habits—those which will lead from true premises to true conclusions most or all of the time. Given the doctrine of fallibilism, we cannot know when we have true premises and true conclusions, but we can know when we have premises and conclusions which cohere with the data and upon which we can safely act. So we might say that good rules of inference lead from stable premises to stable conclusions. Inferences owe their validity to the fact that the method or rule that they follow is reliable.

Peirce thinks that the logic that the ordinary person uses is a reliable method: 'You have to depend upon your natural power of reasoning being better than tossing up a copper to decide which way the truth lies.' (MS 453, p. 27, 1903; see also *CP* 2. 189, 1902; 2. 204, 1902.) Everyone, he says, has an instinctive, vague, unarticulated set of rules or norms which guide their inferences: 'Every agent has a generalized ideal of good reasoning, we all form notions of what is good reasoning and what is not. We carry more or less distinctly in our minds patterns of good and bad reasoning, which may be called Norms.'[8] Logic is the formal study of how to get stable belief, but most inquirers rely on less formal methods. One's implicit logic, however, only takes one part of the way—its reliability is limited. If we are to advance inquiry, we must study logic systematically.[9] Our instinctive logic is better than flipping a coin, but if we want to increase the probability of reaching a true conclusion, we will reason according to the more developed logician's logic.

2. Abduction, Induction, Deduction

Peirce classified inference into three types: deduction, induction, and abduction (which he also called retroduction or hypothesis). Deduction is 'explicative' inference and abduction and induction are 'ampliative'. In explicative inference, the conclusion follows from the premises necessarily; in ampliative inference, the conclusion amplifies rather than explicates what is stated in the premises. Peirce argues that ampliative inference is the only kind that can introduce new ideas into our body of belief.[10] In his early work especially, Peirce wanted to distinguish the three kinds of inference by their form. In the 1878 paper 'Deduction, Induction, and Hypothesis' (*CE* 3, 325), he classifies them as follows. Deduction proceeds from rule and case to result:

[8] MS 453. See also *CP* 1. 606, 1903; 1. 630, 1898; 5. 181, 1903; 2. 753, 1883; 5. 174, 1903; 2. 3, 1902. Peirce calls this body of norms an agent's 'logica utens', as distinct from the 'logica docens', which is what the logician studies. See *CP* 2. 186, 1902; 2. 204, 1902.

[9] See *CP* 2. 178, 1902; 2. 3, 1902; 2. 188, 1902.

[10] See *CP* 6. 475, 1908. Sometimes he says that it is only abduction that can introduce new ideas 'for induction does nothing but determine a value' (*CP* 5. 171, 1903).

Rule: All the beans in this bag are white
Case: These beans are from this bag
Result: Therefore these beans are white

Induction proceeds from case and result to rule:

Case: These beans are from this bag
Result: These beans are white
Rule: Therefore all the beans in this bag are white

Abduction or hypothesis proceeds from rule and result to case:

Rule: All beans from this bag are white
Result: These beans are white
Case: Therefore these beans are from this bag

In the 1883 'A Theory of Probable Inference' (*CP* 2. 704), Peirce characterizes abduction as follows:

Rule: All M's have the characters $P_1, P_2 \ldots P_n$
Result: S has the characters $P_1, P_2 \ldots P_n$
Case: S is an M

But he later classifies these last two inferences as a form of induction—'qualitative induction'. Such an inference samples characters or properties and is not the most reliable form of induction. (See *CP* 8. 233, 1910.)

There is an even weaker sort of induction. A 'crude' induction concludes that all *A*s are *B*s because there are no known instances to the contrary. It assumes that future experience will not be 'utterly at variance' with past experience (see *CP* 7. 756, 1905). As an example, Peirce offers the inference 'No instance of a genuine power of clairvoyance has ever been established: So I presume there is no such thing'. No attempt at enumerating instances is made in this sort of induction. Rather, it is the absence of instances to the contrary which provides the basis for the inference. This is, Peirce says, the only kind of induction in which we are able to infer the truth of a universal generalization. Its flaw is that 'it is liable at any moment to be utterly shattered by a single experience' (*CP* 7. 157, 1905). It does, however, go some way to saving us from surprises.

But Peirce thinks that it is a mistake to think that all inductive reasoning is aimed at conclusions which are universal generalizations (see *CP* 2. 775, 1901). The strongest sort of induction (the sort that best saves us from the unanticipated) is 'quantitative induction' and it deals with statistical ratios. For instance:

Case: These beans have been randomly taken from this bag
Result: 2/3 of these beans are white
Rule: Therefore 2/3 of the beans in the bag are white

That is, one can argue that if, in a random sampling of some group of Ss, a certain proportion r/n has the character P, the same proportion r/n of the Ss have P. One concludes from an observed relative frequency in a randomly drawn sample a hypothesis about the relative frequency in the population.

Quantitative induction can be seen as a kind of experiment. We ask what the probability is that a member of the experimental class of the Ss will have the character P. The experimenter then obtains a fair sample of Ss and draws from it at random. The value of the proportion of Ss sampled that are P approximates the value of the probability in question. This sort of induction is the one that Peirce takes to be the most important and his characterization of it is constant throughout his writing.[11]

In the 1900s Peirce explicitly takes the three types of inference to be 'stages' of inquiry in a way that is very much like the hypothetico-deductive model of science.[12] The first stage is abductive—a hypothesis is identified as a plausible conjecture or an explanatory hypothesis is formed. In the 'Minute Logic' of 1902, Peirce sees that the way in which he construed abductive inference in 'A Theory of Probable Inference' 'could not be the reasoning by which we are led to adopt a hypothesis . . . I was too taken up with considering syllogistic forms' (*CP* 2. 102, 1902). He restricts abductive inference to another way he characterized it in the 1878 'Deduction, Induction, and Hypothesis'. It is 'where we find some very curious circumstance, which would be explained by the supposition that it was a case of a certain general rule, and thereupon adopt that supposition' (*CE* 3, 326, 1878). The form it takes is:

---

[11] See *CP* 6. 473, 1908; 2. 703, 1883; *CE* 3, 312, 1878.
[12] See *CP* 6. 469, 1908; 7. 672, 1903; *CE* 3, 326, 1878.

The surprising fact, C, is observed;
But if A were true, C would be a matter of course.
Hence, there is reason to suspect that A is true. (*CP 5.* 189, 1903;
    see also 2. 624, 1878.)

So abduction is 'the process of forming an explanatory hypothesis' (*CP 5.* 171, 1903). These hypotheses, however, are merely conjectures; we must 'hold ourselves ready to throw them overboard at a moment's notice from experience' (*CP 1.* 634, 1898; see also 6. 470, 1908). Peirce stresses that 'Abduction commits us to nothing. It merely causes a hypothesis to be set down upon our docket of cases to be tried.' (*CP 5.* 602, 1903.) And that is the first stage of inquiry: arriving at a conjecture or an explanatory hypothesis.

The second stage is to deduce consequences or predictions from the hypothesis. The 'purpose' of deduction is 'that of collecting consequents of the hypothesis'. The third stage is that of 'ascertaining how far those consequents accord with Experience' (MS 841, p. 44, 1908). By induction we test the hypothesis: if it passes, it is added to our body of belief.[13]

Whereas abduction begins with some (surprising) experience and turns to a hypothesis, induction begins with a hypothesis and turns to experience (for testing). (See *CP 2.* 755, 1905.) When we test, we infer that if a sample passes the test, the entire population would pass the test. Or we infer that if 10 per cent of the sample has a certain feature, then 10 per cent of the population has that feature.

So the three kinds of inference are three stages of inquiry— they form the core of the scientific method. What makes the scientific method successful in providing beliefs that fit with experience is the possibility of arriving at hypotheses via abduction, deducing consequences from them, and testing them by induction. To say that a true hypothesis would be believed at the end of inquiry is to say that it would be abducted to, has consequences, and would survive all tests. In the rest of this chapter, I will be mostly concerned with Peirce's account of inductive inference, as it is usually taken to be intimately connected with his theory of truth. But first, abduction needs some elucidation.

[13] See *CP* 2. 755, 1905; 6. 469, 1908.

Abduction, being a form of ampliative inference, allows us to add to our body of belief; it allows us to infer, or at least conjecture, from the known to the unknown. We can infer a hypothesis to explain why we observed what we did. Peirce thinks that it is a regulative assumption of inquiry that, whenever any observation C obtains, there will be some hypotheses which entail C or make C probable. And one of these hypotheses is the best explanation of C. That is, we must assume that every observation has an explanation. Abductive inference will provide us with candidates for that explanation; it is inference to the best explanation.

Peirce argued with Paul Carus about when an explanation is called for. Carus claimed that irregularity demands an explanation and Peirce disagreed. Nobody, he says, is 'surprised that the trees in a forest do not form a regular pattern, or asks for any explanation of such a fact' (CP 7. 189, 1891). Peirce suggests that irregularity is 'the over-whelmingly preponderant rule of experience, and regularity only the strange exception'. A mere irregularity, where no definite regularity is expected, he says, creates no surprise; it excites no curiosity. And it is a surprise or an anomaly that throws us into doubt or demands an inquiry to explain the phenomenon. It is an *unexpected* regularity or the breach of an existing regularity that makes a demand for explanation. It is the interruption of a habit of expectation (a belief) that calls for an explanation.

Peirce is anxious to remind us that this is not a psycholo-gical principle, but a logical one; the strength of an emotion of surprise is not the measure of a 'logical need for explanation' (CP 7. 190, 1901). This emotion 'is merely the instinctive indication of the logical situation. It is evolution . . . that has provided us with the emotion.' (CP 7. 190, 1891.) Peirce wants to offer 'a purely logical doctrine of how discovery must take place' (CP 2. 107, 1902). So in 'Reason's Conscience', he distinguishes between an 'unconquerable disposition' and the genuine compulsion of experience. He does not think that 'if the human race like moths had an unconquerable disposition to get into the fire (and some of the dispositions of young men are much like that)' the conduct would be reasonable. For 'on trying the experiment we should meet with a surprise. Now I think that sound reasoning is constituted by its leading us to believe what will reduce our surprises to a minimum. For sound reasoning seems to me to be reasoning that tends toward the truth as much as possible.' (MS 693, p. 162, undated.) The bruteness of experience can, he thinks, be distinguished from other sorts of things that we think are irresistible. It has an undeniable status that psychological compulsions lack. And only a surprising brute experience demands an explanation.

The addition of abduction to the standard two types of inference (deduction and induction) does a great deal of work in Peirce's system. For one thing, it allows us to infer (some sorts of) metaphysical hypotheses, hypotheses about the past, and hypotheses about unobservable entities. Peirce does not adopt the extreme empiricist position that these sorts of hypotheses have a lower status than those which are empirically verifiable.[14] He thinks that they can be true or false in the same way that hypotheses about the observable can. They can be, or they can fail to be, permanently settled. Peirce refuses to say of any kind of hypothesis that it is not a candidate for a truth-value. And he argues explicitly for the candidacy of hypotheses about the unobservable. For abductive inference will frequently infer the existence of something unobservable. Physicists, he says, do not confine themselves to a

'strictly positivistic point of view'. Students of heat are not deterred by the impossibility of directly observing molecules from considering and accepting the kinetical theory; students of light do not brand speculations on the luminiferous ether as metaphysical . . . All these are 'attempts to explain phenomenally given elements as products of deeper-lying entities'. (*CP* 8. 60, 1891, Review of James's *Principles of Psychology*.)

Peirce insists that it is only the premises, not the conclusions, of science which must be directly observable (*CP* 6. 2, 1898). The data will be observable data, but the explanations of the data need not be empirical hypotheses.

Abduction also goes a long way in solving an intractable

---

[14] See van Fraassen (1980) for an extreme empiricist position about theoretical entities. See Ellis (1985) for a Peircean position.

contemporary philosophical problem—Goodman's recharacterization of Hume's problem of induction.[15] Peirce virtually ignores Hume's problem of induction; he simply is not interested in it. Part of the reason for this is that Peirce argues that induction tests a hypothesis that answers a question. And the fact that the hypothesis already has this going for it gives us a reason to make inductive inferences.

Goodman illustrates his 'new riddle of induction' by the following sort of example. Suppose we define a predicate 'grue': an object is grue if it is observed to be green and first examined before 1 January 1998 or it is first examined after 1 January 1998 and it is observed to be blue. The hypothesis 'all emeralds are grue' has just as much inductive support as does the hypothesis 'all emeralds are green'. For, on the grue hypothesis, any emerald that I examine now which is green is also grue. Goodman asks why we should select 'green' rather than 'grue' as the appropriate predicate to apply to objects. Why do we expect that if an emerald were to be first found in 1999, it would be green rather than blue?

Goodman's point is that not all regularities result in the formation of a habit of expectation. We do not expect first-examined emeralds after 1998 to be blue, despite the fact that we have 'confirmed' the grue hypothesis by observing all emeralds thus far to be green. The problem is to spell out some principled way of determining which inductive inferences are good and which are not. But inductive inference rests solely on the enumeration of observed instances and so we cannot appeal to non-enumerative considerations to bolster one inductive conclusion over another. Since the inductive evidence underdetermines the 'grue' and the 'green' conclusions, it is going to be hard to cite reasons for preferring one over another.

On Peirce's account, the choice between the 'green' and 'grue' hypotheses is a matter for abduction, not induction. The inference to 'all emeralds are green' is not an induction from the premise 'all observed emeralds have been green'.

[15] See Goodman (1955). See Harris and Hoover (1980) for a similar discussion of Peirce and Goodman. David Wiggins, in lectures given at the University of Oxford in 1987/8, has emphasized Peirce's account of abduction in a way that lends itself to the following treatment.

Rather, we would, if we were interested enough in the matter, infer 'all emeralds are green' as an abduction—as the best explanation of the observed regularity that they have all thus far been green. And then we would test the hypothesis by induction and find that it passed all tests. But the abductive origin of the hypothesis gives it a weight that not just any inductively tested generalization would have.[16]

Like Goodman, Peirce sees that regularities abound, and argues that only some of them want explanations. Only unexpected or surprising regularities demand us to make an abductive inference to an explanation. And what is unexpected is that by which our body of background belief would be upset. Thus, if in 1999, we observe only blue emeralds, we might conjecture the grue hypothesis. But until we are surprised, we will not conjecture that emeralds are grue. Abduction does not in fact throw up the hypothesis 'all emeralds are grue' and that is why the hypothesis is ignorable. The boring regularity that, thus far, all emeralds have been observed to be green will not lead us to infer the grue hypothesis.

So Peirce holds that we must assume that every observation has some explanation. An inference to the best explanation produces a real candidate for belief. The hypothesis which is the best explanation of a phenomenon is not only a candidate for testing, but it shows itself to be a reasonable or plausible conjecture.

This brings us to the murky issue of what makes one explanation better than another. Peirce offers us some guidelines, but his primary thought is that we have evolved such that we have developed an instinct or tendency for making good abductive inferences.[17] He says

---

[16] Notice that this point illuminates the discussion of Russell's five minute hypothesis in Ch. 1. We do not infer the hypothesis 'the world and everything in it was created five minutes ago' as an explanation of anything. Scientists have, on the other hand, inferred a different hypothesis. That hypothesis has something going for it by virtue of being the conclusion of a number of abductive inferences and by virtue of having survived so far as a hypothesis. Thus, we are justified in condemning the five minute hypothesis as empty—its consequences are indistinguishable from those of a hypothesis which already has something going for it.

[17] See *CP* 1. 630, 1898; 6. 531, 1901; 5. 591, 1903.

Nature is a far vaster and less clearly arranged repertory of facts than a census report; and if men had not come to it with special aptitudes for guessing right, it may well be doubted whether in the ten or twenty thousand years that they may have existed their greatest mind would have attained the amount of knowledge which is actually possessed by the lowest idiot. (*CP* 2. 753, 1883.)

But we can improve on our instinctive ability by studying logic. Peirce suggests that we ought to:

(*a*) choose hypotheses that are capable of being tested by induction (*CP* 5. 599, 1903; 7. 220, 1901);

(*b*) construct our hypotheses so as to explain the surprising observations we have before us; deduce the observations from the hypothesis or choose a hypothesis which 'renders the facts likely' (*CP* 7. 202, 1901; 7. 220, 1901);

(*c*) derive consequences before testing (2. 775, 1901);

(*d*) choose hypotheses that are 'economical in money, time, thought and energy' (*CP* 5. 602, 1903; 7. 220, 1901; 1. 93, 1896; 2. 511, 1867; 3. 528, 1896; 6. 408, 1877; 6. 413, 1877; 2. 780, 1901);

(*e*) ensure that the experimental sample does not include members on whose basis the abductive hypothesis was formed (*CP* 2. 758, 1905);

(*f*) 'make our hypotheses as broad as possible' (*CP* 7. 221, 1901);

(*g*) choose 'simple' hypotheses; abide by Ockham's razor (*CP* 5. 60, 1903; 6. 535, 1901);

(*h*) choose highly falsifiable hypotheses (*CP* 1. 120, 1896);

(*i*) choose hypotheses that bring 'the most facts under a single formula' (*CP* 7. 410, 1893);

(*j*) not attach too much importance to subjective 'antecedent probabilities' (*CP* 2. 777, 1901; 1. 120, 1896; 7. 220, 1901).

Whatever we think of the merits of this particular list, we should see, with Peirce, that the validity of abductive inference is going to be hard to characterize. Its conclusion is not even asserted to be true, for it is a mere conjecture. He says:

The hypothesis which it problematically concludes is frequently utterly wrong in itself, and even the method need not ever lead to the truth; for it may be that the features of the phenomena which it aims to explain have no rational explanation at all. Its only justification is that its method is the only way in which there can be any hope of attaining a rational explanation. (*CP* 2. 777, 1901; MS 652, p. 13, 1910.)

He argues that the reason we are justified in making abductive inferences is that, if we are to have any knowledge at all, we must make them. A logician, Peirce says, should have two goals—he should 'bring out the amount and kind of *security* . . . of each kind of reasoning' and he should bring out the 'uberty, or value in productiveness, of each kind' (*CP* 8. 384, 1913). Abduction is such that 'though its *security* is low, its *uberty* is high' (*CP* 8. 388, 1913).

It is the other two kinds of inference to which the notions of security and validity more aptly apply. In order to understand Peirce's account of validity, we must take a quick glance at his theory of probability.

3. Probability

The two most widely held interpretations of probability are the empirical (or objective) and the subjective (or personalist) accounts.[18] The empirical interpretation takes a probability statement to be a statement, which is true or false, about the world. We arrive at probability measures by observing actual relative frequencies and probability is about the frequencies or about things that manifest the frequencies. One type of empirical interpretation is the relative frequentist one, which takes the probability of the hypothesis '*A* is *B*' to be the limit of relative frequency of *B*s among *A*s in a hypothetically infinite series.[19] Another type is the propensity theory, which takes probability assignments to be predicates of certain kinds of events or things—'propensities' or 'chance set-ups'. On this account, probability is a disposition which can be expressed or manifested by relative frequencies, and observed relative frequencies constitute part of the evidence for

---

[18] The logical and the ignorance (or classical) interpretations will not concern me here.

[19] See, for instance, Reichenbach (1949) and von Mises (1928).

something's having the disposition. The disposition explains why one observes the frequencies that one does. On Popper's (1960) view, an object (for example a coin) has a certain propensity (to land heads) whether or not any trials are performed. For Hacking (1965) 'chance' is a property not of an object, but of a 'chance set-up'—an experimental device on which one can perform trials.

Subjectivists allow many different, yet correct, probability assignments. They construe probabilities as concerning actual degrees of belief which are interpreted behaviouristically; they are measured by looking at what people's betting practices would be. Probability assignments can vary from agent to agent, as they merely express an agent's degree of belief or credence in the truth of the hypothesis. The one constraint is that the set of degrees of belief which an agent actually has must be 'coherent'. A person's set of degrees of belief must be such that there is no sure-win strategy that could be played against it and modifications must conform to the probability calculus.

Peirce argues for an empirical and against a subjective interpretation of probability.[20] He usually puts his theory in terms of relative frequencies and sometimes he turns it into a propensity theory.[21] But there is a twist in Peirce's account, for he says that probability 'belongs exclusively' to the principles which govern inferences, not to events or to the hypothesis in question.[22] A rule will have a probability p of giving the correct conclusion and this probability is characterized or manifested by the relative frequency with which the argument type would produce true (stable) conclusions from true (stable) premises among the total number of cases in which the premises were true (stable) in a hypothetically infinite series. He says: 'in the long run, there is a real fact corresponding to the idea of probability, and it is that a given mode of inference sometimes proves successful and sometimes not, and that in a ratio ultimately fixed' (*CE* 3, 280, 1878; see also *CE* 3, 286, 1878, 'Doctrine of Chances'; *CP* 2.

---

[20] See *CP* 2. 747, 1883. In 1910, Peirce says that he arrived at his conception of probability in 1864. See MS 660.

[21] See *CP* 8. 225, 1910; 2. 664, 1910.

[22] *CE* 3, 290, 1878; see also *CP* 5. 169, 1903; *CE* 3, 290, 1878; *CE* 3, 280, 1878.

697, 1883). Probability is a matter of the relative frequency of arguments of the type with true premises to arguments of the type with true premises and true conclusions. Since probability is a matter of relative frequency, it is empirical or objective; it is 'a thing to be inferred upon evidence' (*CE* 3, 295, 1878).

Notice that this account of probability is a pragmatic account. We would expect certain things if the hypothesis 'the probability of *H* is 0.95' were true. We would expect that, in inferences which the hypothesis governs, we would draw true conclusions from true premises 95 per cent of the time. Probability is a matter of what we can expect of inferences.

Peirce's account of probability does not conflate things that one might expect such an account to conflate. For instance, he does not conflate assigning a probability to the success rate of arguments and assigning one to the conclusion of an argument on the basis of the evidence expressed in the premises. He is wary of assigning a probability to the conclusion or assigning a degree of belief to the hypothesis in the conclusion. But he allows that, as long as we are aware that we are speaking very loosely, we can assign such measures. They must, however, be identical with the measure of the ratio of success of the argument type.[23] A probability assignment is a representation of a 'general statistical fact' or a 'real objective fact' (*CE* 2, 100, 1867) and so degrees of belief and measures attached to conclusions of arguments must be 'intimately connected' to objective probabilities (*CE* 2, 293, 1878). Our degree of belief in a hypothesis 'does and ought to vary with the chance of the thing believed, as deduced from all the arguments' (*CE* 3, 293, 1878). Towards a hypothesis that has an even chance of being true, or a probability of 0.5, we ought to suspend judgement. We may also, he says, loosely speak of the chance of an event 'absolutely': the chance of an event will be related to the combination of all relevant arguments which exist for us in our present state of knowledge.[24] So probabilities of hypo-

---

[23] See *CE* 3, 281, 1878. Peirce says that such degrees of belief are closely connected to betting behaviour. See *CP* 7. 314, *c*.1873.

[24] This sense of chance bears some similarity to Carnap's (1945). Carnap

theses, degrees of credence, and 'absolute' or prior probabilities are all to be inferred upon the evidence—observed relative frequencies of the success of argument types.

4. Validity and Leading Principles

Peirce argues that the validity of an inference depends on it being of the type that possesses a 'truth-producing virtue'. He suggests that 'leading' or 'guiding' principles license the drawing of conclusions of Type *B* from premises of Type *A* and they thus define a genus of argument. Good principles confer validity upon arguments. (See *CE* 2, 23, 1867.) If you rely on a good leading principle, you will draw true conclusions from true premises in the type of inference which it governs. And it is to these principles that probability measures attach. A principle with a high success rate or high probability will be a principle that governs valid arguments. Peirce defines validity as follows: 'a genus of argument is valid when from true premises it will yield a true conclusion invariably if demonstrative, generally if probable' (*CE* 2, 99, 1867; see also *CE* 2, 267, 1869).

Inquirers, Peirce argues, have habitual rules which they use to govern inferences. These rules will be more or less sophisticated, depending on whether the agent is relying on her instinctive set of leading principles, or whether she has studied and adopted logic's set of leading principles. As Ian Hacking (1980) says, Hume was right in thinking that induction is a matter of habit, but wrong not to see, with Peirce, that we can assess our habits. If we are rational, we will adopt good habits and will recognize the active leading principle (and hence the genus of argument defined by that principle) of an argument. If we do not recognize the governing principle of an inference, we cannot give an account of how we arrived at the conclusion. And Peirce thinks that the sort of uncontrolled 'reasoning', where the

suggests that we look at all the possible arguments (whose premises are compatible with our knowledge) and arrive at a prior probability. For Peirce the absolute chance of something happening is the chance of it happening relative to all the arguments available.

agent cannot identify the leading principle, is not reasoning at all, or at least it is the 'lowest kind of reasoning' (MS 736, 'Ch. II', p. 2, undated).

Peirce was not generous with examples of leading principles for any of the types of inference. Sometimes he says that they are 'maxims of logical procedure', or rules of inference, and are good or bad, not true or false. Sometimes he says that they are 'cerebral habits'.[25] And sometimes he says that any general proposition is a leading principle. So it is not clear whether he intends us to view leading principles as inference rules of the type 'when you have x, infer y', or major premises in arguments, such as $(P \& Q) \rightarrow Q$. He intends to leave the notion vague: 'I call it a rule, although the formulation may be somewhat vague; because it has the essential character of a rule of being a general formula applicable to particular cases.' (*CP* 1. 606, 1903.) Rules, habits, and universal generalizations are all such that they are general principles which govern particular cases. We can leave the characterization vague and view leading principles as either rules or general propositions which the inquirer habitually employs. For the general propositions which are major premises of deductive arguments can be recast as rules which say, for instance, 'when P is true and Q is true, infer P'.[26]

So, in deductive inferences, a general statement or law will be the leading principle. Peirce also suggests that the theorems of what we would now take to be a natural deduction system function as logical leading principles for the appropriate type of deductive arguments. They will be

[25] See *CP* 3. 160, 1880; see also *CE* 3, 245, 1877; *CP* 7. 460, undated; 1. 606, 1903.
[26] Peirce distinguishes two kinds of leading principles: logical and non-logical. A logical (or formal) leading principle cannot be false, and a material (or factual or non-logical) one can. Leading principles, Peirce says, contain whatever is necessary besides the premises to determine the truth of the conclusion (*CE* 2, 23, 1867). Content is transferable between the leading principle and the premises, but there is something uneliminable or untransferable in every leading principle. What is uneliminable is the logical leading principle, which is 'empty' (*CE* 2, 23, 1867). These principles imply those facts which are presupposed in all discourse (*CE* 3, 246, 1877). For instance, the inference 'Socrates is a man, therefore he is a sinner' has as part of its leading principle 'all men are sinners'. This is a material principle and can be transferred to the premises. But 'all men are men' is part of the logical leading principle. It does not need to be set forth as a premise yet it is assumed in the argument.

correct sequents of the sort $A \rightarrow B$, A, $\vdash B$. The validity of deductive arguments rests on the fact that if the premises are true, the conclusion must be true. Deduction is justified because 'the facts presented in the premises could not under any imaginable circumstances be true without involving the truth of the conclusion' (*CP* 2. 778, 1901). So the validity of deductive inference is due to its being sure-fire or such that it cannot lead to a false conclusion from true premises.

If leading principles for deductive inferences are exemplified by correct sequents of the deductive calculus, it seems natural to turn to the calculus of probability to find leading principles for inductive reasoning. This, though not in these terms, is what Peirce does. It is the job of induction to provide the means for testing a conjecture. If a particular sort of inductive inference is a reliable method of testing, then it is valid. It fulfills its function in inquiry and it has a leading principle with a high probability measure attached to it. The testing of hypotheses is largely a matter for statistics and Peirce directs his discussion of induction accordingly. Sampling and other features to do with chance set-ups form the core of inductive inference. (See *CP* 2. 726, 1883; 6. 40, 1891.)

He tells us what the leading principle of a probabilistic or statistical deduction (today called statistical syllogism or direct inference) is. These inferences are deductive inferences with statistical hypotheses, rather than universal laws, as major premises. They take the form:

[*Rule:*] The proportion r of the Ms are Ps
[*Case:*] S_1, S_2, S_3, etc. are a *numerous* set, taken at random from among the Ms
[*Result*] Hence, *probably* and *approximately*, the proportion r of the Ss are Ps (*CP* 2. 700, 1883.)

Of these syllogisms, Peirce says, 'The principle of statistical deduction is that these two proportions—namely, that of the *P*'s among the *M*'s, and that of the *P*'s among the *S*'s—are probably and approximately equal.' (*CP* 2. 702, 1883; see also 2. 718, 1883; *CE* 2, 268, 1869; *CE* 3, 305, 1878.) This principle allows you to make two sorts of inferences. As in the above schema, it allows you to move from a hypothesis about relative frequencies in a population to a conclusion about relative frequencies in a randomly drawn sample. But it also allows you to conclude, from an observed relative frequency in a sample, hypotheses about relative frequencies in the population from which it was randomly drawn. And this is the job of quantitative induction. Peirce sees that the same principle governs both sorts of inferences: 'These two forms of inference, statistical deduction and induction, plainly depend upon the same principle of equality of ratios, so that their validity is the same.' (*CP* 2. 703, 1883.)

The principle is that, given random sampling, predesignation of the character to be tested, and large enough samples and populations, the composition of the population is approximately the same as the composition of the observed sample. In Peirce's words, 'there is a certain vague tendency for the whole to be like any of its parts taken at random because it is composed of its parts' (*CE* 1, 470–1, 1866). Now this is a loose way of stating a theorem of the calculus of probability—the weak law of large numbers.[27] It states that, given a large population, the majority of decently large samples drawn from it will have, with high probability, nearly the same composition as the population. A high proportion of samples drawn from a large population will have the roughly same ratio of any property as the population. Hence, both statistical deductions and inductions (i.e. inferences from trials to populations) will lead from true premises to true conclusions in a high proportion of the cases. And this is just what Peirce required of valid inductive inferences.

So, for Peirce, the validity of an inference is characterized in terms of a long run relative frequency. We 'know that if we were to reason in that way, we should be following a mode of inference which would only lead us wrong, in the long run, [say] one in every fifty times' (*CP* 2. 697, 1883). Validity is a matter of the ratio of arguments with true Type *A* premises

---

[27] See also *CE* 2, 1, 2, 48, 217 and 263, 1867–9; *CP* 2. 758, 1905. Peirce intended to devote a lecture to 'The Law of High Numbers: Important consequences of certain numbers being large in different branches of science' (see MS 745, undated). For a discussion of the law of large numbers and Peirce's theory of inductive inference, see Cheng (1966).

and true Type *B* conclusions to the total number of arguments with true Type *A* premises. And because probability, on Peirce's account, is a matter of objective relative frequencies, the validity of inference does not depend on an agent's recognizing the inference type as valid—validity is a 'question of reality, and has nothing at all to do with how we may be inclined to think'.[28] Validity depends on the relative frequency of success of the kind of inference. The ratio of success for a valid deductive inference will be 1:1, and for a valid inductive inference it will be some relatively high ratio. It will be high because the leading principle of inductive inference is the weak law of large numbers. It will be sure-fire (see *CP* 2. 781, 1901) for deductive inference because the leading principles will be theorems of the deductive calculus.

But there is also a difference in kind, as opposed to one of degree, between the validity of deductive and inductive inference. When we test a hypothesis in quantitative induction, we infer that the observed relative frequency in a sample is 'probably and approximately' the same proportion that would be found in the whole population. Peirce was aware of the ambiguity of 'probably and approximately'; it could be a part of the conclusion or an indication of 'the modality with which this conclusion is drawn and held for true' (*CP* 2. 720 n. 1, 1883).

He favours the latter. For the degree of credence we ought to have in a hypothesis depends partly on how that hypothesis was inferred. In probable reasoning, 'we only know the degree of trustworthiness of our proceeding' (*CE* 3, 305, 1878) and so 'account has to be taken of various subjective circumstances' (*CP* 2. 696, 1883). Peirce mentions requirements concerning the size of sample, the random drawing of the sample, the predesignation of the character we are testing for, and additional knowledge we may have regarding the trial (see *CE* 2, 215, 1868). Unlike deduction,

---

[28] *CP* 5. 161, 1903. Peirce argued against psychologism in logic. He claims that Mill, for instance, holds that the way an agent ought to reason is based on how he must reason. Peirce says that while 'compulsion attaches to that subconscious thought over which we have no control', it does not attach to conscious reasoning. (See *CP* 2. 47, 1902) He argues that 'Logic does rest on certain facts of experience among which are facts about men, but not upon any theory about the human mind or any theory to explain facts.' (*CP* 5. 110, 1903.)

induction does not have a purely formal form of validity; in
order to be valid, all sorts of contingent circumstances have
to be fulfilled.

5. The Single Case Problem

One difficulty that Peirce's account of the validity of
induction must overcome is a standard objection to relative
frequency interpretations of probability. Peirce argues that
only if the agent can ground a judgement in knowledge of
relative frequencies can she have knowledge of a probability.
But the frequency theory provides no grounds for thinking
that the probability on a single trial is the same as the long-
run success rate—and it is the long-run success rate that
determines validity on Peirce's account. As Hacking has put
it, how can long-run virtues justify short-run policies?

Peirce is aware of this problem: he discusses it in the 1869
'Grounds of Validity of the Laws of Logic' and the 1878 'The
Doctrine of Chances' (*CE* 3, 284). He sees that:

> According to what has been said, the idea of probability essentially
> belongs to a kind of inference which is repeated indefinitely. An
> individual inference must be either true or false, and can show no
> effect of probability; and, therefore, in reference to a single case
> considered in itself, probability can have no meaning. (*CE* 3, 281,
> 1878; see also *CE* 2, 270, 1869; *CP* 2. 661, 1910.)

But it does seem legitimate to make isolated probability
assignments and the frequentist must make sense of this.
Peirce offers the following illustration (*CE* 3, 281 ff., 1878).
Someone is faced with two decks of cards, one containing
twenty-five black and one red, the other containing twenty-
five red and one black. He must draw a card, and is told that
if he draws a red one, he will go to heaven, and if he draws a
black one, he will suffer eternal damnation. Peirce notes that
it would be 'folly' to pick from the deck with twenty-five
black cards. But because the very nature of the gamble is such
that it could not be repeated, the frequency theory gives no
justification of what is obviously the best choice.

Contemporary advocates of the propensity interpretation
of probability invoke propensities to solve the single case

problem. Peirce, although he sometimes puts his interpretation of probability in terms of a propensity, does not. The
contemporary thought is that we can make sense of a single
case regarding the probability that 'this bottle will break if I
drop it from a height of two feet' by saying that the bottle (or
any bottle of this type) has a disposition to break under a
certain impact.

Since Peirce is a realist about dispositions, he could have
dealt with the single case problem in this way.[29] For instance,
he remarks that, when discussing probability, he sometimes
wrote as if the ratio was the ratio that is or will be
determined. He repudiates those statements and insists that
probability is the ratio that *would* manifest itself in the
indefinite long run.[30] And he says that the ratio that *would be*
manifested in the long run is a habit, propensity, or
disposition. A coin has a certain 'would be' to turn up heads
half the time and the probability of getting a six is a habit of
the die.[31] But although Peirce's realism about dispositions
does give him the materials with which to talk about the
probability of a single case, he seems to resist such a
formulation. Instead, he gives the following striking solution
to the single case problem.

He says that, since individuals have finite lives, they cannot
help themselves to the notion of the 'long run' or the infinite
series which is at the core of the frequency theory. Thus

It seems to me that we are driven to this, that logicality inexorably
requires that our interests shall *not* be limited. They must not stop
at our own fate, but must embrace the whole community . . . He
who would not sacrifice his own soul to save the whole world, is, as
it seems to me, illogical in all his inferences, collectively. Logic is
rooted in the social principle. (*CE* 3, 284, 1878; see also *CP* 2. 661,
1910.)

We are warranted in making probability assignments or
inferences which depend on a relative frequency in the long
run because we can see that, if everyone made them, then, in

---

[29] Hacking (1980) makes this point.
[30] No problem arises if the lot being sampled is finite, for a finite lot can be
sampled as an infinite one, if you throw back the items sampled. See *CP* 2. 731,
1883.
[31] See *CP* 2. 664, 1910, 'Notes on the Doctrine of Chances'.

the long run, they would be correct. But since our inferences and lifetimes are limited, we cannot be guaranteed that we will arrive at correct conclusions. We must make these inferences with the assurance that, while our own may lead to error, the community will arrive at the correct conclusion in the long run.

In both papers in which he offers this solution, Peirce immediately renders the talk of altruism innocuous: inquirers do not actually have to adopt such attitudes about self-sacrifice nor do they have to assume that the community will exist indefinitely. They need merely to regard their inductive inferences and probability assignments as being valid only if they would be authorized by such a hero. As Levi (1980) puts it, they must simulate heroic reasoning. An agent must recognize that validity depends on an identification of oneself with the community 'even if he has not it himself' (CE 2, 271, 1869). I should choose the mostly red deck now for if everyone did the long-run rate of success would be extremely high.

Notice that Peirce's appeal to sociality is not a way of assigning a probability measure to the single case. Probability does not apply to the single case. The appeal to sociality is an account of how it is none the less rational for agents to behave in certain ways when faced with single cases. There is a right thing to do, but there is no probability attached to any particular outcome. Perhaps this thought might be general-ized to provide a theory of rational action; a theory which holds that rational action is applicable to single cases only as instances of general principles.[32] Such a generalization would bear some resemblance to Kant's universalizability principle: 'I should never act in such a way that I could not will that my maxim should be a universal law' (Kant 1785, sect. 402). Analogously, is rational for me to do A if and only if I could recommend that everyone similarly situated do A. Thus, in order to recommend a certain procedure I must, in some sense, assume that there would be indefinitely many other persons persisting indefinitely into the future. The reason I am justified in doing A is that if everyone did A, then, for the most part, they would not be surprised by experience. Experience would shock them only in a fraction of the cases.

[32] Calvin Normore suggested this to me.

In Peirce's example of the two decks of cards, it would be mad of someone to *recommend* choosing from the mostly black deck. In the long run, twenty-five out of twenty-six of those who did would end up in hell. Since the recommendation to choose from the mostly red deck would be a sensible one, it would be rational for me to choose from the mostly red deck.

Notice that we need to assume realism about 'would bes' here as well; the fact that a rule would be successful justifies us in using it here and now. This account of rationality suggests that we shift focus from the justification of a particular instance to the justification of a general rule. A justified rule is a rule which would prove reliable for an indefinitely prolonged community of inquirers. It is too much to ask of someone who recommends a reliable method or a rule of inference to say to every putative user that she will not suffer for using it. The method will rather let us down in as few instances as possible. This is all that one can ask. It is what makes it rational to make judgements of probability in single cases and it is what confers validity upon inductive inference.

6. The Problem of Induction

The reader familiar with Peirce may wonder why I have not taken into account Peirce's frequent statement that

The true guarantee of the validity of induction is that it is a method of reaching conclusions which, if it be persisted in long enough, will assuredly correct any error concerning future experience into which it may temporarily lead us. (CP 2. 769, 1905; see also 5. 576, 1898; 5. 145, 1903; 2. 775, 1901).

Much has been made of such statements of Peirce's. Some philosophers see in them a response to Hume's problem of induction. And others see a picture of the progress of science. In what follows, I shall take up these claims.

Hume suggested that no rational justification for inductive inference can be provided. The following sort of inference is not deductively valid:

All observed *A*s are *B*s
Therefore all *A*s are *B*s.
[*Or*] Therefore the next *A* I observe will be a *B*
And if one tries to justify such an inference on the grounds
the it is reliable, then one is relying on an inductive
conclusion (it has proved reliable in the past) to justify
inductive inference.

Notice that the problem of induction, as Hume characterizes it, is about what Peirce called 'crude induction'. It is a
problem for inferences that conclude, from an observed
constant conjunction, a universal generalization. We have
seen that Peirce thinks that this is a very weak sort of
inference for reasons similar to those given by Hume—it is
apt to be overthrown by a single experience. Peirce, however,
is not very interested in crude induction. His concern is
always with quantitative induction—with statistical syllogism or direct inference. Peirce never mentions Hume with
respect to induction. His concern with induction is how
inductive inference forms a part of the scientific method; how
inductive inferences can fulfil their role as the testing ground
for hypotheses.

One might think that Peirce's talk of leading principles
governing inductive inference is reminiscent of attempts to
justify induction by invoking a 'supreme' major premise. Mill
thought that such a premise was needed, namely, the
principle of the uniformity of nature. But this is not how
Peirce avoids Hume's problem, for he argues explicitly
against Mill. We have seen that Peirce thinks that 'Nature is
not regular . . . It is true that the special laws and regularities
are innumerable; but nobody thinks of the irregularities,
which are infinitely more frequent.' (*CE* 2, 264, 1869,
'Grounds of Validity of the Laws of Logic'.) And even if
nature were uniform, adding a major premise stating that fact
would not be the right way to justify induction. Induction,
Peirce says 'needs no such dubious support'.[33]

Hume's problem, Peirce assumes, is settled by fallibilism
and critical commonsensism. We do, and should, believe that
the sun will rise tomorrow, yet it is by no means certain that
it will. And the probability of a fair coin landing tails on an

---

[33] *CP* 6. 100, 1901; see also 2. 102, 1902; 2. 784, 1901.

infinite number of tosses is 0.5, but this does not rule out an infinite run of heads. Showing that induction is valid is not showing that we can be certain about the correctness of inductive conclusions. Fallibilism holds that this is a pipe dream. What we have to show is that induction is a reliable method in inquiry.

Moreover, we have seen that Peirce thinks that law and necessity are operative in nature, and so he is not very interested in Hume's suggestion that there might not be any laws or necessary connections. He thinks that this thesis is a pernicious feature of nominalism and he wants no truck with it.

But the response to Hume which is usually attributed to Peirce concerns probability. Reichenbach says that Peirce 'expressed the idea that a solution of the problem of induction is to be found in the theory of probability' (Reichenbach 1938, p. 339). Reichenbach himself tried to develop a probabilistic solution to Hume's problem and, ever since, popular philosophical opinion has it that Peirce was a forerunner to Reichenbach's 'vindication' of induction.[34] This is due to the fact that both make heavy use of the notion of the 'self-correcting' nature of induction. But their accounts are not straightforwardly similar.

Reichenbach suggested that Hume was right to see that induction could not be justified; for all we know, the world may be irregular and we cannot know anything about the future. He argued, however, that induction could be vindicated. If we want to have knowledge, we should use inductive inference, for it, if anything, will give us knowledge. This vindication is based on a frequency account of probability. Suppose we have a sequence of events (coin tosses), and some of these have the property A (tails) and some have $-A$ (heads). Reichenbach construed the principle of induction as stating that for any prolongation of the series, the relative frequency of A-type events to the total number of observed events will remain within a small interval: in this case, the relative frequency will hover around 1:2. The heads to total

---

[34] See e.g. Madden (1964), Haack (1976), Laudan (1974), Ayer (1968), Lenz (1964), Skyrms (1966). Reichenbach himself could not see his position clearly stated in Peirce's work. See Reichenbach (1949), p. 446.

tosses ratio may fluctuate dramatically at the beginning of the series; we might, for instance, come up with three tails in the first three tosses, making the heads to total tosses ratio 0:1. But the method, Reichenbach says, will correct itself. The next ten tosses might turn up six heads and four tails, making the heads to total ratio closer to the eventual limit of 1:2. The point is that eventually the bouncing around of frequencies of divergence from the centrepoint will stabilize and stay within a limit: 1:2 plus or minus some small *e*. The relative frequency account of probability holds that this limit or convergence is the probability of the event in question.

Now if, in the long run, the relative frequency of outcomes of a trial will stabilize towards some limit, the true value of the ratio of heads to tails will emerge. Reichenbach argued that this entails that at some point in the series we can infer that in any future prolongation of the series, the relative frequency which we have observed will hold. And this is a warranted inductive inference. We can say, once we have made a good number of tosses, that the relative frequency of heads in the future will remain more or less the same as it has been in the past. So, on Reichenbach's account, the reason we are vindicated in our use of inductive inference is that if there is a truth of the matter in a set-up like this—if there is a true probability assignment—then we will converge upon it. If knowledge of the future is possible, then there must be a series of events with properties whose frequency of occurrence converges to a limiting value. Hume's point, Reichenbach says, is that there might not be any series of events with this property. But if there are, then the method of induction will arrive at their limits.[35]

We saw that Peirce offered this sort of vindication for abductive inference. He argued that we must hope that every observation has an explanation and that we will arrive at it.

---

[35] There is a powerful objection to Reichenbach's account (made by Salmon 1957 and Lenz 1958, and noticed first by Reichenbach himself). The principle of induction is not the only rule that is justified by his argument. It is possible to construct an infinite number of rules or policies which give you the same limiting value, but which give different values for any finite part of the sequence. Thus, they tell us to infer different things and they assign different probabilities to the occurrence of the event in question. There is, moreover, no non-arbitrary and non-question-begging way of choosing one of these methods over the others.

Otherwise, we cannot argue from the known to the unknown. If we are to have any hope of gaining knowledge about the unknown, we must make abductive inferences. And at times Peirce's account of induction does sound like Reichenbach's. He repeats again and again that the justification of induction is that it is a self-correcting method and:

As we go on drawing inference after inference of the given kind, during the first ten or hundred cases the ratio of successes may be expected to show considerable fluctuations; but when we come into the thousands and millions, these fluctuations become less and less; and if we continue long enough, the ratio will approximate towards a fixed limit.[36]

It is not clear, however, just what this claim amounts to. The notion of self-correction was the talk of philosophy of science in Peirce's day[37] and he used it with a free and liberal hand. For instance, sometimes he means the following. If one is making a crude induction from observed instances to the universal generalization 'All As are Bs', the method 'must correct itself if it were wrong'. For if you were persistent in your observations, you would, if the conclusion were wrong, come across an A that was not a B. (See CP 7. 215, 1901; 7. 111, 1903.) That is, sometimes he says that a method is 'self-correcting' if it produces falsifiable conclusions. At other times, he seems to suggest something like Reichenbach suggests. And at other times he seems to suggest what Levi (1980) and Hacking (1980) take his writings on probability and statistical inference to be about.

They argue that Peirce's notion of self-correction anticipates not Reichenbach, but the Neyman-Pearson confidence interval approach to testing statistical hypotheses. Neyman and Pearson (1933) saw the problem in testing statistical hypotheses (such as 'the proportion r of Ms are P', where r is the unknown parameter) as that of deciding what kind of tests imply that a particular hypothesis should be rejected. A good rule does not tell us whether in a particular case H is true or false or what the probability of H is. It tells us when we should reject the hypothesis. It may often be proved that if

---

[36] CE 3, 281, 1878; see also CP 2. 758, 1905; 5. 565, 1901; 8. 112, 1900.
[37] See Laudan (1974).

we adopt a certain rule, we shall reject *H* when it is true not more, say, than once in a hundred times. In the long run of experience, we shall not be too often wrong. If we follow good rules, we will make the correct decisions most of the time. So on the confidence interval approach, the inductive procedure is self-correcting, but not self-correcting in Reichenbach's sense. It is not that probability measures attached to hypotheses mathematically converge upon a limit. As Peirce says:

> it may be conceived, and often is conceived, that induction lends a probability to its conclusion. Now that is not the way in which induction leads to the truth. It lends no definite probability to its conclusion. It is nonsense to talk of the probability of a law, as if we could pick universes out of a grab-bag and find in what proportion of them the law held good. (*CP* 2. 780, 1901.)

Rather, if we choose good rules, then if a particular conclusion is inaccurate, the conclusion of the next inference of that type drawn will be accurate with an overwhelming probability.

Thus not only did Peirce show a remarkable lack of interest in solving 'the problem of induction', but a number of distinct theses about the self-corrective nature of inductive inference are discernible in his work. My motive for blurring the connection between Peirce and Reichenbach on this score is to highlight the inadequacy of a certain sort of reading of Peirce's account of truth. These interpretations take Peirce's doctrine of truth to be virtually one and the same with his account of inductive inference as self-correcting. They are inadequate interpretations because, as we have seen, Peirce's account of inductive inference is by no means as straight-forwardly Reichenbachian as these commentators suggest. And, secondly, Peirce generally maintains a healthy distance between his doctrines of truth and induction. It is hard to individuate these different readings about Peirce's construal of truth, but in what follows I will mention some frequently suggested ones.

Some commentators conflate Peirce's claims about validity with his claims about truth. Rescher (1978, p. 10), for instance, says that Peirce takes a true theory to be a theory that has a probability of 1; its success rate is 100 per cent. By 'success rate', Rescher means the rate at which the theory works when we employ it for prediction and control. A theory, on this account, will more closely approximate the truth as its success rate or probability gets closer to one. But Peirce is quite clear that probability measures attach to leading principles and success rates to inferences. He thinks that assigning a probability to a hypothesis or a theory leads to ridiculous results. (See *CP* 5. 169, 1903.) While it is right to say that, on Peirce's account, a theory that would never disappoint us in prediction and control would be true, it is misleading to suggest that this point rests on his claims about probability and the self-correcting nature of induction. A true belief or theory is not one which has a probability of 1. Beliefs and theories do not, on Peirce's account, have probability measures at all, never mind probability measures which converge upon the truth.

Another mistaken interpretation is that Peirce claims that whatever the continued use of induction will have us believe is the truth.[38] That is, because induction is self-correcting, it is guaranteed to deliver the truth eventually. But Peirce thinks that, although inductive inference is a part of the method (the scientific method) that would eventually produce true beliefs, nothing about it makes it automatically produce the truth.

Other commentators take Peirce to hold that science as a whole is self-correcting in Reichenbach's sense, and then go on to criticize him on the grounds that science, as Peirce construes it, is *not* really self-correcting.[39] On Reichenbach's account, which we have seen Peirce sometimes approximates, the reason why probability assignments are supposed to get more accurate involves facts about sampling, randomness, and other statistical features of chance set-ups. Thus the hypotheses with the self-correcting feature will always be statistical. Reichenbach thinks that most hypotheses in science are statistical, so he can claim that science, or the hypotheses of science, will get closer to the truth. That is, he

---

[38] See Lenz (1964) and Madden (1981).
[39] See Laudan (1974), Shimony (1970), p. 127.

thinks that 'the method of scientific inquiry may be considered as the concatenation of inductive inference',[40] and so he holds the scientific method to be self-correcting and continually getting closer to the truth. But Peirce does not identify induction with the scientific method and he only occasionally claims that science itself is self-correcting.[41] His central argument is that science, utilizing the method of abduction, deduction, and induction, would eventually reach the truth because it is connected to experience. Peirce thinks that there is a major difficulty in identifying science with induction—we have to think up the hypotheses that we want to test, and this is the province of abductive inference. Induction and deduction alone provide an inadequate characterization of the scientific method.

Other commentators argue that Peirce thinks that inductive inference leads to beliefs which correspond to reality. Peirce does sometimes say of induction that it is a method which, because it is self-correcting, must lead to the truth. But it is important to keep in mind that by 'the truth' he means that which would not be overturned by doubt. He makes a parallel claim about abductive inference. It leads to the truth: 'intelligent guessing may be expected to lead us to the one (hypothesis) *which will support all tests*, leaving the vast majority of possible hypotheses unexamined' (*CP* 6. 530, 1901, my emphasis). His claim is not that we have an ability for guessing The True Hypothesis (the one which corresponds to reality), but rather for guessing in a manner that will turn up the hypothesis that will prove permanently to be doubt-resistant. Similarly, he says that a reasoner must be conscious that the leading principle of an inference is

conducive to true knowledge. By true knowledge, he means, though he is not usually able to analyze his meaning, the ultimate knowledge in which he hopes that belief may ultimately rest, undisturbed by doubt, in regard to the particular subject to which his conclusion relates. (*CP* 2. 773, 1901, see also 1. 609, 1903.)

---

[40] Reichenbach (1938), p. 364

[41] Peirce occasionally says that in science we 'sample' predictions, and so all inference in science is inductive. (See *CP* 7. 216, 1901.) And he occasionally claims that science and reasoning are self-correcting. (See *CP* 5. 579, 1898.) But he usually does not make so much of the method of induction.

So when Peirce says that induction is such that it must lead to the truth, he means that it must lead to beliefs which would encounter no recalcitrant experience. The 'essential condition' of inductive inference is that of 'saving me from surprises both positive and negative; that is from the happening of things not anticipated and the non-occurrence of imaginary disasters' (*CP* 2. 757 n. 1, *c.*1902, see also 2. 775, 1901). Induction, happily, is a reliable method in inquiry because it tends to lead from doubt-resistant beliefs to other doubt-resistant beliefs. If it sometimes leads to beliefs that fall to recalcitrant experience, we must, Peirce argues, stick with the method. We must continue to test, and eventually we will correct the mistake and end up with a doubt-resistant belief.

The upshot is that one needs to be careful, in interpreting Peirce's account of truth, to stay clear of identifying his account of inductive inference with his account of truth. Because both are concerned with what would be the case in the long run, it appears to be an easy identification. But the brief glance we have taken at Peirce's theory of induction and probability should rid us of this temptation. Although Peirce's account of probability is complex, this much is simple: it does not entail that truth is what would be believed in the long run. Peirce's account of truth does not follow from his account of induction. Rather, there is a connection between (*a*) arriving at hypotheses by abduction, deducing consequences from them, and testing those consequences by induction, and (*b*) an opinion that cannot be improved upon. Because the scientific method (abduction, deduction, induction) takes experience to constrain beliefs, our beliefs, we hope, will get closer to the truth; they will result in fewer and fewer surprises.

7. The Growth of Knowledge

Along with the mistaken interpretation of Peirce's account of truth often comes a mistaken interpretation of his view of the growth of knowledge. He is supposed to hold that science systematically gets closer and closer to the truth. Quine, for instance, says:

Peirce was tempted to define truth outright in terms of scientific method, as the ideal theory which is approached as a limit when the (supposed) canons of scientific method are used unceasingly on continuing experience. But . . . there is faulty use of numerical analogy in speaking of a limit of theories, since the notion of limit depends on that of 'nearer than' which is defined for numbers and not for theories. (Quine 1960, p. 23.)

He says that Peirce's theory is untenable because it 'depends on a notion of successive approximation on the part of theories, and this supposes that we know what it means to compare theories in respect to degree of similarity' (Quine 1981, p. 31).

The thought that science gets closer to the truth has many forms. Some think that knowledge, or at least scientific knowledge, marches towards the truth in a cumulative fashion. A naïve version of the accumulation view would have us getting closer to the complete truth simply by adding more and more truths to our growing body of knowledge. This picture, however, fails to take into account the fact that once-prized theories get discarded. The radical changes that have taken place through the history of inquiry indicate that science is not a mere serial accumulation of truths. The following pessimistic induction seems to be warranted: every theory in the past has eventually been shown to be false, so our current theories may well be shown to be false. Peirce clearly rejects the accumulation picture of inquiry, for his fallibilism is based in large part on this pessimistic induction.

So if a philosopher wants to argue that our theories are getting closer to the truth, she needs to specify some traits which make one false theory more like the truth than another. If no traits are specified, then there is a trivial way to get close to the truth—we can assert only truisms, such as 'there are nine planets or it is not the case that there are nine planets'. Clearly, some notion such as content, information, or strength must be included in the construal or verisimilitude. It is not truth *simpliciter* that we are after on such an account, but rather it is something like 'interesting truth' or 'complete truth' or 'the complete true description of the world'.

Notice that seeking truth alone is, anyway, not an adequate aim for inquiry. For if we wanted simply to maximize truth, we would believe everything. We also want to avoid believing what is false. But if we merely wanted to avoid error, we would believe nothing. And if we wanted 'truth and nothing but the truth', we would believe only the evidence and its deductive consequences, for to go inductively beyond the evidence is to risk error. Since we are prepared to risk error in order to obtain information, many have suggested that these two objectives trade off against each other in inquiry—the goals of inquiry are truth and the avoidance of error.[42]

Some philosophers have said that this is what they mean when they say we are getting closer to the truth. Our aim in inquiry is to add hypotheses which are closer to the truth to our body of belief and weed out the falser ones. But, as Quine suggests, the project of making sense of measuring theories for truthlikeness is very difficult. No one has yet been able to give a satisfactory account of the notion of verisimilitude. Popper (1963) provides the most famous attempt. He advises the scientist to make bold conjectures—conjectures with lots of content so that they run a high risk of falsification. The more a hypothesis rules out, the stronger it is, or the greater its content. He defines the content of a theory as the set of statements derivable from the theory, the set of its deductive consequences. The truth content of a theory is the intersection of the content of the theory and the set of all false statements. His definition of verisimilitude is: a theory T_1 has less verisimilitude than T_2 if and only if the truth content of T_1 is less than the truth content of T_2, and the falsity content of T_2 is equal to or less than the falsity content of T_1.

There is, however, a devastating and well-known objection to this intuitively pleasing verisimilitude measure: Popper's definition never holds for two false theories.[43] One false theory will have both true and false consequences which the other lacks. So T_1 is closer to the truth than T_2 only if T_1 is true. Since the point of arriving at a measure of verisimilitude is to be able to compare false theories with each other, Popper's measure is not of much use. Much energy has been

---

[42] See Levi's work for a discussion which goes along these lines.
[43] See Miller (1974) and Tichy (1974).

spent trying to come up with an unproblematic successor, to no avail.

But, despite the passages in which Peirce speaks of hypotheses approaching a limit and induction correcting itself, it is not true to Peirce's spirit to construe him as being engaged in the project which seeks an account of verisimilitude. He can indeed be seen as construing the aim of inquiry as truth and the avoidance of error, for we have seen that he holds that the aim of inquiry is to get beliefs which would result in a 'maximum of expectation and a minimum of surprise' (MS 693, p. 166, undated). We might construe a maximum of expectation as true belief and minimum of surprise as avoidance of error. But this is not identical with the aim of getting theories which are more and more like the truth.

To see why Quine is mistaken, the little-noticed distinction between the notions of consensus and convergence must be respected.[44] Convergence is a mathematical notion: measures converge when, for two parameters with different measures, the difference between the measures gradually diminishes until it is as small as is desired. A notion of verisimilitude such as Reichenbach's or Popper's leads to a thesis about convergence. The error involved in theories (with some sort of truthlikeness measure attached to them) diminishes as the measures get closer to the truth. The gap between our theories and true theories diminishes as the measures get closer to the limit.

Consensus, on the other hand, is a matter of agreement (remember that in Peirce's case it is agreement of those engaged in experience-constrained investigation). The notion of consensus does not implicitly involve the notion of getting closer to a limit, although the consensus concept does not rule out a situation in which there would be a convergence towards agreement. Of course, if consensus is to be achieved, there will be a point at which the beliefs of inquirers converge. But 'converge' here just means 'coincide': the convergence does not have to be systematic.

Quine thinks that Peirce had something like convergence in

---

[44] Susan Haack reminded me of this distinction; Jardine (1986) also sees its importance (see p. 17).

mind when he wrote of truth—theories will get mathematically closer to the one true theory. But Peirce does not think that hypotheses are getting closer to a limit. Opinion, he insists, may oscillate for generations without any permanent settlement: 'The perversity or ignorance of mankind may make this thing or that to be held for true, for any number of generations, but it cannot affect what would be the result of sufficient experience and reasoning. And this it is which is meant by the final settled opinion.' (*CE* 3, 79, 1873.) Inquiry can go very wrong for generations and so a given point in inquiry is not a point in a convergent process. Rather, Peirce's view of truth has it that a true hypothesis is one which would be agreed upon if inquiry were to be pushed sufficiently far, if inquiry were to be pushed to its limit. And those hypotheses that would be so agreed upon would be those that produced the maximum of expectation and the minimum of surprise. Mathematical metaphors are out of place here, which is a good thing, for it seems that Quine is right in suggesting that no content can be given to a mathematical measure of the verisimilitude of theories.

It is only by paying attention to Peirce's fallibilism and critical commonsensism that we can get an accurate picture of how he conceived of the growth of knowledge and the progress of science. (The reader will notice that Peirce's picture is very similar to Quine's.) Peirce's position is that science 'is not standing upon the bedrock of fact. It is walking upon a bog, and can only say, this ground seems to hold for the present. Here I will stay till it begins to give way.'[45] Critical commonsensism insists that any discussion of the growth of knowledge must be conducted from the perspective of our current body of knowledge. Accepted hypotheses and theories are stable until they are upset by experience. They are as good as they can be, given the state of evidence, technology, argument, etc. Knowledge is rebuilt bit by bit when experience forces inquirers to revise their beliefs. The rebuilding principle is to modify in the light of recalcitrant experience and Peirce argues that we cannot help but adopt this principle.

---

[45] *CP* 5. 589, 1898. See Skagested (1981) for a similar discussion of this 'bog' metaphor.

We do have some reason to believe that, in rebuilding, we are in some sense getting closer to the truth. For the new beliefs will get along with experience better than the old ones. True beliefs are those which would, in the end, get along with experience and one explanation of our beliefs achieving better and better fit with experience is that a good number of them are true. A good number of them would be permanently doubt-resistant.

But Peirce's picture is not one of placing indubitable building blocks upon each other as we progress towards the truth. Rather, the picture is one of doubt (recalcitrant experience) forcing us to inquire until we reach another tentative doubt-resistant belief. The ground upon which inquiry walks is not solid and it is only the danger of losing our footing that makes us go forward. Doubt and uncertainty provide the motive for inquiry. All our beliefs are fallible, and when an agent accepts a belief she does so with the knowledge that it might very well succumb to surprise. But if the agent knows that the belief is the result of a reliable method (for instance, the method of abduction, deduction, induction), then she is warranted in accepting it, asserting it, and acting upon it. Whereas a true hypothesis would impinge upon us were inquiry to have run its course, hypotheses which are here and now the result of a reliable method are rational beliefs. A true belief is one that would be agreed upon and although we cannot know what would be agreed upon 'what *would* be can . . . only be learned through observation of what happens to be' (MS 200, p. 39, 1908). Beliefs which are settled upon are the best beliefs given the available evidence and argumentation. While we are waiting for the ultimate discovery of truth we can say, 'oh well, philosophical science has not by any means said its last word yet; and meantime I will continue to believe *so and so*' (CP 1. 644, 1898; see also MS 602, p. 6, 1908).

4

Objectivity, Bivalence, and Truth

Introduction

We saw in Chapter 1 that the pragmatic project is a unique philosophical enterprise—it is a specification of the consequences of hypotheses containing the notion in question. It is thus committed to providing an account of the notion which does not go beyond experience and which has 'wholesome' effects on practice. Peirce suggests that the following is a consequence of '*H* is true'. (T–I): if *H* is true, then, if inquiry relevant to *H* were pursued as far as it could fruitfully go, *H* would be believed. And he argues that we had better not add anything to the notion of truth over and above the specification of the relationship between truth and inquiry. That is, he adds another conditional. (I–T): if, if inquiry were pursued as far as it could go, *H* would be believed, then *H* is true. For if we attempt to pack more than this into the notion of truth, our account will go beyond experience.

Each of these conditionals, however, seems to put at risk what is sometimes called 'objectivity'. The I–T conditional seems to suggest that inquirers, with all of their human faults and contingencies, create the truth. One argument against this thought was articulated in Chapter 2: we saw what it is about inquiry and about belief that makes it appropriate to think that, if a hypothesis were to be believed at the end of a sufficiently prolonged inquiry, it would be true. It would be the very best it could be. In this chapter I shall take a closer look at the I–T conditional and show how it preserves four other well-understood senses of objectivity.

The T–I conditional puts objectivity at risk because it seems to entail that all of the many hypotheses which will never be settled by inquiry do not have objective truth-values. The principle of bivalence seems not to hold on Peirce's account of truth. I shall argue that Peirce thinks that both T–I and the principle of bivalence have an unusual status. He argues not that they are true, but that they are regulative assumptions of inquiry. We must hope or assume that if H is true, then if inquiry were to be prolonged as far as it could fruitfully go, we would arrive at H. And we must hope or assume that every hypothesis in an objective area of inquiry eventually would have its truth-value settled by inquiry.

We shall see, however, that the contemplation of the possibility that some hypotheses might escape this hope does not endanger what is worth preserving in Peirce's account. It does not endanger the relationship he has seen between truth and inquiry.

1. Truth, Reality, and Objectivity

Most philosophers think that Peirce cannot incorporate a very intuitive thought about what is called 'objectivity'. Peirce thinks that the meaning of the term 'objective' has undergone a 'perversion' and so he rarely uses it.[1] Things are no better now—'objectivity' is used in a startling number of ways in contemporary philosophy. It is hard to talk about it without sinking into a mire of metaphor and, as Peirce says, 'jargon,—slang jargon, at that' (*CP* 7. 195, 1891). Nevertheless, I will attempt to show how, despite first impressions, Peirce holds that whether a hypothesis is true or false is an objective matter, in some plain and respectable senses of that word.

Let us say, as a first approximation to an objectivity requirement on an account of truth, that an account of truth must have it that whether a hypothesis in a legitimate area of inquiry is true or false is not a matter of what some inquirer or group of inquirers happens to think. Someone's believing that the earth is flat does not make it so. And the community of scientists' believing that the earth is round does not make it so. This must be right. And it is the thought which motivates the correspondence theorist. But she thinks that if someone's believing H does not make H true, then *something else* must

---

[1] See *CP* 5. 501 n. 1, 1905.

make *H* true—she suggests that 'correspondence with the world' is that something else. The correspondence theorist will think that Peirce is committed to saying that what makes a hypothesis true is the agreement of inquirers. And that sounds like a straightforward denial of the first intuition about objectivity.

Other philosophers think that one can capture the intuition about objectivity without specifying correspondence with the world as what makes a hypothesis true. The intuition can be captured by a minimal requirement modelled on Tarski's work. An account of truth for a language *L* will be adequate if and only if it entails for each sentence *H* in *L* that: '*H*' is true in *L* if and only in *H*.[2] Such an account will entail that 'the earth is flat' is true in English if and only if the earth is flat. Our philosophical inquiry into the nature of truth should stop at this adequacy condition—nothing mysterious (such as the correspondence relation) should be added to it. That is, these philosophers agree with Peirce about the defects of a position which turns on a notion which we cannot grasp. Their offering for a plain and graspable account of truth is the Tarski-style definition.

Again, it is hard to see how the adequacy condition could be wrong and it has seemed to many that Peirce must think it is wrong. For it seems that Peirce goes beyond the plain adequacy condition and specifies agreement as the thing which makes a hypothesis true. Rather than asserting that '*H*' is true if and only if *H*, Peirce seems to assert that '*H*' is true if and only if it would be agreed upon.

The Peircean response here turns on the distinction between a definition and a pragmatic elucidation. Peirce would want to retain something like the adequacy condition but retain it only as a nominal or trivial definition. Certainly, he would agree with the claim that 'the earth is flat' is true if and only if the earth is flat. But he would quarrel with anyone who wanted to make such a thought the centrepiece of a substantive account of truth. For Tarski leaves open what it takes for a given sentence (or object) to satisfy the condition. We can agree that '*H*' is true if and only if *H* and ask what 'if

[2] See Tarski (1949) and (1956).

and only if *H*' amounts to.[3] The Tarskian will take a principled silence on this question.

But Peirce would argue that, while it is laudable to refrain from adding to a nominal definition anything which is metaphysically spurious, *something* must be added. For, as it stands, the Tarski-style definition tells us nothing substantial about the property truth. Like the correspondence formula, it does not tell us what to expect of true hypotheses and it does not tell us how to go about inquiring into the truth of hypotheses. Nor does it, for instance, tell us what it is about the property truth that makes it sensible to suggest that some statements are the sort which are true or false and some are the sort which are not. In its efforts to refrain from invoking anything mysterious it fails to engage the notion of truth with *anything* so as to give us a grasp of the predicate 'is true'.

The correspondence theorist will jump in here and argue that what lies behind the Tarski formula is the thought that ' "*H*" is true if and only if it corresponds to the world'. She will think that if the Tarskian account has any content at all, it coincides with the correspondence theory. The pragmatist will conclude that as soon as the Tarski-style definition engages the notion of truth with something—as soon as it is given content—it becomes identical with the correspondence theory. It engages truth with something which we cannot grasp.

So Peirce would argue that a theory which does not go beyond the adequacy condition is not up to much and a theory which elaborates the adequacy condition in terms of correspondence is up to too much. He would accept the Tarskian adequacy condition as a nominal definition of truth without trying to improve upon or refine it. Recall that he says:

So what is truth? Kant is sometimes accused of saying that it is correspondence of a predicate with its object. The great analyst was guilty of no such puerility. He calls it a nominal definition, that is to say, a suitable explanation to give to a person who has never before seen the word 'Wahrheit'. (MS 283, p. 39, 'assorted pages', 1905.)

---

[3] The same point can be made against the redundancy theory, which holds that '*H* is true' is equivalent to the assertion of *H*. We can ask just what assertion amounts to.

A nominal definition is good enough for certain purposes, but for those of us already familiar with the word 'true' something more must be offered. What Peirce adds to a nominal definition of truth is an account of the relationship between truth and inquiry. He engages the notion of truth with the notion of inquiry. But he does not do this by replacing the Tarskian biconditional with one that equates '*H* is true' with '*H* would be agreed upon'. We have seen that his thoughts about the relationship between truth and the agreement of inquirers are not expressed in terms of a biconditional.

He spells out the relationship between truth and inquiry not with a statement of logical equivalence, or a statement of equivalence of meaning, but with two conditionals—conditionals which spell out the relationship between a belief-worthy hypothesis and a true hypothesis. Peirce *asserts that* if *H* would be believed at the hypothetical end of inquiry, then *H* is true. And we shall see that he argues that we must *hope* that a consequence of *H* being true is that, if we were diligently to inquire into *H*, its truth would impress itself upon us. If we inquired long and hard about it, it is the sort of hypothesis that we would find irresistible.

In addition, Peirce is a fallibilist—he cannot take even the conditional he does assert to be a necessary or an analytic truth. He says that inquiry would arrive at the truth with a probability 1, not with absolute certainty—i.e. it is possible that the I–T conditional is false. But this does not prevent one from arguing for it, believing it, and asserting it.

So, because Peirce's view of truth does not make use of an equivalence between truth and what would be agreed upon at the end of inquiry, it is not in direct competition with the Tarskian account. Peirce's theory is not in tension with that objectivity requirement. He can absorb something like a Tarski-style definition[4] of truth and add that it is much more interesting to notice the relationship between truth and a sufficiently prolonged experience-constrained inquiry.

Let us now turn to how Peirce maintains the initial intuition about objectivity—the thought that someone's

---

[4] If the principle of bivalence is built into Tarski's account, then Peirce will not be able to absorb that particular account. For, as we shall see, Peirce maintains the principle of bivalence only as a regulative assumption of inquiry.

believing a hypothesis to be true does not make it true. We can see the issue most clearly if we look at how the notion of objectivity surfaces in Peirce's account of reality, for there is a parallel notion in his account of truth.

Peirce argues that there are two different views about reality which ought to be seen as being compatible. They are set out in his 1871 review of Fraser's edition of *The Works of George Berkeley* (CE 2, 462). He thinks that the following is a good enough definition of reality: 'The real is that which is not whatever we happen to think it, but is unaffected by what we may think of it.'[5] This definition captures the first objectivity requirement set out above—whether a thing is real cannot be a matter of what someone thinks. Peirce thinks that this is a nominal definition, 'a verbal definition, not a doctrine' (CP 5. 525, 1905). There is more to the real than that, just as he would think that there is more to the truth than the Tarski-style adequacy condition. He says that 'there are two widely separated points of view, from which *reality*, as just defined, may be regarded'. The first of these substantial views is the more 'familiar' one, which Peirce labels 'nominalist'. It specifies what it is that is unaffected by us—external objects. Our thoughts 'have been caused by sensations, and those sensations are constrained by something out of the mind. This thing out of the mind, which directly influences sensation . . . is independent of how we think it, and is, in short, the real' (CE 2, 468). The nominalist view of reality takes reality to be the set of external physical entities which impinge upon us.

But this view of reality, Peirce thinks, only captures part of what is real. There is another view of reality which fulfils the independence condition imposed by the definition of reality: 'it is not in respect to this immediate insistence alone that the real is as it is independently of how we think it to be' (CP 7. 666, 1903; see also CE 2, 469).

That view, unsurprisingly, is a pragmatic one.[6] The consequence of a thing's being real is that the hypothesis

---

[5] CE 2, 467, 1871; see also CE 3, 271, 1878; CP 1. 578, 1902; 6. 495, 1906.

[6] Peirce calls it the 'realist' view, as opposed to the nominalist one. To avoid confusion with what is currently called 'realism', I will refer to this view as the pragmatic view. Peirce says that 'after forty years experience in this way of using the word [real], I find it remarkably satisfactory' (MS 200, p. 96, 1908).

asserting its reality would be, if inquiry relevant to it were pursued, perfectly stable or doubt-resistant. If we were to inquire into issues for which the hypothesis is relevant, it would in the long run force itself on our attention. The pragmatic view of reality is that reality is the 'object' of true beliefs—it is what true beliefs are about.[7] Reality is what beliefs in the final opinion would fix on.[8]

This view of reality, Peirce argues, fulfils the definition of reality as that which is independent of whatever 'you, I, or any number of men' think. We have seen that Peirce is a realist about subjunctives. What would be believed to be real is thus independent of what is believed to be real at any particular point. The real 'is that which, sooner or later, information and reasoning would result in, and which is therefore independent of the vagaries of you and me'.[9] So Peirce thinks that reality as construed pragmatically—that 'permanency, that fixed reality'—is 'an objective point' (*CE* 3, 29, 1872).

He makes the same point about truth. What would be ascertained to be true would be so ascertained whatever anyone here and now thinks. A hypothesis may be believed, then doubted, and then believed again, but this does not alter whether it would be believed at the end of a prolonged inquiry. Independently of whatever any 'definite' group of

---

[7] Notice that it does not follow from Peirce's position that if thinking beings had not evolved, there would be no reality. For if thinking beings had not evolved, it would not have been a consequence of '*x* is real' that *x* would finally be believed to be real. Moreover, the predicate 'is true' applies only to beliefs (or to sentences or some other bits of language) and beliefs must be believed by humans or some other suitable sort of being. So if there were no thinking beings, 'truth' would be an uninstantiated property. There would be no true *beliefs*. But there would be the brute existence of reality.

[8] Sometimes, when Peirce accepts the correspondence theorist's nominal definition of truth, he insists that the reality to which our beliefs correspond must be construed pragmatically. He says, 'the only object to which inquiry seeks to make our opinion conform is itself something of the nature of thought; namely, it is the predestined ultimate idea, which is independent of what you, I or any number of men may persist, for however long, in thinking, yet which remains thought after all.' (*CP* 8. 103, 1900; see also 5. 553, 1905; 5. 565, 1901.) If a hypothesis is 'a safe basis for prediction' ('safe' in that it would not be upset by surprising experience, and hence would be believed at the end of inquiry) then you can say that it 'corresponds to a reality' (*CP* 5. 96, 1903).

[9] *CE* 2, 239, 1868, 'Consequences of Four Incapacities'. Notice the use of the subjunctive in this (early) 1868 statement. See also *CE* 2, 469, 1871; MS 393, p. 1, undated; MS 409, p. 182, 1883; *CP* 8. 144, 1901.

inquirers may think about the truth-value of H, H either would be or would not be a member of the final opinion (*CP* 5. 565, 1901). Thus the truth-value of H is an objective matter—it does not depend on what anyone happens to think. This point about objectivity also comes out within Peirce's doctrine of fallibilism. It holds that because truth is what would be believed at the end of an indefinitely prolonged inquiry, we cannot be sure that any current belief of ours is true. What we now take to be true and what our inquiries are now concerned with might be very different from what is taken to be true and interesting as inquiry progresses. Hence the final beliefs are independent of us.

One might object that, if time T_f is the hypothetical end of inquiry, then any stage T_{f-n} will play a causal role in determining what would be believed at T_f. That is, the final opinion would arise from a step-by-step process, and any given time T_{f-n} is a stage in that development. What we inquire into now will affect what questions get asked in the future and it will thus affect what questions get settled. Truth, on Peirce's account, does seem to be dependent on what we think here and now.

But Peirce's point is that what is believed at any T_{f-n} may be radically different from what would be believed at T_f. Hence, we cannot infallibly infer from what is believed at any T_{f-n} what would be believed at T_f. In this sense, what would be believed is independent of what is now believed.

None the less, truth is a property of *our* beliefs. And truth is what we would find *ourselves* with at the end of a sufficiently resolute inquiry. Thus, in some other sense of 'dependent', truth is dependent on us. The predicate 'is true' applies to the beliefs (or sentences if you like) of a certain kind of being. Once beliefs are as good as they possibly could be for that sort of being, they are true.

We have seen that Peirce holds that there are 'two views of the real—one as the fountain of the current of human thought, the other as the unmoving form to which it is flowing' (*CE* 2, 471). And both views are committed to the thought that reality is, in one sense or another, independent of what anyone thinks about it. The difference between the two is that pragmatism 'emphasizes the permanency and

fixity of reality' whereas nominalism 'emphasizes its externality' (*CE* 3, 29, 1872).

Each of these positions articulates a conception of objectivity and although Peirce favours one articulation, he does
not want to jettison the other. And here we find another sense
in which objectivity is preserved in Peirce's account. He
argues that although we should 'regard reality as the normal
product of mental action, and not as the incognizable cause
of it', the two views are nevertheless compatible[10] The
pragmatic view encompasses the nominalist view, which is
'convenient for certain purposes'. It is just that the pragmatist
is unhappy with the thought that what nominalism offers is
an account which can stand on its own.[11] For in appealing in
such a cavalier way to external objects as the cause of belief,
the nominalist is making the correspondence theorist's
mistake—she is appealing to something which we cannot
grasp. This view is pragmatically empty and will thus have no
'wholesome effects' upon inquiry. It is only useful to those
who have never encountered the term 'real' before.

Peirce asks what it is that the nominalist view is really
committed to. It holds that a real thing is something in the
physical world which impinges upon our senses. He asks
'What is the *power* of external things, to affect the senses?'
(*CE* 2, 469.) The way in which we discover such a power or
the existence of a real thing, he suggests, is by noticing a
regularity and expecting it to hold for future events. And then
he says:

to assert that there are external things which can be known only as
exerting a power on our sense, is nothing different from asserting
that there is a general *drift* in the history of human thought which
will lead it to one general agreement, one catholic consent. And any
truth more perfect than this destined conclusion, any reality more
absolute than what is thought in it, is a fiction of metaphysics. (*CE*
2, 469.)

That is, if you ask the nominalist how the existence of a real
physical entity will manifest itself, she will reply that, if we
inquire into it, it will impinge upon us. Pragmatism, far from

---

[10] *CE* 2, 471. He sees that, on the surface, the two views seem to be incompatible.
See *CE* 3, 30, 1872.
[11] Similarly, what the Tarski definition offers is not an account which can stand
on its own.

denying this, holds that this is just what the consequence of a thing's existing would be. Thus the pragmatic view 'is also highly favorable to a belief in external realities' (*CE* 2, 470). These are not, however, 'the unknowable cause of sensation', for we can have knowledge of them—we can have permanently settled beliefs about them. External entities would be believed to be real at the end of inquiry; they will be among 'the last products of the mental action which is set in motion by sensation' (*CE* 2, 470).

Thus the pragmatic view subsumes the nominalist view. The pragmatist agrees that the real is the fountain of human thought but insists that we can say nothing about its nature. All we can say is that a consequence of something being real is that it would impinge upon us—it eventually would be believed to be real. And external entities, we think, would be believed to be real. Pragmatists 'need not, and should not deny that the reality exists externally to the mind' (*CE* 3, 29, 1872). Idealism—that it is a 'mere fairy tale to say that outward objects *exist*, the only objects of possible experience being our own ideas'—is 'completely false'. For 'Secondness jabs you perpetually in the ribs' (*CP* 6. 95, 1903).[12] The bruteness of experience cannot be ignored and we take this experience to be an index of the existence of things. But we must not make the nominalist's mistake and leap from this indication of reality to the assertion that reality consists of external objects which are utterly independent of inquirers and which cause inquirers to form beliefs about them.

Pragmatists, moreover, should deny that *all* reality exists externally to the mind. For although external reality may cause some sensations and these sensations can cause doubts, this does not entail that true beliefs can only be about physical sensations and objects. The 'hardness of fact' is not due to its externality; it is due to 'its resistance to being ignored' (*CP* 2. 139, 1902). Nominalists deny the predicate 'is real' to anything other than actual existing objects. Pragmatists maintain that there is more to reality than the physical world.

---

[12] Sometimes, however, Peirce called pragmatism a brand of idealism. See *CP* 8. 284, 1904. For passages connecting reality with brute compulsion, see *CP* 1. 175, 1897; 1. 325, undated; 2. 337, 1895; 6. 340, 1908; 8. 156, 1901; 5. 564, 1900.

As we saw in Chapter 2, Peirce's categories admit three grades of reality—the possible, the actual, and the general. Only the second category is the category of existence and brute force. A law, a possibility, and a right are not existing objects, and yet could be believed, at the end of inquiry, to be real. The real is thus a wider notion than the existent. Peirce says:

It is perfectly true that all white things have whiteness in them, for that is only saying, in another form of words, that all white things are white; but since it is true that real things possess whiteness, whiteness is real. It is a real which only exists by virtue of an act of thought knowing it, but that thought is not an arbitrary or accidental one dependent on any idiosyncrasies, but one which [would] hold in the final opinion. (*CE* 2, 470, 1871.)[13]

So when Peirce says that dispositions, generals, possibilities, etc. are real, he does not mean that they actually exist as objects or entities. Holding that x is real does not commit one to holding that x is an existing thing in the world. Rather, it commits one to holding that at the end of a prolonged inquiry, x would be believed to be real or at the end of a prolonged inquiry, some hypotheses about x would be believed. There would be all sorts of beliefs about the external world in the final opinion but there would be other sorts of beliefs as well.

We have seen in this chapter that Peirce's I–T conditional accommodates objectivity in a number of ways. First, an unsubstantial Tarski-style adequacy condition can be subsumed. Secondly, inquirers, at any given stage of investigation, do not determine or create the truth; truth is not a matter of what inquirers happen to think. The objective truth of the matter is that which inquiry *would* determine. Thirdly, 'immediate insistence' provides a kind of objectivity: the brute impinging of experience indicates that something 'is'. And we saw in Chapter 2 that because of the nature of genuine inquiry and genuine belief, the beliefs which inquiry would determine would have all of the virtues belief can have. Not just any old beliefs would be found in the final opinion. This point might lead us to discern a final way in which objectivity is found in Peirce's position. Although

---

[13] I have replaced a 'will' with Peirce's considered 'would'.

reality is not, on his account, just the physical world, unless our beliefs cohere with external experience we will doubt them. Hence, that which would be believed at the end of inquiry would cohere with experience—with our indices of the external world.

Peirce, however, is indeed set against one conception of objectivity. Some philosophers take the issue about objectivity to be as follows: 'How do we tell when we are discovering objects "as they really stand in nature", and when we are doing some other thing, such as projecting onto them our own subjective sentiments?'[14] This way of stating the issue connects objectivity to 'nature' or to the physical world. Those who endorse this conception of objectivity tend to think that the only objective area of inquiry is empirical or scientific inquiry. Unsurprisingly, they conclude that only when we hypothesize about the external world are we making claims about objects as they really stand in *nature*; the rest of the time we are 'doing some other thing'. Hypotheses about possibilities, generalities, probabilities, or morals are not objective on such an account.

We have seen that the pragmatist, on the other hand, does not focus on the sense of 'objectivity' which is connected to 'nature' or to the physical world. Rather, the most important sense of objectivity is that which is connected to what would prove resistant to doubt and thus to what inquiry would eventually decide. Those hypotheses which are such that they would be determined to be either true or false are objective. Those which are such that they would not be settled are not objective.

Peirce refuses to offer an opinion about which sorts of hypotheses are objective and which are not. He articulates his position with conditionals only. If, after a sufficiently prolonged inquiry into the matters, we were to agree on the truth-values of '*A* is morally wrong' and '*B* is not a possibility', then these hypotheses would be objective ones. If there would be no such agreement, then the hypotheses would not have objective truth-values. And Peirce's generous

---

[14] Blackburn (1984), p. 145. Blackburn calls himself a 'quasi-realist' because he is willing to give some sort of legitimacy to non-objective 'stances'. But he draws a sharp line between objective stances (empirical matters) and stances for which we 'project' properties onto the world (moral matters, probabilities, etc.).

notion of experience invites hypotheses about non-physical matters to try and qualify themselves as candidates for truth-values. So we must remember not to conflate undecidability and unverifiability. To decide or agree that something is the case is not the same as to verify by observation that it is the case.[15] For the reasons for deciding upon something might have little to do with sensory evidence. Hypotheses about matters which do not lend themselves to direct observation might eventually be settled. Peirce says, for instance, that 'The truth of the proposition that Caesar crossed the Rubicon consists in the fact that the further we push our archaeological and other studies, the more strongly will that conclusion force itself on our minds forever—or would do so, if study were to go on forever.' (*CP* 5. 565, 1901.) Statements about the past, unobservable entities, and morals can, in principle, be candidates for the truth predicate, despite the fact that they have no direct link with empirical observation. They may be the sort of hypothesis that would be believed at the end of inquiry, for we have seen that abductive inference is frequently going to infer these sorts of hypotheses to explain certain phenomena. As an example, Peirce cites the documents and monuments referring to Napoleon Bonaparte: although we have not seen the man, we cannot explain what we have seen (the documents and monuments) 'without supposing that he really existed'. Thus history or inquiry about the past is a matter for abduction. (*CP* 2. 511 n. 1, 1883.)

2. Buried Secrets

Peirce, we have seen, thinks that an objectively true hypothesis would have as a consequence that which is spelt out by

---

[15] Nor is it the same as to prove that it is the case. Nothing like a mathematical *proof* is required in order for a hypothesis to be true. For instance, we assume that if we were to inquire into it, the pragmatically defunct hypothesis about the recent creation of the world would be decided upon. No experience could tell us that it is false, yet we would not be able to bring ourselves to believe it. Common sense settles the matter. Similarly, the fact that there are mathematical proofs that certain mathematical questions cannot be proved is of no great worry. If we can recognize a hypothesis as reasonable to believe, that is enough.

his T–I conditional: if inquiry relevant to it were pursued, it would be agreed upon. An objectively false hypothesis would have the following consequence: if inquiry relevant to it were pursued, it would be agreed to be false. And only those questions which would have determinate answers or those hypotheses which would have their truth-values determined by inquiry are objective. He says, 'as to an inquiry presupposing that there is some one truth, what can this possibly mean except that there is one destined upshot to inquiry with reference to the question in hand—one result, which when reached will never be overthrown?' (*CP* 3. 432, 1896.) Peirce thinks that what we aim for in inquiry is the objectively correct answer to the question at hand. And we have seen that he takes that aim to amount to the aim

to get a settlement of opinion, that is; some conclusion which shall be independent of all individual limitation, independent of caprice, of tyranny, of accidents of situation, of initial conditions, a conclusion to which every man would come who should pursue the same method and push it far enough. (*CE* 3, 19, 1872; see also *CP* 5. 494, 1907).

An objective question is one which 'has one answer which is decidedly right, whatever people may think about it . . . there is *something* that is *so*, no matter if there be an overwhelming vote against it' (*CP* 2. 135, 1902).

But many will think that this is an impoverished account of objectivity and thus an impoverished account of truth. For many philosophers these days think that an adequate account of truth must preserve the following sort of objectivity: an objective hypothesis is one which is either true or false, whether or not we will in fact, or could ever, know which it is. I will call this the realist intuition. It maintains that the principle of bivalence holds for all hypotheses in an objective area of inquiry. The principle of bivalence is a semantic principle: a hypothesis is either true or false, but not both. (Its syntactic partner is the law of the excluded middle: $Pv\text{-}P$.) That is, every significant statement in the indicative mood has a truth-value.[16] And if the principle of bivalence holds, then if the truth-value of a significant hypothesis cannot or would

[16] The reader will recognize this as part of the issue between 'semantic'

not be settled, we still know that it is in fact either true or false. The knowledge that it is either true or false goes beyond our ability to determine the application of the predicates 'is true' and 'is false'.

We have seen that Peirce does not hold that there is an equivalence between truth and final agreement. But final agreement plays a role in a way that distinguishes his account from others who would altogether sever truth and objectivity from inquiry. These positions hold that the objective truth-value of a hypothesis is not the value which would be assigned to it by a sufficiently pursued and experience-constrained inquiry, for the value which such an inquiry would assign might be the wrong one. We saw in Chapter 2 that Peirce could not accept this suggestion. He thinks that it is spurious to hold that our best hypotheses could be false. In 4.6, I shall argue that Peirce is right in linking truth and inquiry in this way. He is right to assert the I–T conditional: if, if inquiry were to be pursued as far as it could fruitfully go, then *H* would be believed, then *H* is true.

But the philosophers who unlink truth from the final upshot of inquiry will also want to dispute the T–I conditional. They will want to dispute the claim that if a hypothesis is true, then it would have the consequence of being agreed to be true after a prolonged inquiry. They will argue that the claim entails a denial of the realist intuition. Some hypotheses which we think must have determinate truth-values will not, it seems, be agreed to be true or false, no matter how far inquiry is prolonged.

We surely think, for example, that the issue of how many times Churchill sneezed in 1949 is an objective one: the hypothesis 'Churchill sneezed exactly fifty-two times in 1949' is either true or false. But it is extremely unlikely that inquiry would ever settle the issue of how many times Churchill sneezed in a given year.[17] It is not, it seems, a consequence of the true hypothesis that Churchill sneezed some *n* times that inquiry would finally settle upon that. And thus it seems that,

---

realists and anti-realists. Although I will articulate Peirce's position on the principle of bivalence, I will not explicitly discuss its relevance to this debate. For Peirce does not fit neatly into either of these camps.

[17] See Smart (1986) for this objection.

on Peirce's account, the hypothesis has no truth-value. The principle of bivalence does not hold in a case in which it seems that it should hold.

Peirce anticipates the challenge:

> But I may be asked what I have to say to all the minute facts of history, forgotten never to be recovered, to the lost books of the ancients, to the buried secrets . . . Do these things not really exist because they are hopelessly beyond the reach of our knowledge? (*CE* 3, 274, 1878, 'How to Make Our Ideas Clear'.)

We saw in Chapter 2 that Peirce's response to these sorts of questions is that it is a regulative assumption of inquiry that inquirers hope or assume that, if we were to inquire diligently into any given question, there would be an upshot to our inquiry. He argues that 'the only assumption upon which [we] can act rationally is the hope of success' (*CE* 2, 272, 1869). Thus his response to the challenge is to remain optimistic about inquiry; he suggests that we remain optimistic that, for any hypothesis in a legitimate domain, a prolonged inquiry would declare it to be either true or false.

The notion of a regulative assumption requires some analysis. The Peircean point is not about the logical status of the principle of bivalence (i.e. that it is a logical truth) nor is it about the nature of the world (i.e. that the world is such that the principle of bivalence must hold). It is a point about inquiry and what those engaged in inquiry must assume. For to say that something is a regulative assumption is to make a statement about a practice. A certain practice—in this case inquiry—requires for its sensible continuation that inquirers assume something. But to say that something is a regulative assumption is not to say that it is true. Peirce says that we are 'obliged to suppose', but we 'need not assert', that there are determinate answers to all of our questions.

The assumption, like everything else, is subject to Peirce's fallibilism:

> We cannot be quite sure that the community ever will settle down to an unalterable conclusion upon any given question. Even if they do so for the most part, we have no reason to think the unanimity will be quite complete, nor can we rationally presume any overwhelming *consensus* of opinion will be reached upon every question. (*CP* 6. 610, 1893.)

The fact that the assumption is indispensable to inquiry should not convince us of its truth. He says: 'I do not admit that indispensability is any ground of belief. It may be indispensable that I should have $500 in the bank—because I have given checks to that amount. But I have never found that the indispensability directly affected my balance, in the least.' (*CP* 2. 113, 1901; see also 3. 432, 1896.) We must make the assumption 'for the same reason that a general who has to capture a position or see his country ruined, must go on the hypothesis that there is some way in which he can and shall capture it' (*CP* 7. 219, 1901; see also *CE* 2, 272, 1869).

So Peirce's claim is that if we are to inquire rationally about some particular issue, then we must assume that there is at least a chance of there being an upshot to our inquiry. Otherwise, there really would be no point in inquiring into the matter. Refusing to make the assumption is to block the path of inquiry and that, Peirce maintains, is the cardinal philosophical sin. But the justification for the regulative hypothesis is merely one of 'desperation'—if we do not make it, we will 'be quite unable to know anything of positive fact' (*CP* 5. 603, 1903). Such an assumption is one we must 'embrace at the outset, however destitute of evidentiary support it may be' (*CP* 7. 219, 1901).

The claim, notice, is not that anyone who refuses to assert bivalence for some domain or for some hypothesis is irrational. That would be prematurely to condemn intuitionist mathematicans and those who deny bivalence for statements such as 'Rocky Road ice cream is delicious'. The Peircean point is about areas of inquiry which are thought to be objective. The inquirer must assume, for a hypothesis which is thought to be objective, that there is a chance that inquiry would eventually settle on its truth-value. Of course, on Peirce's account, whether an issue is indeed objective can only be known in the long run. But we can have more or less reasonable beliefs here and now about which matters are objective and which are not.

It remains to be seen, however, whether Peirce's appeal to a regulative assumption is the best way for the pragmatist to deal with the realist intuition. To see just what Peirce is and should be committed to about the principle of bivalence, Nicholas Jardine's *The Fortunes of Inquiry* (1986) provides a useful backdrop. For Jardine develops a pragmatic[18] conception of truth which is similar to Peirce's and he is very concerned to block challenges that arise from the realist intuition.

3. Peirce and Jardine on the Fortunes of Inquiry

Jardine does not have a general pragmatic account of how to go about unpacking philosophical concepts but none the less, he offers the following neo-Peircean biconditional definition of truth (p. 28): 'S is *true* if, and only if, there is an absolute inquiry series from the standpoint of which it is true.' A hypothesis is true if and only if it would be the product of (a certain sort of) inquiry.

Jardine spends much energy trying to block objections about the principle of bivalence, for he says that the most obvious challenge to his (and any) pragmatic account of truth is the fact that it seems to go against the grain of the realist intuition.[19] In order to preserve that intuition, Jardine makes it a condition of his special inquiry series that it have an unlimited capacity to resolve questions.[20] If a question is well posed, it ought to be answerable—'no genuine question for ever resists settlement'.

Jardine thinks that the realist intuition is so powerful that if an account of truth denies it, the denial is a *reductio ad absurdum* of that account. Since he defines truth and falsity as what would be believed to be true or false at the end of inquiry, he is thus committed to arguing the following. The inquiry series whose endproduct is the truth must be capable of resolving (or dissolving) all questions. At the end of inquiry, all questions which had been asked would have had to have been answered or shown to be illegitimate.

---

[18] Jardine considers and rejects what is commonly taken to be Peirce's theory and goes on to 'improve' upon it. Peirce is discussed only in one footnote (p. 14), and is taken to hold an account based on convergence, not consensus. We saw in Ch. 3 that this is not the best interpretation of Peirce.

[19] See Jardine (1986), p. 29.

[20] Jardine (1986), p. 26. The other two features of a truth-producing inquiry series, which I shall not discuss, are (i) the special inquiry must 'transcend error' and (ii) it must 'dominate' all other inquiry series.

Jardine identifies different sorts of problematic questions. There are three sorts of challenges to his claim that all questions would be resolved or dissolved at the end of inquiry or to Peirce's assumption that the consequence of a true hypothesis is that, in a prolonged inquiry, its truth would impinge upon us. The first sort are of the Churchill type, 'factual' questions for which some indispensable data is inaccessible:

how many coelacanths swam in the deeps, how many pterodactyls flitted the skies and how many tyrannosaurs roamed the earth eighty million years ago today? That many such questions have determinate answers is an assumption that we are exceedingly unlikely to revise. But it is practically certain that almost all such questions would remain unresolved even were human inquiry (or, for that matter, the inquiries of whatever other inquirers the universe may sustain) to continue for ever. (Jardine 1986, p. 29.)

These are 'genuine questions' (i.e. questions which cannot be dissolved) whose answers could have been determined by inquirers who had possessed evidence which is now inaccessible. Jardine responds to this challenge by recommending 'counterfactual bravado': a counterfactual thought experiment involving time travel. We are to 'imagine an indefinitely prolonged human inquiry in which, *per impossibile*, our evidence-gathering capacities are entirely unrestricted' (Jardine 1986, p. 56). Jardine wants us to conceive of inquirers as having an ability they in fact do not have. Inquirers, construed with counterfactual bravado, can travel back in time to gather evidence.

So he thinks that the question 'How many tyrannosaurs were there exactly eighty million years ago?' has a determinate answer. It is either true or false that there were exactly 2,006. There is a determinate answer because, were we able and willing to travel back to the time in question, we would count some number n of them. If we broaden the notion of inquiry in this manner, the pragmatist can cope with the first sort of problematic question.

The second kind of challenge is the type of question for which we are unable to arrive at explanatory theories and hypotheses. For instance, we might not see how we could explain the origin of consciousness, of life, or of the universe. Jardine responds by pointing out that 'The history of science is well stocked with examples of questions once thought on such grounds to be entirely intractable, but from the standpoint of current theories either resolved or well on the way to resolution . . . '(Jardine 1986, p. 47). He points to research involving syntheses of organic macromolecules under circumstances which simulate the 'primeval soup' as the beginning of an answer to one of these intractable questions.

Thirdly, there are 'philosophical' or enigmatic questions which seem to be well posed, but are such that we have no conception of evidence relevant to them. One such type of question, he says, transcends inquiry by virtue of its generality—for instance, 'Why is there something rather than nothing?'.

Another sort is the kind of question for which there are equally balanced considerations pro and con; perhaps the issue of free will versus determinism is such a question.[21] Jardine suggests that we try to break some of these down into smaller soluble questions, and he recommends dissolving the others. It is instructive to look at the latter strategy, for it appears to be similar to the pragmatic method of disqualifying certain questions.

The thesis that Jardine needs to maintain is that all questions have determinate answers or else they are dissoluble. Dissolving a question, he says, is showing it to be ill posed. One way of doing this is to show that the question rests on false presuppositions. For instance, from the standpoint of our current theories, questions about what type of weather corresponds to a particular bodily disease are dissolved. We would not expect inquiry to answer questions which assume a false framework.

But another way of dissolving an issue, he says, is to show it to be 'not susceptible to any evidential considerations'.[22] He would presumably say that the hypothesis 'the world and

---

[21] This question seemed to be a stock example of a potentially unanswerable question in Peirce's day. Peirce mentions it (*CP* 5. 565, 1901) and so do Du Bois-Reymond (1882) and Haeckel (1899).

[22] Jardine (1986), pp. 21, 25, 121.

everything in it, including memories and fossils, was created five minutes ago' is such a hypothesis. No evidence relevant to the resolution of the question could be available, and hence it is ill posed and dissoluble. Here, however, Jardine seems to be involved in considerable question-begging. The challenges posed by undecidable questions all appeal to the realist intuition. The questions are problematic because it seems that we have no evidence for them—because the evidence is inaccessible (the tyrannosaur type), because we do not yet have the evidence (the origin of life type), or because there just could not be any evidence for the claim in question (the worst sort of philosophical type). Surely, the challenges go, the pragmatist does not want to say that these hypotheses have no truth-values. The first sort, Jardine responds, do indeed have truth-values—we must merely exercise counter-factual bravado in thinking about them. At least we can imagine how, if certain counterfactual conditions were to obtain (if we could go back in time and check), we could decide the truth-values of the hypotheses. The second sort also have truth-values—we must merely be optimistic about future inquiry discovering them. The third sort, however, do not seem to be relevant even to counterfactually construed evidence, nor to any future evidence. So Jardine insists that they are not genuine.

But to argue that some questions are dissoluble, not resoluble, because no evidence would be relevant to their resolution, is just to repeat the reason for them being problematic. They are problematic (we cannot seem to answer them) because no evidence seems to be relevant to their resolution. To claim that they are dissoluble for this reason is to sentence them for no crime other than that they are a nuisance.

Notice that the first of Jardine's dissolution strategies— dissolving questions because their presuppositions are false— is a principled means of sentencing questions to the dissoluble realm. There is something wrong with questions that are based on false presuppositions, and we can hardly expect those questions to be answered in the final, true, opinion. They do not pose a serious challenge to the resolution hypothesis because they are defective. That is, we can say 'question Q does not count as undecidable (it does not refute

the resolution hypothesis) because——', where in place of
'——', we have considerations about the inadequacy or
falsity of its presuppositions. And for the tyrannosaur type
questions, we fill the blank with 'if we exercise counterfactual
bravado we can see that they are, in principle, indeed
decidable'.[23] But saying, for the philosophical questions, that
no evidence would be relevant to their resolution is to replace
the'——'with the blatantly unsatisfactory 'it is undecidable'.
That is, 'question Q does not count as being undecidable (it
does not refute the resolution hypothesis) because nothing
can decide it'.[24]

If Jardine had a good independent argument for the
inadmissibility of questions which are not amenable to
evidence, his response to the challenge posed by philosophical questions would be satisfactory. Then there would be
good reason for making 'susceptible to evidential considerations' a necessary condition for non-defective hypotheses.
The arguments might be the pragmatic ones sketched in the
first chapter, contemporary 'manifestationist' arguments,[25]
or the logical positivist's arguments. Jardine, however, does
not seem to want to be associated with any of these positions.
But one cannot detach the pragmatic account of truth from
the pragmatic account of significance and be left with a viable
position.

So, like Jardine, Peirce would respond to the challenge
posed by the worst sort of 'philosophical' questions by saying
that many of them should be dissolved.[26] Unlike Jardine, he
offers an argument for connecting the undecidable with the
non-genuine. The realist intuition is of course only going to

---

[23] I do not want to support this reason here, but merely to say that at least it is a
reason; i.e. some reason is given for not counting the sort of question as undecidable.

[24] Another way of putting this point is as follows. Jardine defines a 'well-posed'
question as one which has true presuppositions and is susceptible to evidential
considerations. Then he says (p.26) 'An inquiry series S is *infinitely resolutive of
questions* just in case, for all Q? such that Q? is well posed from the standpoint of S,
Q? is determined by S.' But his definiton of 'well-posedness' does away with the most
problematic type of questions for the resolution hypotheses.

[25] See Dummett (1978), Luntley (1988), Peacocke (1988).

[26] Peirce does not suggest, with Jardine, that we can break them down into
soluble bits or dissolve them by showing that they rest on false presuppositions. He
might well agree with these claims, but in general he thinks that philosophy's
incompetence at settling belief is a measure of its immaturity as a method of inquiry.

range over non-spurious hypotheses: no one would say that a hypothesis which failed the test of significance was determinately either true or false. The pragmatic maxim will declare some philosophical questions to be suspicious, and hence they will not form a part of the challenge based on the realist intuition. The hope that a hypothesis has a determinate truth-value applies only to hypotheses that are pragmatically significant:

> though in no possible state of knowledge can any number be great enough to express the relation between the amount of what rests unknown to the amount of the known, yet it is unphilosophical to suppose that, with regard to any given question (*which has any clear meaning*), investigation would not bring forth a solution of it, if it were carried far enough. (*CE* 3, 274, 1878, my emphasis.)

And

> If our hope is in vain; if in respect to some question—say that of the freedom of the will—no matter how long the discussion goes on, no matter how scientific our methods may become, there never will be a time when we can fully satisfy ourselves *either that the question has no meaning, or that one answer or the other explains the facts*, then in regard to that question, there certainly is no *truth*. (*CP* 5. 565, 1901, first emphasis mine.)

If a hypothesis has no pragmatic meaning, then it has no consequences and its truth would not impinge upon us: 'As for questions which have no conceivable practical bearings, as the question whether force is an entity, they mean nothing and may be answered as we like, without error.' (*CP* 8. 43, 1885, Review of Royce's *The Religious Aspect of Philosophy*.) The reason for there not being any settled belief about a question might be that there is no truth of the matter (*CP* 5. 565, 1901). The phenomena, as it were, refuse to point in one direction. So, with respect to Jardine's worst sort of 'philosophical' questions, Peirce can retain the hope of bivalence and have his pragmatic maxim ensure that those hypotheses which are in principle not amenable to evidential considerations are ruled out as pragmatically meaningless.

Both Peirce and Jardine appeal to optimism with respect to the second sort of question, those for which we cannot seem to arrive at explanatory hypotheses. Peirce argues that science has resolved all sorts of questions that once looked hopeless, and hence we ought to be hopeful:

in all our gropings, we bump up against problems which we cannot imagine how to attack, why space should have three dimensions, if it really has but three . . . why atoms should attract one another at a distance, if they really do . . . how or by what kind of influence matter came to be sifted out . . . why certain motions of the atoms of certain kinds of protoplasm are accompanied by sensation, and so on through the whole list.[27]

Our science, he says, is still superficial; even more so 'when we consider within how narrow a range all our inquiries have hitherto lain'. We hope that (eventually) we will strike upon the best explanation of these phenomena, and if that explanation would fit with the rest of our stable theories and would not be overturned by experience, the matter would be settled.

Peirce mentions one type of problematic question which Jardine does not—questions which would be undecided not because of lack of sufficient evidence, but rather because of lack of sufficient interest.[28] If a question does not 'excite sufficient interest' in inquirers so that they pursue inquiry, then the question of truth does not arise for it. It may have an objective truth-value, for were inquiry relevant to it pursued, it might be decided upon. Again, we must appeal to realism about subjunctives. Peirce argues that if H has a truth-value then this conditional holds: if inquiry were to be pursued, H would either be agreed to be true or agreed to be false. If the antecedent of the conditional is not fulfilled, we cannot conclude that the consequent is false; i.e. we cannot conclude that H does not have a determinate truth-value. What we can say, however, is that the question of truth does not *arise* for these hypotheses. That is, there is a difference between (*a*) hypotheses which, were inquiry to be pursued, would not be resolved and (*b*) hypotheses for which inquiry is not pursued.

---

[27] CP 5. 586, 1898, see also CP 6. 556, 1905. The issue of whether some things were destined always to be riddles was raging in Peirce's day. As Jardine notes, Du Bois-Reymond (1882) set out a number of enigmas including the origin of motion, the basis of sensation, the origin of life, the reason organisms adapt to environments, the genesis of reasoning and language, and the problem of free will. Haeckel (1899) immediately proceeded to outline potential solutions to most of them.

[28] See CP 8. 43, 1885, Review of Royce's *The Religious Aspect of Philosophy*.

Hypotheses of type (*a*), on Peirce's account, do not have truth-values; for hypotheses of type (*b*) the question of truth-value will be contingently unanswerable. Thus the following objection to Peirce's position is not a good one. This objection is that if science would never come to a settled belief about some issues, the final opinion will not be the entire body of truths. Peirce would say here that it is misleading to talk of the truth as being the complete body of truths, as being the one true complete description of the world. We must talk of truth question by question, and complicate the subjunctive conditional: if a particular non-spurious issue were to excite sufficient interest, and were to be pursued as far as it could fruitfully go, then what would finally be believed about it would be the true belief. Peirce does not think that at the end of inquiry we would have discovered every truth, but rather, for any question we think of and diligently inquire into, if it admits of an answer, then in the end we would have arrived at that (correct) answer. To the objection that 'investigation does not suppose that it can solve *all* questions', Peirce replies: 'it will at least never positively conclude any question to be absolutely insoluble so that it may as well assume them [all] to be soluble after an indefinite time' (*CE* 3, 18, 1872). We shall never know the true answer to *every* question, but with respect to any question which is in doubt, we assume that a sufficiently prolonged inquiry would produce a true belief. Because 'there is nothing to distinguish the unanswerable questions from the answerable ones', we must 'proceed as if all were answerable' (*CP* 8. 43, 1885).

So Peirce easily wards off those who, like Harman, object to any 'idealized theory of truth' for this reason:

> it is perfectly obvious that truth cannot be identified with an idealization of rational acceptance, since there are many trivial truths it would be irrational to accept. It is irrational to clutter one's mind with useless information . . . So, even if the ideal result of rational inquiry must be counted as true, there will be other truths as well that are not included in the ideal result of rational inquiry. (Harman 1982, p. 574.)

The ideal result must not be pictured as a body of statements which constitute the complete truth. If we were interested enough to inquire into genuine but trivial hypotheses, we would uncover their truth-values.

The most problematic sort of question remains to be dealt with. These are the tyrannosaur or Churchill type, for which the evidence is buried or inaccessible—questions for which Jardine recommends counterfactual bravado.

4. Counterfactual Bravado and the End of Inquiry

It might seem natural at this juncture for Peirce to adopt some form of counterfactual bravado in order to preserve the principle of bivalence for such statements. For not only does Peirce think that subjunctive conditionals can be correct or incorrect, but he thinks that counterfactual conditionals can be as well. We have seen that he thinks that since laws are efficacious, we can know that a diamond that will never be scratched is none the less hard. If we know that a law (all diamonds are hard) holds, then we can infer that, if the diamond were to be scratched, it would resist, and that if it had been scratched, it would have resisted.

Thus we could characterize the consequence Peirce derives from '*H* is true' with a little counterfactual bravado. If *H* is true then: either if inquiry were to be pursued, *H* would be agreed upon, or if inquiry *had been* pursued, *H would have been* agreed upon. That is, we can add to the forward-looking subjunctive in Peirce's account a backward-looking counterfactual. But this move, however natural it may seem, ought to be resisted. Not only is it against the letter of what Peirce says about buried secrets, but it is against the spirit of his account of truth.[29]

Let us first look at a mundane form of counterfactual bravado—mundane because it does not rely on time travel.[30]

---

[29] I thank David Wiggins for making me stick to this point.

[30] There are difficulties with Jardine's use of the notion of time travel. Some philosophers argue against the very conceptual possibility of time travel. And those who think that time travel is conceptually possible tend to think that the only coherent form it could take is a form that is not available to Jardine. (See Newton-Smith 1989.) And what if we propose to send an inquirer back to a time when the earth was unable to sustain human life? Or what if sending an inquirer back in time would most likely alter the situation she was inquiring about? These issues, however,

We can think of inquiry as embracing inquiries that could have taken place, but in fact did not. For the reader who likes the terminology of possible worlds, this possible world is closer to the actual world than is the possible world in which we can travel back in time. In the mundane possible world, inquirers who actually were in a position to have inquired at time *t*, but did not, simply inquire at time *t*. We do not have to imagine fancy machinery that can transport people back in time. We simply imagine that, say, Churchill's friends and acquaintances conspired to count his sneezes.

This brand of counterfactual bravado, however, results in a view of truth that everyone ought to eschew. We have seen that the pragmatic account of truth is first and foremost a thesis about the relationship between truth and inquiry: the aim of inquiry is to get true beliefs and true beliefs are those which are the very best that inquiry would produce. If we were to keep at inquiry and seek to fix genuine belief, we would, we hope, end up with beliefs that would encounter no recalcitrant experience.

Now mundane counterfactual bravado has it that the evidence that would have been gathered when it was available counts as evidence for or against a hypothesis about the past. And if there is no additional non-counterfactual evidence, that means that an inquiry in 1949 would have determined the truth about Churchill's sneezes. But if we allow this, we try to connect truth and inquiry in a very unsatisfactory way. It seems that a hypothesis is true if those who had been around at the right time would have believed it. This makes the truth about Churchill's sneezes rest on what his friends and acquaintances would have thought. We have seen that Peirce found this view repugnant. It is a denial of the first commonsense objectivity requirement set out in 4.1: the truth of a hypothesis cannot be a matter of what some inquirer or group of inquirers think. Jardine must also find it repugnant; he does not want the number of Churchill's sneezes there were at a given time and place to depend on

---

will not concern me. For my suggestion is that even if we assume that the notion of time travel is coherent and available to the pragmatist, there is good reason to resist Jardine's strategy. It might be argued, however, that the difficulties with time travel bravado are such that Jardine must rely on mundane bravado.

someone's fallible method of inquiry and upon the bit of evidence which that person would have collected. The view is hardly improved by making the counterfactual situation more exotic by taking as relevant evidence not that which would have been collected at the appropriate time, but that which would be collected if we could now send intelligent investigators with sophisticated equipment back in time to inquire. For Jardine should not want a true hypothesis to be a hypothesis that he or I or some group who travelled back in time would believe. What if a tyrannosaur managed to hide from the time travellers? What if the equipment they used was not sophisticated enough to detect a muffled sneeze?

Again, the point is that the methods, equipment, and background theories that today's inquirers use will, we assume, be immature in comparison to those which would be adopted if inquiry were allowed to run its course. And the evidence that we would gather in our time travels might be misleading or might only be a fraction of the evidence that would be relevant to the matter if we had an indefinitely long time in which to inquire. What inquiry would turn up if it were prolonged is one thing but what inquiry would have turned up at a given time, or would turn up if we could now go back in time to check, is another. The latter two notions do not involve progression, improvement, and getting as much evidence as would be possible. And it is notions like these which confer respectability on the pragmatic account of truth. To propose to send today's inquirers back to gather lost evidence is not a proposal in which the pragmatist should be especially interested. For we do not know whether the hypotheses they would believe have the advantage of being the sort of hypothesis that inquiry would not improve.

It is important to see that the objection to backward-looking proposals is not an objection to taking the evidence at some particular time seriously. Consider, for instance, questions for which the evidence is merely diminishing as time goes on, as opposed to the evidence being utterly inaccessible. It might be asked whether statements such as 'Churchill was a prime minister' or 'Cheryl Misak drank four pints of beer on 3 November 1989' are true on Peirce's account. There is evidence now that leads us to believe that they are true, but this evidence (especially for the second hypothesis) will diminish as time goes on. Are these hypotheses in trouble as well?[31]

The Peircean should say here that such hypotheses are ones which we have reason to believe now. For the evidence is in their favour and a reasonable belief, on the pragmatic account, is one which it is best to believe, given the available evidence and argumentation. The hypotheses are true if the following conditional is true: if inquiry were to be pursued on these matters, they would not be overturned. If inquiry were to be continued and no contrary evidence would come to light, then they are true. This is forward-looking, not backward-looking, and so does not suffer from the defect of mundane counterfactual bravado. They are hypotheses which would not be improved upon. It is the (forward-looking) fact that all of the evidence is in favour of the hypotheses and that no evidence would overturn them which makes them the sort of hypotheses worthy of belief.

Let us look now, however, at what Jardine must have surely intended his counterfactual bravado strategy to be—a forward-looking rather than backward-looking proposal. For this will point to an important objection against any counterfactual strategy and to the feature of pragmatism which is perhaps the most worthy of preservation. Jardine's proposal must be to send back at regular intervals inquirers who keep up with the latest theories and methods. That is, inquirers in an indefinitely prolonged inquiry would be the inquirers who would gather the lost evidence.

I suggest that if we appeal to even this sort of counterfactual bravado in order to preserve the principle of bivalence, our grip on the relationship between truth (the aim of inquiry) and inquiry will slip. For when counterfactual bravado is added to the pragmatist's account of truth, the resulting view does not engage the notion of truth with the notion of what inquirers would actually have to take account of if they were to fix belief which would have all of the virtues belief can have—virtues such as empirical adequacy, explanatory power, etc. A strategy involving counterfactual bravado abandons the pragmatist's commitment to say

---

[31] John Upper put this sort of question to me.

something about the relationship between truth and inquiry (how it is and should be conducted) and replaces it with a claim about what the relationship between truth and inquiry would be if inquiry were something it is not. But pragmatism is interested only in the actual world and what would be the case in it. It is not interested in what inquiry might have produced if it were a different sort of thing, but in what inquiry would produce if it were diligently pursued under favourable conditions.

So the appeal to counterfactual bravado undermines something which is important and interesting in Peirce's account of truth. Peirce's distinctive contribution to debates about truth is to see that, if the aim of inquiry is to get true beliefs, then truth must be thought of as the best that inquiry would do, given as much time and evidence as it takes to reach beliefs which would not be overturned. I shall examine this argument in the next section. The point here is that the relationship Peirce saw between truth and the fixation of belief is sacrificed if counterfactual bravado is adopted. The pragmatist should assume that inquiry, as it actually is, will uncover the answer to any given question. She should insist that it is pointless to assume that an inquiry that in fact did not or could not take place would have uncovered it. Jardine provides the pragmatist with a trivializing temptation and we should follow Peirce in resisting it.

So if the principle of bivalence is to be preserved, it must be preserved in some other way. It is in Peirce's thought about optimism that the pragmatist's proper stance on the principle of bivalence lies. The response that Peirce actually makes to the challenge posed by buried secrets is that it is a regulative assumption of inquiry that the answer would turn up in the end.[32] We must hope or assume that, if we were moved to inquire about such a question, abduction would throw up a hypothesis that eventually would be settled upon.

Now for some questions (such as the Churchill and

[32] Blackburn (1980) argues for a similar position. The non-realist, he says, can 'mimic' the intellectual practices supposedly definitive of realism (p. 353). The non-realist can (and must) act as if the principle of bivalence is true, for it is a regulative assumption of discourse and of judgement-making. Blackburn finds the roots of this position in Hume (with respect to causal and moral beliefs). Ramsey (1929) also puts forward such a view.

tyrannosaur questions), the assumption will seem *ridiculously* optimistic. Does the pragmatist not have to admit that, despite our hopes, and despite the fact that we might (psychologically) have to make the assumption, some questions will not be answered? Does the pragmatist not have to admit that, for some genuine statements, the principle of bivalence will not hold? Peirce considers the possibility and does indeed suggest that if a question would not be answered, then the hypotheses in question have no truth-values: 'if nothing [would be] ever settled about the matter, it will be because the phenomena do not consistently point to any theory; and in that case there is a want of that "uniformity of nature" (to use a popular but very loose expression) which constitutes reality, and makes it differ from a dream'.[33] And:

Truth is the opinion which sufficient inquiry would establish and fix forever . . . This I later modified by adding that there is no reason whatsoever entitling us to any confidence that the pendulum of opinion will not, in regard to any given question you please, continue to oscillate back and forth forever, in which case, in regard to such [a] question, there is no *real* truth, at all.[34]

Here Peirce is referring to questions such as the enigmatic philosophical ones rather than 'factual' questions such as the Churchill or tyrannosaur ones. But the point remains the same. He does not straightforwardly assert the principle of bivalence. He does not assert that all genuine hypotheses are either true or false. We must merely assume that any given hypothesis is. So Peirce cannot *assert* the T–I conditional—he cannot assert that if *H* is true then inquiry would eventually settle upon it. For some Churchill and tyrannosaur type

---

[33] CP 8. 43, 1885. I have replaced an 'is' in this passage with Peirce's considered 'would be'. In this 1885 review of Royce's *The Religious Aspect of Philosophy*, Peirce was not yet a committed realist about dispositions and instead argued that the community of inquirers will in fact continue indefinitely.

[34] MS 300, p. 6, 1905. The passage continues: 'Today, however . . . I say that in such a case (if such there be) the real truth would be of an *indefinite* nature, that is, would in some measure violate the principle of contradiction, being as much *pro* as *con*.' For instance, the question whether Hamlet had a birthmark on his left arm would not, we think, be answered. Peirce says that Hamlet is 'indeterminate in this respect' (*NE* iv, xiii, undated). But I suggest that, whereas it is plausible to think that the world of fiction is indeterminate, what is at issue is whether facts about Churchill's sneezes and the number of tyrannosaurs are indeterminate. It is better to stick with Peirce's original response.

hypotheses are true and perhaps their truth would not impinge upon us. But it does not follow that the pragmatist must deny the principle of bivalence nor even be suspicious of it. And it does not follow that the pragmatist must say that the hypothesis 'Churchill sneezed exactly fifty-two times in 1949' is neither true nor false. For Peirce countenances the possibility that the hypothesis would not be decided upon *only as a (subjunctive) conditional statement*. That is, he says that *if* inquiry with respect to *H* were pursued as far as it could fruitfully go, and *if* belief were still to be unsettled about *H*, then *H* has no determinate truth-value. But since the antecedent of this conditional is about what would be the case if inquiry were pushed indefinitely far, we can never assert that it is fulfilled. We cannot assert that some hypothesis will never have its truth-value determined. Peirce does not say that there is in fact a genuine question about which the pendulum of opinion will swing forever; for any legitimate question, he assumes that it will eventually cease to swing. He refuses to say '*H* has no determinate truth-value' or that 'hypotheses of type *A* have no determinate truth-values'. For his stance on the principle of bivalence is couched in a subjunctive conditional which has an antecedent about the indefinite future. He will never assume that the antecedent is true; he is only committed to contemplating that it might be true for some issues.

Now we see exactly why the pragmatist cannot, even if that was what was desired, offer a biconditional definition of truth. For the status of one of those purported conditionals— the T–I conditional—is a mere hope or assumption. Since the pragmatist must contemplate hypotheses which escape this hope, the status of the pragmatic account of truth is an unusual one. Rather than a definition, what is being offered is more like a specification of the chief symptoms or expectations of truth. We can expect true hypotheses to have certain properties, such as being the sort of hypothesis which would figure in the final opinion, being the sort of hypothesis which would not fall to recalcitrant experience, etc. These are properties that true hypotheses typically have, not accidentally but essentially. Just as it is essentially typical of cats to have four legs (but not all do), it is essentially typical of true hypotheses to have the property of being those that would figure in the final opinion (but not all have it).[35]

No account of essentialism or natural kinds is required here. The point is merely that it is no accident that, unless something unusual has happened, a cat has four legs. And it is no accident that, unless something unusual happens, a true hypothesis, were investigation relevant to it prolonged, would impinge upon us. The pragmatic project is less formal and less ambitious than that standardly undertaken by a 'theory of truth'. But, as we shall see, it is ambitious enough to provide us with a substantial account of truth.

So the principle of bivalence and the T–I conditional are regulative assumptions, not logical truths or even assertions. Peirce says: 'Logic requires us, with reference to each question we have in hand, to hope some definite answer to it may be true. That *hope* with reference to *each* case as it comes up is, by a *saltus*, stated by logicians as a law concerning *all cases*, namely the law of excluded middle.' (*NE* iv, p. xiii, undated.) He does not fit into any of the categories that Rorty speaks of in the following passage: 'the pragmatist denies bivalence for all statements, the "extreme" realist asserts it for all statements, while the level-headed majority sensibly discriminate between the bivalent statements of, e.g., physics and the non-bivalent statements of, e.g., morals'.[36]

Finally, notice that the issues for which the pragmatist must contemplate the possibility of the failure of bivalence will not be live ones. The fact that the regulative assumption is foolish with respect to a particular issue will coincide with the fact that no one will inquire into that issue. No one investigates the question of the exact number of Churchill's sneezes or the exact number of tyrannosaurs at the end of the last ice age. If investigation were to take place about these matters, the inquirers would have to have some reason to think that they could be successful in their endeavour. What this suggests is that, for any issue that is actually a subject of inquiry, we should hold out the promise of bivalence.

[35] David Wiggins encouraged me to put the point this way.
[36] Rorty (1982), p. xxvii, attributes this thought to Dummett.

Inquiry, as it is actually conducted, is governed by the (reasonable) assumption that the principle of bivalence holds.[37]

And we have seen that the pragmatist is interested in just that: the relationship between truth and inquiry, as it is actually conducted. We are brought again to the pragmatist's view of the character of good philosophy. We saw in Chapter 1 that the pragmatist insists that philosophical notions (of truth, probability, etc.) must connect with inquiry They must have consequences for experience and 'wholesome effects' on the way in which we go about some practical business. With respect to the notion of truth, this insistence is particularly forceful, for truth is the aim of inquiry. A good 'theory' of truth is a theory which makes it clear what we are and should be doing when we engage as a community in inquiry or the pursuit of truth.

Now if an account delivers this but is subject to objections or counterexamples which rest on situations which do not actually occur in the course of inquiry, those objections will not have maximum force. The pragmatist will attach minimal importance to them. It is not that the objections are dismissed: they do damage to the pragmatist's view of truth, but the damage is limited.[38] What all of this suggests is that the Peircean view of truth requires the accompanying pragmatic view of philosophy. Those who will be attracted to Peirce's account of truth will be those who take the pragmatic insight seriously.

Those who do not think that pragmatism has any insights to offer should not, however, too quickly disregard the Peircean thoughts about truth. For in the next section I shall

---

[37] Peirce would say the following of an issue which is live but seemingly underdetermined by the evidence: we must assume that one of the competing theories would in the end be agreed upon. If it transpired that the theories were underdetermined by the evidence, no matter how far inquiry were pursued, then either the theories are pragmatically equivalent or there is no truth of the matter at stake.

[38] What would count most against a pragmatic proposal would be the following sorts of points: we cannot really expect of x what the proposal suggests we can expect of x; the suggested expectations are in fact pragmatically spurious; the proposed account of x is not recognizably an account of x at all, but an account of some other notion, etc. We shall see that the most pressing objection for the pragmatic proposal about truth is the last sort.

articulate Peirce's basic insight about truth—an insight which should be acceptable even to those who eschew the broader context of pragmatism. In 4.6 pragmatism will be taken seriously—I shall give the arguments in favour of accepting the pragmatic context with respect to the elucidation of truth. Those who see the force in these arguments will want to extend the basic claim to a full-fledged pragmatic account of truth.

5. Truth and the Inquirer: The Uncontentious Claim

We have seen that, because of the regulative status of the T–I conditional, Peirce does not assert the equivalence: *H* is true if and only if, if inquiry relevant to *H* were pursued as far as it could fruitfully go, then *H* would be believed. However we have also seen that the possibility of there being buried secrets should not discourage the inquirer from thinking of truth in terms of that equivalence. For the inquirer should assume that the T–I conditional holds for whatever issue is in question. We must now turn more explicitly to the reasons why Peirce's account of truth is the account that the inquirer ought to adopt. In the next section we will see what reasons there are for thinking that Peirce's account is also the account that the philosopher ought to adopt.

One does not have to hold a pragmatic criterion of significance in order to think that we need to have a conception of truth which is able to guide inquiry and deliberation. For truth is the aim of inquiry and the aim of any activity ought to be a comprehensible guide to that activity. But only a pragmatically legitimate conception of truth will be able to serve as this guide, for only it will result in a set of expectations. An inquirer who accepts such a conception of truth can incorporate those expectations into the practice of inquiry.

Peirce is looking for an account of truth that the investigator can and ought to adopt. 'Real pragmatic truth' is 'truth as can and ought to be used as a guide for conduct' (MS 684, p. 11, 1913). He suggests that the investigator should think of truth in terms of the above biconditional. That is (I–T): truth is the property of those beliefs which would encounter no recalcitrant experience, broadly construed. Truth is the property of those beliefs that a sufficiently pursued experience-constrained inquiry would turn up. And (T–I): we must assume that if a hypothesis is true, then if we were to inquire about it, eventually something would impinge upon us to convince us of its truth.

This view of truth has (at least) three advantages for the investigator. First, it provides the rational context for inquiry to proceed. The only way in which we can rationally inquire about *H* is to assume that something would eventually impinge upon us to settle the issue of *H*'s truth or falsity.

Secondly, it makes sense of the practice of inquiry as the search for truth. With the adoption of the Peircean account of truth, the inquirer can see how it makes sense for her to aim for true beliefs. On this account, true belief would lie at the end of the inquiry process of which the investigator is a part. Truth is in principle not beyond investigation; it is in principle accessible.

Thirdly, Peirce's view of truth provides and justifies a methodology. It encourages the inquirer to put her beliefs to the test of experience and argument, applying the methods described in Chapters 2 and 3. For the best way to get beliefs which are the sort that would never be upset by experience, broadly construed, is by applying a method something like that of abduction, deduction, and induction.

So Peirce's basic claim is that the inquirer who aims to get the truth ought to think of her aim as the acquisition of beliefs which would never be overturned by doubt or recalcitrant experience, as beliefs which would be the best that inquiry would produce. This fact itself, Peirce thinks, should go a long way to persuading the philosopher that his is the best conception of truth. The onus of justification is on the philosopher who thinks she needs a different account of truth than the inquirer. But the claim, as it stands, is a claim about inquirers, not yet about truth.

It is important to see that anyone can accept Peirce's basic claim. For the positions opposed to the pragmatic view of truth will not be concerned with the view of truth that investigators ought to adopt. Rather, they will be concerned with specifying necessary and sufficient conditions for truth —conditions which the philosopher is supposed to adopt. That is, Peirce's opponents will think it beside the point to focus on what inquirers ought to think. They may be happy enough with Peirce's suggestion about what inquirers ought to think but they will be eager to address what they take to be the philosophical question.

For instance, philosophers who oppose the Peircean view might hold the following position. The definition of truth is the correspondence definition.[39] What Peirce has given us is an account of what, optimally, the relationship between truth and inquiry would be. That is, if everything goes very well, the hypotheses which would be agreed upon at the end of inquiry would correspond to the way the world is. Peirce is right to suggest that we must hope that our investigations will be such that they will produce true beliefs. The inquirer ought to assume or hope that inquiry will arrive at beliefs which correspond to the world. But it may be the case that it would not. It may be the case that some hypotheses, or perhaps even all hypotheses, will be such that inquiry will get their truth-values wrong.

Peirce's opponents might suggest that Peirce is right to think that if the inquirer is to have any hope of achieving her aim (getting the truth), she ought to think of the aim of inquiry in terms of the Peircean biconditional. It might even be agreed that it would be foolish or pointless for the investigator to refuse to call beliefs that were as good as they could be 'true'. But these opponents will insist that, despite all of this, if the philosopher is to get the notion of truth right, something additional must be said. It must be said that *H* really is true if and only if it really does get the world right.

6. The Pragmatic Arguments

We have seen that the following claim ought to be acceptable to anyone: (1) an inquirer who seeks to fix belief should

---

[39] Alternatively, one could hold that the correct definition is the Tarskian definition.

envisage truth as the property possessed by the beliefs that would be thrown up by a sufficiently resolute process of inquiry. Pragmatism's distinctive thesis is the additional claim: (2) nothing else can be (or had better be) said about truth, over and above (1). The arguments which strengthen Peirce's first claim (about inquirers) into a claim about truth depend on taking the pragmatic insight seriously. If one agrees with Peirce about the criterion for what is spurious and for when two hypotheses are equivalent, one will want to offer the account of *truth* which Peirce offers. One will want to refuse to add the transcendentalist's claim that truth really does go beyond inquiry, even if investigators might best think of it as what would lie at the end of inquiry.

The pragmatic account of truth pays special attention to the fact that, pre-theoretically, we think that inquiry aims at truth. What we know about truth is that truth is what we aim for in inquiry. That is what our grasp of the notion of truth amounts to: our access to it is via the concept of investigation. So not only must our philosophical account of truth be linked to the concept of inquiry, but we can enrich our understanding of truth if we determine the relationship between it and inquiry. That relationship, Peirce suggests, is epitomized by his biconditional. True beliefs are beliefs which are as good as they possibly could be and a true belief, it must be assumed, would eventually be uncovered by inquiry.

So the pragmatic account of truth has at its centre the following thesis about the relationship between truth and inquiry: the aim of inquiry is to get true beliefs and the beliefs which would be produced if inquiry were to run its unhindered course would be true. For if inquiry would no longer be able to improve upon a belief, then that belief would satisfy all of the aims we might have in inquiry. It would, for instance, cohere with the rest of our belief network and with all of the data, and it would play a part in explaining the data. For if our beliefs do not have these features, then inquiry will not be at rest. Inquirers will take it that there is more work to be done. If inquiry were to be at its natural rest, our beliefs would have these features; they would be the very best beliefs we could have. The pragmatist then suggests that there would be no point in withholding the title 'true' from these beliefs. The beliefs satisfy not only the proximate aims of inquiry (empirical adequacy, explanatory power, and the like) but also the ultimate aim of inquiry—truth.

Now I suggested in the last section that anyone, even the correspondence theorist, might find it acceptable to say that there would be no point to the investigator refusing to call the best possible beliefs true. The pragmatist, however, is distinguished from other philosophers in that she attaches special weight to the fact that there is no point in refusing to call something x. If there is really no point in refusing to call a certain sort of hypothesis true, then the pragmatist insists that it really is true.

Thus the Peircean pragmatist does not think, with James and perhaps Rorty, that 'truth' is merely an honorific term which we bestow upon warranted beliefs. Nor does the Peircean accept that we ought to think of truth in whatever way we find useful or convenient. Rather, the Peircean looks to what our access to the concept of truth must be. The only grasp that we have on the notion of truth is that it is what we aim for in inquiry. Once we get what we aim for in inquiry—the very best that inquiry could produce—we have true beliefs. There is no further step to be taken—there is nothing further to aim for in the search for truth.

Let us return to Peirce's transcendentalist opponent—the philosopher who argues that truth transcends inquiry. She will resist the step that tries to turn Peirce's claim about how the inquirer ought to think of truth into a claim about truth itself. Four transcendentalist theses can be distinguished and ordered in strength:

(1) truth goes beyond inquiry here and now;
(2) there are truths that inquiry would not catch;
(3) the best that inquiry would do might not be the truth;
(4) the notion of truth has nothing to do with the notion of inquiry.

The last is the strongest, for no one who thinks that truth is the aim of inquiry will assert it. The first is the weakest and Peirce clearly affirms it. Truth, he argues, would be the product of a sufficiently prolonged inquiry: it is not the product of inquiry here and now. We have seen that Peirce cannot straightforwardly deny (2), which is the denial of the T–I conditional. Since he has to entertain the possibility that the principle of bivalence might fail to hold, he has to entertain the possibility that there may be truths that would fail to be captured by inquiry. What he says is only that we must assume that (2) is false. The third thesis, the denial of the I–T conditional, is the most important point of dispute between Peirce and the transcendentalist. For the transcendentalist denies that a hypothesis that would be believed at the end of an indefinitely pursued inquiry must be true. The best hypotheses that inquiry would produce might be false.

There are two sorts of transcendentalists who might deny the I–T conditional. The first is the sceptical transcendentalist who thinks that the best that inquiry would do might be false because of some bare possibility, such as the possibility that we are all brains in a vat. We saw in Chapter 2 how Peirce disarms this sort of position; it is, he suggests, based on a paper doubt. The transcendentalist who is of most interest here is the second sort—the scientific sort who thinks that inquiry aims at and achieves a measure of truth. But she still insists that truth is more than the best that inquiry would do.

The scientific transcendentalist does not deny Peirce's basic point about how the inquirer ought to think of the aim of inquiry—as the acquisition of beliefs which would stand up to experience. But she wants to resist Peirce's stronger claim that that is all there is to truth. Truth is the aim of inquiry, but there is more to truth than what can be got out of inquiry.

If this account is to be coherent, inquirers must adopt a set of proximate aims—they aim for beliefs which fit with experience, have explanatory power, etc. But they should see that the fulfilment of these proximate aims is not coextensive with the ultimate aim of getting the truth. Inquirers should indeed adopt something like the methodology and aims which Peirce's construal of truth suggests. But they should think of truth as being correspondence, *because common-sense tells us that truth is correspondence.*

So inquiry, on the transcendentalist's account, should proceed as if the only thing that matters is the fixation of beliefs which would encounter no recalcitrant experience, broadly construed. But the philosophical debate begins only after we have agreed to this basic claim of Peirce's. And Peirce, it is charged, does not have commonsense on his side in that further debate. He has said something about what the inquirer ought to aim for, but he has not said anything about truth; he got the proximate aim of inquiry right, but he should not have called it truth. 'Real pragmatic truth' is not truth at all, for it simply does not fit our pre-theoretical conception of truth.

But Peirce, notice, does think that he is taking commonsense seriously. Pragmatism requires that the philosopher take 'truth' to be more than a technical term in philosophy. For it is also a term used by those engaged in the practice of inquiry. And so a philosophical account of truth must at least roughly square with what, before theorizing about truth, we would recognize as a conception of it, as opposed to a conception of some other property.

Every philosopher,[40] however, thinks that we might want to go beyond our pre-theoretical conception and remedy any defects we might find in it. But how, it might well be asked, do we determine which aspects of our pre-theoretical conception to maintain and which to abandon? How do we know that we are not simply maintaining a prejudice and should, as a result, revise our ordinary concept of truth?

Pragmatism can be of service here. It provides a methodological maxim for unpacking concepts and thus provides some guidance as to when a revisionary approach is required. Peirce argues that, if a philosopher wants to be more than a gratuitous metaphysician, the hypotheses she puts forward must result in a set of expectations. If our ordinary conception of truth does not result in expectations which guide us in inquiry and deliberation, then it is defective and should be revised. And Peirce suggests that the transcendentalist's account of truth, just because it is transcendental, is defective in this way.

Peirce would argue that commonsense is on his side because he, and not the transcendentalist, can make sense of

---

[40] Perhaps an exception is the 'ordinary language' school of philosophers.

ordinary everyday inquiry. On Peirce's account, inquirers can happily say that they aim for truth. Even if they do not reach any true hypotheses during their lifetimes, they are part of a process that would reach truth. Truth is such that if the inquirer is to make sense of inquiry, she has to think of it in terms of the Peircean biconditional. Truth is not beyond inquiry—if inquiry would no longer be able to improve on a hypothesis, then that hypothesis is true. In no practical sense could we be mistaken—no experience and no argument would change our minds. What more could we aim for? What is added by wondering whether the hypothesis is *really* true?

The position of the transcendentalist, on the other hand, is strained. Those in the midst of inquiry aim for beliefs which account for the data, have explanatory power, etc. That is, in actual inquiry and deliberation, inquirers have to adopt some proximate goals such as empirical adequacy and explanatory power. They then must assume that empirical adequacy and explanatory power are connected to the ultimate goal of transcendental truth. They must assume that if they were to get beliefs which explain, which would encounter no recalcitrant experience, etc., they would get beliefs which are likely to be true.

But for the transcendentalist, the link between beliefs with these worthy features and the truth is unfathomable. On her account, a belief that would be forever empirically adequate and explanatory might still be false. As long as this is a possibility, the connection between the proximate goals and the ultimate goal is tenuous. The transcendentalist owes us an account of why empirically adequate and explanatory beliefs, produced by a method something like that of abduction, deduction, and induction, are likely to be true. The transcendentalist who claims that she too can hope that hypotheses which would be believed at the end of inquiry would be true (would correspond to the world) must provide a ground for that hope.

Thus the scientific transcendentalist wants to claim that the methodology of scientific inquiry is a guide to or leads to the truth. But no reason is given for why this is the case. Until such a reason is given, the leap that inquirers must make from empirical adequacy and explanatory power to truth will be a leap of faith. And until such a reason is given, the inquirer cannot appeal to the ultimate aim of truth to justify any methodology.

So if there is a gap between the best that inquiry would do and the truth, then inquiry cannot be made sense of as the attempt to fix true beliefs. Because Peirce closes the gap, he can make sense of inquiry. He thus thinks that his account is a 'highly practical and common-sense position' (*CE* 2, 471, 1871). No leap of faith is required in his secular view of truth and inquiry. That view is a coherent account of how inquiry is related to truth and how inquirers ought to think of truth. Inquiry is that which aims at truth and truth is that which would be the product of inquiry.

Now the transcendentalist might adopt a Humean strategy at this point and hold that there is indeed no link between truth and empirical adequacy. (Hume, for instance, might say that there is no link between constant conjunctions in the past and what we might expect in the future.) But Humean naturalism will not look like an attractive position to the scientific transcendentalist. For it will entail that she abandon the claim that science aims at and approximates the truth. The transcendentalist will more likely want to dig in here and rely on a certain intuition about what truth must be like. But she has no real argument against Peirce. She will merely repeat that commonsense forces us to add something to the notion of truth over and above what inquiry would result in.

But the transcendentalist's addition, Peirce would argue, should be written off as a piece of 'metaphysical surplusage'. On both accounts, inquirers aim for the same thing—fit with experience, explanatory power, etc. There is thus no non-terminological difference between Peirce's view and the transcendentalist's.[41] The addition—the claim that truth is something that is in principle over and above inquiry—adds nothing at all.

Thus Peirce insists that there is no point adding anything to

---

[41] It might be suggested that there is a difference: one refuses to assert bivalence and the other asserts it. But the Peircean will assume bivalence as a regulative assumption and so will behave in the same way and expect the same things as one who asserts bivalence.

the notion of truth over and above what can be squeezed out of inquiry. Nothing metaphysical should be added to this conception: truth is that feature belonging to all beliefs that are as good as they can be, beliefs that would be permanently settled upon or 'indefeasible' (*CP* 6. 485, 1908). This is all that we require of a conception of truth.

5
Ethics

Introduction

We have seen that Peirce's account of experience and truth is broadminded about the kinds of beliefs which might be responsive to experience and hence, about the kinds of beliefs which might be candidates for truth and falsity. A true belief is one which would satisfy all of our aims in inquiry—it would be indefeasible or would stand up to experience and argument. We shall see in this chapter that Peirce argued that the character of indefeasibility will vary from inquiry to inquiry—beliefs in mathematics must measure up to the standards of mathematics, beliefs in ethics must measure up to the standards of ethics, etc. We saw in Chapter 2 that Peirce gave careful consideration to mathematics, arguing that it is an experience-driven inquiry. Indeed, he carried out significant first-order inquiry in logic and mathematics, experimenting upon diagrams, just as his conception of experience for that kind of inquiry requires.[1]

In contrast, Peirce's remarks about ethics can seem so tension-ridden and crude that one's first inclination is to simply dismiss them as entirely unhelpful, as I did in *Truth, Politics, Morality*.[2] The cognitivist position I articulate there is presented very much on Peirce's behalf—as one which he ought to have held, not as one that he actually held. For much of what he says about ethics or 'vital matters'[3] seems

---

[1] He developed a logic of relations and quantifiers independently of, and at roughly the same time as, Frege; discovered the Sheffer Stroke twenty years before Sheffer; and invented a notation (utilizing normal forms) very similar to the one still in use. In mathematics, he anticipated Dedekind on the difference between finite and infinite sets and independently developed arguments about infinity similar to Cantor's. See Dauben (1982), Dipert (1981, 2004), and Putnam (1982) for details.

[2] See also the preface to the 1st edn. of *Truth and the End of Inquiry* and p. 52.

[3] As Chris Hookway pointed out to me, the category of vital matters is, for Peirce, wider than the category of ethical matters. Vital matters include any urgent question—any question which requires action and so can not wait for a final

to open up a gulf between science and ethics, a gulf so great that it is hard to think of both as sharing a general aim—that of getting beliefs which would not be overturned by experience and argument. In a certain mood (Hookway 2000: 22 locates it in the 1880s), Peirce says that in vital matters we need to get ourselves a belief—something upon which we can immediately act. Hence we are to go on instinct or gut reaction, keeping reasoning and inquiry out of the picture. In science, on the other hand, we do not aim at a belief upon which we can immediately act, but at getting a theory which in the long run would stand up to reasoning and experience. Hence science is not concerned with practice and is devoid of beliefs.

These remarks clearly do not suit my purposes, for I would like to see Peirce as setting out a unified picture of inquiry on which all genuine inquiry takes belief to be responsive to experience and argument. And I would like to see Peirce as a moral cognitivist—as one who holds that moral belief falls under the scope of truth, knowledge, and inquiry.

The proposed gulf between science and ethics (or between theoretical and practical matters) is problematic in its own right, even if one does not share my purposes. Even those who do not think that ethics can be construed as a truth-directed inquiry will none the less find the view of science Peirce articulates in this mood highly implausible. The thought that scientists are divorced from practice, do not hold beliefs, do not act on their theories, and stand ready to throw their theories overboard in the face of a single recalcitrant experience has irritated philosophers of science who are otherwise sympathetic to Peirce. (See, for instance, Levi 1983, 1984*b*.)

In this chapter I show what I had previously thought to be impossible: Peirce himself, despite some confusing twists in his presentation, presents us with a coherent and sophisticated cognitivist account of ethics—an account on which moral judgement is brought under the scope of truth, know-

---

answer. He takes, for instance, the question of the existence of God to be vital. This makes his attempt to trace and then test consequences of the belief in God even more interesting. See pp. 31 ff.

ledge, and inquiry. Contrary to first appearances, Peirce does not distinguish science and ethics on the grounds that science aims at truth and ethics at a quick belief. Both science and ethics aim at the same thing: true belief or belief which would stand up to experience and argument.

This kind of cognitivism fits with much of what we find in moral deliberation. We try to get things right, we distinguish between thinking that one is right and being right, we criticize the beliefs, actions, and cognitive skills of others, we are bothered by disagreement, and we think that we can improve our judgements. Indeed, the practice of moral deliberation seems to satisfy Peirce's primary requirement for an inquiry aimed at truth: it seems to be responsive to experience and argument, broadly construed. When we deliberate about what we ought to do, we take ourselves to be sensitive to reasons, argument, and thought experiments. We try to put ourselves in the shoes of others, to broaden our horizons, to listen to the arguments of the other side. That is part of what it is to make a moral decision and part of what it is to try to live a moral life. It would not be a moral life—it would not be engaged with the complexities of moral requirements—if we simply made our decisions about how to treat others by following an oracle, or an astrologer, or the toss of the dice.

We must, of course, be prepared for the possibility that, as Bernard Williams thinks, 'ethical thought has no chance of being everything it seems' (1985: 135). But the commitment to keeping philosophy in touch with experience and practice is such that we should not be too quick to jump to this conclusion.

One thing that causes trouble for the cognitivist project is that there is much disagreement in moral deliberation. We often find issues to be contestable, thorny, and underdetermined. Another is that much work must be done to make plausible the idea that moral judgements are responsive to something uniform enough to be called experience. There is no guarantee in advance that these challenges can be met. I try to meet them in *Truth, Politics, Morality*. Here I shall merely gesture at those arguments and will be content if I show how Peirce was in fact very much open to them.

1. The Tension Between Vital Matters and Science

At times Peirce wholeheartedly embraces the cognitivist view I have wanted to attribute to him—he happily extends his view of truth and inquiry to moral judgements. Here are two passages in which his cognitivist intentions are apparent. In the first, after saying that a true belief is one which would survive the rigours of inquiry, he says that beliefs in ethics can be true or false. In the second, he suggests that moral judgement draws upon experience—experience which is not identical to that which is found in science, but experience nonetheless.

But what else, when one considers it, can our 'truth' ever amount to, other than the way in which people would come to think if research were carried sufficiently far? That would seem to be all that *our* truth ever can be. So good morals is the kind of human behavior that would come to be approved if studies of right behavior were carried sufficiently far. Would it not be a good idea to begin a text-book of ethics . . . with this definition: Ethics is the theory of how to do as one would like if one had considered sufficiently the question of what one would find satisfactory? (MS 673, pp. 12–13, 1911.)

Ethics as a positive science must rest on observed facts. But it is quite a different thing to make it rest on special scientific observation . . . The only solid foundation for ethics lies in those facts of everyday life which no skeptical philosopher ever yet really called in question. (CP 8. 158, 1901, see also 1. 600, 1903.)

This last thought, the reader will recall from pp. 29 ff., is remarkably similar to Peirce's view about the kind of experience relevant to metaphysics. Metaphysics, he says, rests on observations 'and the only reason that this is not universally recognized is that it rests upon kinds of phenomena with which every man's experience is so saturated that he usually pays no particular attention to them' (CP 6. 2, 1898). The observation of phenomena in the special sciences requires special instruments, precautions, and skill (CP 1. 242, 1902). The observation of phenomena in metaphysics does not, but metaphysical phenomena are 'harder to see, simply because they surround us on every hand; we are immersed in them and have no background against which to view them' (*CP* 6. 562, 1905).

Given that the place of experts and equipment in moral deliberation is at very best marginal, this kind of commonplace and non-technical observation seems especially appropriate to moral beliefs. We seem to have a nice route here to thinking that moral beliefs are constrained by experience and hence are candidates for truth-values. We often find ourselves compelled in moral matters and, as in mathematics, this compulsion can take two forms. One is what often gets called by philosophers 'intuition' or 'felt response'. Upon observing a group of teenagers bully and torment a younger child, we simply 'see' that it is cruel. The other kind of compulsion in moral deliberation is that we find some reasons, arguments, imagined situations, and thought experiments compelling and may, in light of them, revise our moral judgements. We can learn from debate and discussion, from 'morals' we find in novels, films, Aesop's fables, the parables of the New Testament, and from the philosopher's hypothetical situations and counterexamples to general moral principles. The force of experience can be felt in the course of this kind of argument and experiment.

We need not, and must not, suppose here that we have a special faculty for perceiving right and wrong or that our intuitions are self-evident or indefeasible. We need only suppose that we find ourselves compelled in moral matters. Observation in the moral domain is of course fallible. What is intuitively obvious in any kind of inquiry can be discredited—think of initially plausible stereotypes in the social sciences and the fact that Einstein's relativity theory was taken at the outset by many to be intuitively false. Indeed, our very ability to recognize mistakes like these turns on the idea that what strikes us as obvious is subject to further experience. We can, that is, be critical of our 'intuitions'.[4]

---

[4] See *CP* 1. 404, 1890. As Elizabeth Anderson (1993: 105 ff.) has so nicely argued, we in fact adopt many critical strategies with respect to our intuitions. We can try to get them into reflective equilibrium with our other considered judgements, we can see that they fall short of our ideals, science can show us that a purported fact which underlies a moral intuition is false, and we can be challenged by someone who does not share our intuitions.

But, as is often the case with interpreting Peirce, matters are not quite so straightforward. He was frequently keen to insist that, in 'vital' or ethical matters, one must eschew reason in favour of instinct: 'matters of vital importance must be left to sentiment, that is, to instinct' (*CP* 1. 637, 1898). For in vital matters, we need to reach a definite conclusion promptly. Science, on the other hand, 'has nothing at stake on any temporal venture but is in pursuit of eternal verities . . . and looks upon this pursuit, not as the work of one man's life, but as that of generation after generation, indefinitely' (*CP* 5. 589, 1898). If ethics requires an immediate belief upon which to act, and science does not, then 'really the word belief is out of place in the vocabulary of science' (*CP* 7. 185, 1901). All science concerns itself with is a 'formula reached in the existing state of scientific progress'.

Science is thus concerned with truth—with finding what *would* best stand up to evidence and argument—and ethics is not. Here we seem to have an extreme non-cognitivist thought, where ethics is a matter for gut reaction. The preservation of the status quo seems inevitable. This view, which he at times calls 'sentimentalism', 'implies conservatism' (*CP* 1. 633, 1898). Ethics, he sometimes says, 'is in fact nothing but a sort of composite photograph of the conscience of the members of the community. In short, it is nothing but a traditional standard, accepted, very wisely, without radical criticism, but with a silly pretence of critical examination' (*CP* 1. 573, 1905). We seem to have here the suggestion that our cognitivist practices—debating and reasoning about moral matters and trying to improve our views by expanding our experience—are based on an error, as Mackie (1977) would say, or worse, on a silly pretence.

It is my aim to resolve the tension between the cognitivist and non-cognitivist strands in Peirce's work. My argument shall be that if one looks at Peirce's epistemology, about which he did not waver, one can see that his remarks about instinct must be folded into the cognitivist view. That is, once we understand the place of instinct in Peirce's philosophy, the odd-sounding view that ethics must go on instinct is perfectly consistent with the cognitivist view. And we shall see that the assertion that belief is out of place in science is not the best way Peirce could have put the point he wanted to make. What he was getting at when he made these remarks is that the scientist must keep his eye on the fallible nature of belief.[5]

2. Instinct and the Scientific Method

There is no use denying that the distinction between vital and scientific matters was dear to Peirce. But it is far less damaging to the cognitivist position than it first appears. Once we understand what Peirce means by 'instinct', 'experience', and 'commonsense' and once we understand their roles in what he calls scientific inquiry, we can see that vital matters are indeed matters for scientific inquiry. And we can see that belief is indeed perfectly acceptable in science.

In order to see how the argument goes, we need to remind ourselves of some of the essentials of Peirce's epistemology. We have seen that he argues in 'The Fixation of Belief' that inquiry begins with the irritation of doubt and ends with a stable doubt-resistant belief. If we were to have a belief which would always be immune to doubt—which would forever fit with experience and argument—that belief would be true. Since we can never know when a belief is like that, all our beliefs are fallible. Any one of them might be shown to be false.

Fallibilism, however, does not entail that we ought to try to bring into doubt all beliefs about which error is conceivable. Such doubts would be, Peirce argued, 'paper' or 'tin'—not the genuine article. Our body of background belief is susceptible to doubt on a piecemeal basis, if that doubt is prompted by surprising or recalcitrant experience. Peirce's critical commonsensism has it that we must *regard* our background beliefs as true, until some surprising experience throws one or some group of them into doubt. The inquirer 'is under a compulsion to believe just what he does believe . . . as time goes on, the man's belief usually changes in a manner which he cannot resist . . . this force which changes a man's belief in spite of any effort of his may be, in all cases, called a *gain of experience*' (MS 1342, p. 2, undated).

---

[5] This, in essence, is the resolution offered in Ch. 2 n. 12.

So on the Peircean epistemology, an inquirer has a fallible background of 'commonsense' belief which is not in fact in doubt. It is taken to be 'infallible, absolute truth' (*CP* 5. 416, 1905). All Peirce means by this is that beliefs in that background are stable and believed until they are upset by experience. We have no choice but to take our background beliefs seriously in inquiry; if we did not, inquiry would grind to a halt. Without that stable background belief, one is not empowered to see things, to distinguish, to reason, or to judge new evidence and hypotheses. One of the most fundamental pragmatist premisses is that some beliefs must be held constant if revision of other beliefs is to take place.

Peirce links the scientific method to this critical commonsensist epistemology. The scientific method is the method which pays close attention to the fact that beliefs fall to the surprise of recalcitrant experience. Science 'is not standing upon the bedrock of fact. It is walking upon a bog, and can only say, this ground seems to hold for the present. Here I will stay till it begins to give way' (*CP* 5. 589, 1998). The scientific method is also the method which leads to the truth. We aim at beliefs which would be forever stable—we aim at getting beliefs which would not fall to experience.

This epistemology and its accompanying view of truth are entirely general, despite the fact that Peirce talks of the method of science. That is, what Peirce calls 'science' is extremely broad. Any inquiry which aims at getting a belief which would forever stand up to experience and argument abides by the method of science. We saw in Chapter 1 that Peirce thought that metaphysics (when it is well-conducted) and mathematics are legitimate aspirants to truth. He thought that beliefs in metaphysics and mathematics are such that they are sensitive to experience for or against them. For anything that is compelling, surprising, brute, or impinging is an experience. It is clear that Peirce will not say, with the logical positivists, that only beliefs in the physical sciences meet the pragmatist standard.[6]

It is critical for our discussion to see that instinct does not

---

[6] See Misak (1995) for a discussion of Peirce, the logical positivists, and other 'verificationists'.

only appear in Peirce's account of vital matters—instinct appears as part of any kind of experience-driven inquiry. For one thing, Peirce thinks that instinct drives the immediate perception of rightness in inference: 'when one fact puts a person in mind of another, but related, fact, and on considering the two together, he says to himself "Hah! Then this third is a fact", . . . it is by *instinct* that he draws the inference' (MS 682, p. 19, 1913). If you feel that an inference is correct, that feeling is very much like the feeling that something is red. You do not have to engage in any further reasoning process in order to accept the judgement—it just comes upon you. Instinct is thus a kind of experience or perception in any area of inquiry. For any area of inquiry will involve inferences.

Peirce sometimes makes this point in a slightly different way—by saying that instinct is aligned with our habits of reasoning or our 'logica utens' (see p. 91). Reasoning 'is the principal of human intellectual instincts . . . reasoning power is related to human nature very much as the wonderful instincts of ants, wasps, etc. are related to their several natures' (MS 682, pp. 8–9). Our instinctive and habitual cognitive skills, as Hookway (2000: 255) puts it, guide our inquiries. Of course, these habits can be flawed, but we nonetheless rely upon them until they are shown to be flawed—until we have evidence that they lead us astray or until we can explain what is wrong with them. If we are to continue to inquire, we must assume that our stock of evolved habitual or instinctive cognitive skills is reliable.

The second (related) way in which Peirce builds instinct into every area of inquiry is that he builds it into the very basics of the scientific method—the method of abduction, deduction, and induction. Abduction, recall, is a matter of coming up with or 'guessing at' an explanation for a surprising experience. These guesses, Peirce thinks, are often instinctive. Once we have a hypothesis in hand, arrived at by abduction, we then deduce consequences from the hypothesis and test it by induction. But it is abduction which provides science with new ideas and thus science advances by 'the spontaneous conjectures of instinctive reason' (CP 6. 475, 1908, see also 5. 604, 1901). When a surprising phenomenon requires explanation, instinct plays a central role. It provides the fallible starting points of the scientific method. That is another way in which instinct, rather than being set against science or inquiry which is aimed at truth, is a part of science.

Finally, and most importantly, instinct is, for Peirce, also aligned with that which is not doubted—that which forms our 'commonsense' fallible background body of beliefs. Writing in an entirely general way about belief and inquiry, Peirce says 'the pragmatist will accept wholesale the entire body of genuine instinctive beliefs without any shade of doubt, tossing aside the toy doubts of the metaphysician as unworthy of a mature mind'.[7] 'Instinct', he says, embraces 'traditional as well as inherited habits' (*CP* 2. 160, 1902).

More often than not, it is this last sense of 'instinct' which Peirce intends when he says that in ethics we must go on instinct. We must, he says, go on the status quo or on our stable body of background belief, for we need an immediate decision. Even if you think, for the most part, that trusting instinct is 'treacherous and deceptive', if you don't doubt something and have never doubted it, you will believe it: 'that which instinct absolutely requires him to believe, he must and will believe it with his whole heart'. If something seems perfectly evident, you can try as you will to criticize it, but you will be eventually obliged to believe it. By 'commonsense' and 'instinct', Peirce means 'those ideas and beliefs that a man's situation absolutely forces upon him' (*CP* 1. 129, 1905). Instinct is just belief that is taken to be commonsense. Instinct is just what the whole of past experience has put into place.

The fact that Peirce thinks that ethics must be driven by this kind of instinct does not distinguish ethics from science or from any other domain of inquiry. For he thinks that, in

---

[7] MS 329, p. 12, 1904, see also *CP* 5. 445, 1905. Short (2002) and Hookway (2000: 198, 205) also point out that Peirce took commonsense beliefs to be 'instinctive'. It is important to see that once one thinks of instinct in terms of Peirce's critical commonsensism, my central thesis follows. That is, the fact that Peirce thinks that vital matters must be driven by instinct does not make vital matters special. For he takes all of our inquiries to rely on a background of undoubted belief—belief upon which we act, until experience prompts us to revise.

every domain of inquiry, we need to rely upon our body of background belief. We might wish that Peirce had found a better name for the source of that body of belief, for 'instinct' has all sorts of connotations that he does not intend. We might also wish that he had refrained from using 'instinct' to refer to a number of different phenomena. Indeed, Peirce would have been less misunderstood if he had simply said that our body of background undoubted belief is put into place by abduction, deduction, induction, by upbringing and education, and by experience and argument.

In Peirce's Cambridge Lectures of 1898, one of the places in which the problematic gap between science and vital matters is most stark, he makes himself clear:

We do not say that sentiment is *never* to be influenced by reason, nor that under no circumstances would we advocate radical reforms. We only say that the man who would allow his religious life to be wounded by any sudden acceptance of a philosophy of religion or who would precipitately change his code of morals, at the dictate of a philosophy of ethics,—who would, let us say, hastily practice incest,—is a man whom we should consider *unwise*. The regnant system of sexual rules is an instinctive or Sentimental induction summarizing the experience of all our race. (*CP* 6. 633).

The 'instinctive' prohibition of incest has been put in place by experience and we should not be quick to have it overthrown by a theory. The ethical deliberator tends to be hesitant to revise her beliefs and this hesitation is often justified. But it is not always justified: 'Like any other field, more than any other [morality] needs improvement, advance . . . But morality, doctrinaire conservatist that it is, destroys its own vitality by resisting change, and positively insisting, This is eternally right: That is eternally wrong' (*CP* 2. 198, 1902).

Parker (1998: 50) shows that James too had this view of morality. In 'The Moral Philosopher and the Moral Life', James extends Peirce's view of truth to ethics, saying 'there can be no final truth in ethics any more than in physics, until the last man has had his experience and his say' ([1897] 1979: 184). He argues that society may be seen as a long-running experiment aimed at identifying the best kind of conduct. Its conventions thus deserve respect, for, while remaining fallible, they capture the experience of generations ([1897] 1979: 206).

Peirce and James agree that moral judgements are connected to experience, just as all genuine judgements are so connected. Peirce says: 'just as reasoning springs from experience, so the development of sentiment arises from the soul's Inward and Outward Experiences' (*CP* 1. 648, 1898). As with every other kind of belief: '[t]hat it is abstractly and absolutely infallible we do not pretend; but that it is practically infallible for the individual—which is the only clear sense the word "infallibility" will bear—in that he ought to obey it and not his individual reason, *that* we do maintain' (*CP* 1. 633, 1898).

We saw in Chapter 2 that, for Peirce, this holds for any domain of inquiry: we take our body of background belief to be practically infallible, until the course of experience weighs in against it. The badly named 'instinctual' and 'common-sense' beliefs are subject to revision, but held firm until experience really does prompt that revision (*CP* 5. 444, 1905). That is the Peirce I want to focus upon. Ethics and science are in the same boat, relying on deeply held, but revisable, background beliefs and habits. Instinct, in this sense, has a positive and essential role to play in science and in morality.[8]

Clearly, we can mistakenly preserve the status quo; we can be too reluctant to revise our background beliefs. The only way of guarding against this—in any area of inquiry—is to recognize the possibility and then to try to stay well away from it by listening to challenges to deeply held beliefs and practices. Those challenges can come from within, when my own judgements or principles conflict and I feel a pull towards revising them. And they can come from without— from the senses or when I see that the judgements of others, from within my circle or from afar, conflict with my own judgements and I feel a pull towards reconsidering them. I

---

[8] Trammell (1972) tells us that Peirce did at times innocuously oppose reason and vital concerns. For instance, the more emotionally committed one is to a belief, the harder it is to reason in an unbiased way about it. And highly theoretical or technical science is such that instinct is less reliable than it is in less abstract and less technical inquiry. These points are of course fine by me.

can then revise those beliefs while holding enough stable against which the revision can take place.

But those beliefs which inquiry has not thrown into doubt in such ways are stable and not doubted. What this means for epistemologists and for moral philosophers is that we have no choice but to begin where we find ourselves, with our thoughts about what counts as evidence, with our thoughts about what the standards for justified beliefs are, etc. There is, recall: 'but one state of mind from which you can "set out", namely the very state of mind in which you actually find yourself at the time you do "set out"—a state in which you are laden with an immense mass of cognition already formed, of which you cannot divest yourself if you would' (*CP* 5. 416, 1905).

3. Belief and the Scientific Method

Enough about how the involvement of instinct does not distinguish ethical matters from other matters. Now we need to focus on the flip side of Peirce's problematic thought: the contentious view of science, in which belief is out of place. Let us look at the source of the talk that, while the scientist can wait for an answer and thus does not believe his theories, the deliberator in ethics requires an immediate answer and thus believes and acts on those beliefs. One source is Peirce's 1902 application to the Carnegie Institute, pleading for funds so that he can write his grand work on logic. There are many drafts of this application in the Peirce Papers and they show very clearly that he did not have a settled view about the matter in question. Perhaps his doubts are best expressed on p. 54 of some of the drafts, where we have him saying that the scientist is in a bind—a 'double position':

As a unit of the scientific world, with which he in some measure identifies himself, he can wait five centuries, if need be, before he decides upon the acceptability of a certain hypothesis. But as engaged in the investigation which it is his duty diligently to pursue, he must be ready the next morning to go on that hypothesis or reject it . . . he ought to be in a double state of mind about the hypothesis, at once ardent in his belief that so it must be, and yet not committing himself further than to do his best to try the experiment.[9]

What a wonderful statement of the tension. The inquirer must be ready to believe and to act on the belief, knowing full well that it might not be true. Belief is not *out of place* in science—it is just tempered by falliblism. The scientist must believe, but be constantly aware that her belief might be overturned. This is a classic statement of the narrow path on which the critical commonsense philosopher must tread.

Similarly, in the 1898 'Detached Ideas on Vitally Important Topics', it turns out that Peirce's statement that there is no belief in science is not as alarming as it first seems. It is here that we find the excellent metaphor that science is walking upon a bog. The reason it can only say 'this ground seems to hold for the present: here I will stay till it begins to give way' is that science always starts with an abductive inference. We saw in Chapter 3 that the conclusions of abductive inferences are not to be believed: they are mere conjectures. Peirce goes on to say: 'After a while, as Science progresses, it comes upon more solid ground. It is now entitled to reflect: this ground has held a long time without showing signs of yielding. I may hope that it will continue to hold for a great while longer' (*CP* 5. 589). We can now act upon the hypothesis, for it no longer rests upon a mere abduction. It has been inductively supported. Peirce says: 'In other words there is now reason to believe in the theory, for belief is willingness to risk a great deal upon a proposition.'

The scientist, that is, believes a theory when it rests upon abductive *and* inductive support. The scientist will still be concerned about whether in fact the theory will continue to survive the trials of induction: he will keep his eye on its fallible nature or on the fact that it might not be true. Nonetheless: 'We call them in science established truths, that is, they are propositions into which the economy of endeavor prescribes that, for the time being, further inquiry shall cease' (*CP* 5. 589).

Another source of the contentious view is Peirce's

---

[9] MS L75, pp. 53–5 of the first 88-page variant.

Cambridge Lectures of 1898. These lectures are not the best place for discerning Peirce's considered view about science and vital matters. He was extremely cross with James, who had charitably set up the lectures so that Peirce might be able quite literally to put some food on his table. Upon learning that Peirce intended to address technical questions of logic, James asked him to 'be a good boy and think a more popular plan out'. Perhaps he could rather speak about 'separate topics of a vitally important character'.[10] Peirce, struggling with the shame of having to be rescued by James and having been shut out of an academic job by Harvard, pours scorn on the Harvard philosophers for their lack of training in logic and goes on and on about how he will restrict himself to 'vital matters'. The drafts of the lectures are more scathing and sarcastic than the lectures actually delivered, showing that Peirce, while he thought he ought to try to hold his anger in check, could not altogether manage it. It is in this context that Peirce makes the extreme remarks about the gulf between science and vitally important topics. Reasoning, he sneers, seems not to be necessary for worldly success.

These remarks simply cannot be taken seriously once it is seen that Peirce was wounded about being told, in such an offensive way, to excise the difficult reasoning and logic from his lectures. After James had died, Peirce clearly felt bad that he had been so rude. Unwilling to give up on the point that his dear friend had an 'almost unexampled incapacity for mathematical thought', he nonetheless promises to endeavour 'to substitute a serious and courteous' tone for 'the tone I used at Harvard' (*CP* 6. 182, 1911).

It is instructive to note that, even in the Cambridge Lectures, we find Peirce see-sawing between the idea that belief has no place in science and the idea that it does. First he says:

I would not allow to sentiment or instinct any weight whatsoever in theoretical matters, not the slightest . . . True, we are driven oftentimes in science to try the suggestions of instinct; but we only *try* them, we compare them with experience, we hold ourselves

---

[10] Trammell (1972) presents an excellent account of this dispute. See also Brent (1993: 262–3) and Hookway (2000: 23–4).

ready to throw them overboard at a moment's notice from experience. (*CP* 1. 634.)

This is the 'no belief in science' side of the see-saw. We are not ready to act on belief in science. Science

merely writes in the list of premises it proposes to use. Nothing is *vital* for science; nothing can be. Its accepted propositions, therefore, are but opinions at most; and the whole list is provisional. The scientific man is not in the least wedded to his conclusions. He risks nothing upon them. He stands ready to abandon one or all as soon as experience opposes them. (*CP* 1. 635.)

But in the next breath, Peirce again says that some of the scientist's conclusions are called 'established truths'—'propositions to which no competent man today demurs' (*CP* 1. 635). Established truths are the background beliefs which we take for granted. Even in the Cambridge Lectures, Peirce holds that belief has a place in science.

If we have to choose, on their own merits, which of Peirce's opposing views of science to accept, the choice is easy. As Duhem, Quine, and Kuhn have gone so far to show us, no scientific theory is overthrown in a flash by a lone experience. Scientists tend to insulate their theories from rogue experiences until the theory can bear such insulation no more. It would be a foolish scientist indeed who abandoned a well-supported theory on the basis of one contradictory experiment. Peirce just sometimes makes a mistake here. He sometimes fails to see how the background theories of scientists are accepted as true until recalcitrant experience overwhelms them. But of course, at other times he sees this very clearly.

If we drop Peirce's contentious thought about science, we can discern a coherent and very sensible position. In both scientific and moral matters, we have cherished beliefs which are nonetheless responsive to experience. In ethics, as in science, we act on our experience-driven background beliefs, while realizing that they might yet be overthrown by further experience. Vital matters are not set against reason, experience, and inquiry. And science is not set against belief and action.

4. Moral Deliberation

I have argued that we should not see Peirce as opening up a gulf between science and vital matters. He holds that ethics falls under the scope of truth, knowledge, and what he calls the scientific method of inquiry.

There is, however, another set of tensions in Peirce's thoughts about science and ethics which we would do well to leave in place. For any cognitivist position which fails to incorporate the tensions is, I propose, too simple for the complex phenomena in question. These are the necessary tensions involved in thinking that our human, contingent, historically rooted judgements about how to treat others are such that they might be objectively correct or incorrect. If we are to get right the thought that our moral judgements aim at truth, we need to preserve the tensions. Failure to do so will result in a cognitivism which does not reflect the difficult, problematic, and sometimes tragic nature of moral deliberation.

At one point Peirce distinguishes disagreement in moral matters from disagreement about taste: 'However it may be about taste, in regard to morals, we can see ground for hope that debate will ultimately cause one party or both to modify their sentiments up to complete accord' (*CP* 2. 151, 1902). That is the cognitivist thought I have been trying to preserve for Peirce. But he then delivers a seemingly anti-cognitivist thought: 'Should it turn out otherwise, what can be said except that some men have one aim and some another? It would be monstrous for either party to pronounce the moral judgments of the other to be *bad*. That would imply an appeal to some other tribunal' (*CP* 2. 151, 1902).

At first glance, this looks like a straightforward contradiction. But Peirce here is articulating his rather subtle position on bivalence—a position especially suited to the nature of moral judgement. Should it turn out that there is no possibility of accord—should it turn out that the hope or regulative assumption of inquiry would in some case not be fulfilled—then there is no truth of the matter at stake. We frequently find Peirce saying, in an entirely general fashion:

'It is true that we cannot know for certain that experience, however long and full, ever would bring all men to the same way of thinking concerning the subject of inquiry. But that is the only result that can satisfy us, so that we must forever continue in the hope that it will come, at last.'[11] We must hope, for any question into which we inquire, that bivalence will hold, but we cannot know that it will hold. And here is the point to which any cognitivist must be alert: we may expect that bivalence will fail more often in moral inquiry than in chemistry and less often than in deliberation about matters of taste.

A particularly helpful text here is the 1901 'Truth and Falsity and Error'. Peirce rehearses his general stance on bivalence and says that perhaps the question of whether there is free will is such that no answer would be forthcoming, no matter how long the discussion were to go on and no matter how advanced our methods of inquiry were to become:

Then in regard to that question, there certainly is no *truth*. But whether or not there would be perhaps any *reality* is a question for the metaphysician . . . Even if the metaphysician decides that where there is no truth there is no reality, still the distinction between the character of truth and the character of reality is plain and definable. (*CP* 5. 565, 1901.)

Hookway (2000) has drawn our attention to this distinction in an especially helpful way. Truth, for Peirce, may be indeterminate and the underlying reality determinate. 'Truth' applies to propositions, statements, or beliefs if they would survive all attempts at refutation—if they would never lead to disappointment (*CP* 5. 569, 1901). 'Reality' applies to things as they are irrespective of what any mind or collection of minds takes them to be (*CP* 5. 565, 1901, see pp. 126 ff.).

After distinguishing truth from reality, Peirce very clearly says that the distinction holds not just for science, but also for ethics (*CP* 5. 566, 1901) and for mathematics (*CP* 5. 567, 1901). Elsewhere he says that all of these inquiries aim at the truth:

[11] MS 1342, p. 2 of variants, undated. See also MS 408, p. 147, 1893–5.

Now the different sciences deal with different kinds of truth; mathematical truth is one thing, ethical truth is another, the actually existing state of the universe is a third; but all those different conceptions have in common something very marked and clear. We all hope that the different scientific inquiries in which we are severally engaged are going ultimately to lead to some definitely established conclusion, which conclusion we endeavour to anticipate in some measure. Agreement with that ultimate proposition that we look forward to,—agreement with that, whatever it may turn out to be, is the scientific truth. (*CP* 7. 187, 1901.)

There will be differences between kinds of inquiry: the mathematician, the chemist, and the inquirer into what is the morally right thing to do will not all find themselves engaged in identical methods. Nor will they find that their aspirations have identical prospects. Nor will they all be talking about the same sort of reality. As Hookway puts it:

We might agree that mathematical propositions, ethical propositions, propositions from the more theoretical reaches of science can all be assessed as true or false. Each, we might suppose, can be tested or 'compared with reality'. This might involve looking for a proof, considering how the ethical proposition would appeal to someone who took up a distinctive disinterested viewpoint on things, or making explanatory inferences about what best systematises our other theoretical beliefs and experimental results.[12]

That is, comparing hypotheses with 'reality' is bound to take different forms in different inquiries.

Peirce goes on to explicitly make the point that I have been pressing: what is central and common to all these various inquiries is the surprise of experience, against a background of stable expectations or beliefs. He says: 'Thus it is that all knowledge begins by the discovery that there has been an erroneous expectation . . . Each branch of science begins with a new phenomenon which violates a[n] . . . expectation'. (*CP* 7. 188, 1901.)

---

[12] I prefer this statement of Hookway's position (2000: 97) to the following: 'Some truths can be understood in a "realist" manner, as dealing with a mind-independent reality, while others deal with matters whose character bears more marks of our interests, sentiments or constructive activities' (2000: 77).

Let us look at the mathematical case, about which Peirce is exceptionally clear. In 'Truth and Falsity and Error', he says:

[t]he pure mathematician deals exclusively with hypotheses. Whether or not there is any corresponding real thing, he does not care. His hypotheses are creatures of his own imagination; but he discovers in them relations which surprise him sometimes. A metaphysician may hold that this very forcing upon the mathematician's acceptance of propositions for which he was not prepared, proves, or even constitutes, a mode of being independent of the mathematician's thought, and so a *reality*. But whether there is any reality or not, the truth of the pure mathematical proposition is constituted by the impossibility of ever finding a case in which it fails. (*CP* 5. 567, 1901.)

Peirce himself argued that mathematics does not answer to a *physical* reality—it is not concerned with physical objects, but with possibilities (*CP* 4. 234, 1902, 3. 527, 1896) or the forms of relations (*CP* 4. 530, 1905). As we saw in Chapter 2, Peirce thinks that reality goes beyond the physical—generals and potentialities, for instance, are real. But his point here is that, whatever your metaphysics might be, mathematics aims at the truth in the same way other kinds of inquiry aim at the truth. A true belief would be the best belief, were we to pursue our inquiries as far as they could fruitfully go and what makes for a best belief in mathematics might differ from what makes a belief best in science, or in morals. As Hookway puts it, Peirce held that the idea of truth is metaphysically neutral.

'Truth and Falsity and Error' is thus a wonderful text for the pragmatist who wants to think of moral belief as being truth-apt. We have Peirce saying, very clearly, that a belief can be sensitive to experience even if there is no underlying physical reality. Perhaps a domain of inquiry which rests on an underlying physical reality will contain plenty of statements which are bivalent. But some kinds of inquiry, such as mathematics, will be full of bivalent statements and yet they are such that there is no underlying physical reality.

Moral deliberation presents us with especially interesting phenomena. We might, for instance, think that there are situations in our moral lives where no decision can be right. Such tragic contexts are exemplified by those horrors from Nazi Germany where a concentration camp guard tells a mother that she must choose one of her two children for the gas chamber. If she does so, one child will live; if she refuses to choose, both will die. There seems to be no decent solution to this kind of problem. Perhaps not even a random choice, a flipping of a coin, will be right, for the mother will surely feel that in making the decision in any way, or in refusing to make it, she betrays something that is valuable and fundamental.

We should not want to set up our moral epistemology so that we do away with the possibility that some issues will prove to be impossible—so that we do away with situations in which wretched compromise is the best that we can manage. Ruling out such possibilities would be untrue to the phenomenology or practice of morals. It would be untrue to all those occasions where we feel at a loss, where we feel that, no matter how hard we persevere, there is no right answer to be had, or where we feel regret that, even though we did something acceptable, we were unable to act on the opposing considerations. To aim for precision where there may be none would be to do a disservice to the kind of inquiry we are trying to characterize. The Peircean view of truth, with its explicit accommodation of the possibility of the failure of bivalence, is well-suited to capture this kind of phenomenon.

Another kind of problematic situation which arises in moral deliberation is that in which there seems to be a number of equally good ways of answering a moral question. It can seem, for instance, that those with one cultural and religious background will have one answer to a question about the right thing to do and those with a different cultural and religious background will have an equally good, but different, answer.

Here the Peircean can think of the potential agreement not as agreement about which one way of life is best, but as agreement about which ways of life are reasonable or permissible. What we might agree upon is that a number of conceptions of how best to live are acceptable and these conceptions will produce different, equally acceptable, answers to some moral questions. There is nothing in the Peircean view which suggests we must hope for an agreement which will level all difference.

Peirce's view, that is, is not committed to a melting-pot metaphor. It is not that we need lots of perspectives in order for the best one or the best amalgam to emerge. Rather, one would expect that plurality of belief would sometimes be preserved, were moral deliberation to continue. (*P or Q*) may be true for the whole community of inquirers. This is very different from saying that *P* is true for one subset of the community and *Q* is true for another.

This is also very different from saying that 'anything goes'. Recall that Peirce justifies a methodology. The aim of inquiry is to get true belief, which, on his view, is belief which would forever fit with experience and argument. The best means to this aim is clearly a method by which we test our hypotheses against experience. If truth is that which would best fit with experience and argument, then if we want true beliefs, we should expose them to experience and argument which might overturn them. Better to find out now that a belief is defeated, rather than down the line.

Not only are we justified in exposing our beliefs to experience, but we are justified in exposing them to as broad a variety of experience as we can. A scientist who refused to take into account any of the experimental results of, say, the English or the Italians, would be adopting a very bad method for getting beliefs that would stand up to experience. Similarly, those engaged in moral deliberation who denigrate or ignore the experiences of those with a certain skin colour, gender, or religion are also adopting a method unlikely to reach the truth. Their methods and their beliefs can be criticized in this second-order way (as failing to be sensitive to all the experience and argument or as failing to properly aim at truth), as well as in the usual first-order kind of way (as being disrespectful or as failing to treat others as equals, etc.).[13]

_____

[13] It will be asked whether the second-order reasons are not as culturally specific as the first-order reasons—specific, that is, to those cultures who value argument and the truth. The response, in a nutshell, is that everyone values beliefs which stand up to experience. For a more sustained discussion, see Misak (2000).

So, while (*P* and *Q*) might be equally acceptable, if *R* turns on denigrating some group or other, then it is unacceptable. And the judgements in which it issues are not likely to be true. Peirce's position, while leaving plenty of room for difference and plurality, has the wherewithal to rule out some beliefs and some methods (intolerant ones, for instance) as being on the wrong track.

The upshot is that the fact that the sort of experience relevant to morality is liable to vary from culture to culture need not be destructive for Peirce's position. For that position allows for some failures of bivalence and it allows us to criticize cultures which do not take the moral experience of others seriously. It brings moral deliberation within the scope of an experience-driven and reason-driven inquiry which is aimed at the truth, yet it does not pretend that ethics is identical to science or has the same prospects as science.

Indeed, we are not short of explanations for why we find things as we do in moral deliberation. It might be that moral judgements require more collateral information. The judgement that the bullies are cruel requires, for instance, that we know that they intend to cause distress.[14] Or perhaps science has a more precise theory of error and disagreement there can often be explained by citing malfunctioning or misuse of equipment, for instance.[15] Perhaps the scarcity of goods and resources explains some kinds of irresolvable conflict in the moral and political domain. All these things said, we must be careful also to notice the tremendous amount of underlying agreement in moral matters as well as the diversity of background theory and belief in science and mathematics. As Putnam (1987) has argued, nothing very uniform can be said of the sciences over and above a few thin methodological points—points like Peirce's argument about the need to take experience seriously.

[14] See Wiggins (1996: 278–9). Wright (1992: 101) points out how this is true of the comic—the unintended spoonerisms and muffed anecdotes of the pompous after-dinner speaker are not funny if you know that he is distracted by the fact that his child is seriously ill. Judgements about what is funny, which Wright thinks are not truth-apt, are, on my view, less able to achieve their aim, if indeed they do aim at truth.

[15] See Jardine (1995: 41–2) for the argument that the difference between science and ethics here is not as striking as it first appears.

It is useful in summing up to consider how Peirce puts his view in yet another grand proposed book on logic—yet another systematic outline of his position. Morality, he says, is somehow both subjective and objective. It arises from human predicaments and history—it 'has its root' in 'human nature' (*CP* 2. 156, 1902)—yet is such that we aim to get a right answer. Unlike taste, which seems to be mostly subjective, morals 'has a subjective and an objective side' (*CP* 2. 153, 1902). There is a continuum here: 'taste, morality, rationality, form a true sequence in this order', with taste being 'purely subjective, and morals half subjective, half objective'.

After identifying the half-subjective, half-objective nature of moral judgement, Peirce calls for a correction in moral philosophy: 'It is true that the majority of writers on ethics in the past have made the root of morals subjective; but that best opinion is very plainly moving in the opposite direction' (*CP* 2. 156, 1902). It cannot move too far in the objective direction, for the only ground we have for our moral judgements is feeling: 'our aversion for and horror of' incest 'is simply felt' (2. 171, 1902). The kind of experience relevant to moral judgement is likely to be much less uniform than the kind of experience one finds relevant to belief in logic and in science.

We need to remind ourselves here of the importance of the distinction between belief (which is aimed at the truth) and tenacity. If we hold this distinction steady when we think of moral deliberation, we will want to retain, against the obstacles, the thought that moral judgements are responsive to experience. What it is to assert, to make a claim, to believe, to judge, is to be engaged in a process of justification. It is to commit oneself to giving reasons—to be prepared, in the appropriate circumstances, to justify one's assertion to others, and to oneself. Those claiming to hold a belief, something which has a truth-value, commit themselves to being open to evidence and argument. Those who engage in moral *deliberation*, as opposed to holding on to our moral opinions come what may, must take their beliefs to be responsive to new reasons, arguments, and experiences about what is cruel, kind, odious, just, etc. If one is committed to never revising an opinion, no matter what evidence against it is brought to light, then that is something like blind dogmatism and not a genuine judgement about what is true. Moral deliberation, for those who engage in it, is experience-driven, example-driven, and argument-driven. And we do sometimes, if not always, engage or try to engage in moral deliberation rather than in mere tenacity.

Peirce thus presents us with an extremely sophisticated cognitivism. We ought to expect bivalence to fail more often in ethics than in physical science, but ethical deliberation is nonetheless such that it aims at the truth. We can see that the reality to which moral judgements fit is not physical reality, yet ethical deliberation is still governed by the surprise of experience. Ethics falls somewhere in between the highly subjective domain of taste and the much more objective domain of the physical sciences. We are pulled to think that our moral judgements are true, even if those judgements are products of our history and education. Peirce's account of truth and knowledge goes a long way in saying how all this can be. We have moved very far indeed from the thought that he had only crude things to say about ethics.

Bibliography

I

Editions of works by C. S. Peirce which are cited throughout are listed first, with the abbreviations linked to the publication details. Other works by Peirce follow.

CP *Collected Papers of Charles Sanders Peirce* (Cambridge, Mass.: Belknap Press), i–vi, ed. C. Hartshorne and P. Weiss (1931–5); vii and viii, ed. A. Burks (1958).

CE *Writings of Charles S. Peirce: A Chronological Edition*, ed. M. Fisch (Bloomington, Ind.: Indiana University Press, 1982).

MS Microfilm: *The Charles S. Peirce Papers* (Cambridge, Mass.).

NE *The New Elements of Mathematics*, ed. C. Eisle (The Hague: Mouton, 1976).

Complete Published Works, Including Selected Secondary Materials, ed. K. L. Ketner *et al.* (microfiche collection).

Contributions to The Nation, ed. K. L. Ketner and J. E. Cook (Lubbock: Texas Technical University Press, 1975).

Semiotics and Significs, ed. C. Hardwick (Bloomington, Ind.: Indiana University Press, 1977).

II

Almeder, R. (1982). *The Philosophy of C. S. Peirce: A Critical Introduction* (Oxford: Basil Blackwell).

—— (1985). 'Peirce's Thirteen Theories of Truth', *Transactions of the C. S. Peirce Society*, 21/1.

Altshuler, B. (1978). 'The Nature of Peirce's Pragmatism', *Transactions of the C. S. Peirce Society*, 14/3.

—— (1980). 'Peirce's Theory of Truth and his Early Idealism', *Transactions of the C. S. Peirce Society*, 16/2.

—— (1982). 'Peirce's Theory of Truth and the Revolt Against Realism'. *Transactions of the C. S. Peirce Society*, 18/1.

Anderson, E. (1993). *Values in Ethics and Economics* (Cambridge, Mass.: Harvard University Press).

Armstrong, D. (1973). *Belief, Truth and Knowledge* (Cambridge: Cambridge University Press).

196　　　　　　　*Bibliography*

Arnauld, A. (1851). *The Port-Royal Logic*, trans. T. Baynes (Edinburgh: Sutherland and Knox).

Austin, J. (1950). 'Truth', *Proceedings of The Aristotelian Society*, suppl. vol. 24.

Ayer, A. J. (1946). *Language, Truth and Logic* (New York: Dover).

—— (1959). *Logical Positivism* (New York: The Free Press).

—— (1968). *The Origins of Pragmatism* (London: Macmillan).

Ayim, M. (1974). 'Retroduction: The Rational Instinct', *Transactions of the C. S. Peirce Society*, 10.

Bain, A. (1859). *Emotion and the Will* (New York: Longmans Green).

—— (1868). *Mental and Moral Science* (London: Longmans Green).

Bernstein, R. (1964). 'Peirce's Theory of Perception', in E. C. Moore and R. Robin (eds.), *Studies in the Philosophy of Charles Sanders Peirce*, 2nd series (Amherst, Mass.: University of Massachusetts Press).

—— (1965). 'Action, Conduct and Self-Control', in R. Bernstein (ed.), *Perspectives on Peirce: Critical Essays on C. S. Peirce* (New Haven, Conn.: Yale University Press).

Berry, G. (1952). 'Peirce's Contributions to the Logic of Statements and Quantifiers', in P. Wiener and F. Young (eds.), *Studies in the Philosophy of Charles Sanders Peirce* (Cambridge, Mass.: Harvard University Press).

Blackburn, S. (1980). 'Truth, Realism, and the Regulation of Theory', in P. French, T. Vehling, jun., and H. Wettstein (eds.), *Midwest Studies in Philosophy V* (Minneapolis: University of Minnesota Press).

—— (1984). *Spreading the Word* (Oxford: Clarendon Press).

Boler, J. (1963). *Charles Peirce and Scholastic Realism: A Study of Peirce's Relation to John Duns Scotus* (Seattle: University of Washington Press).

Braithwaite, R. B. (1932). 'The Nature of Believing', *Proceedings of the Aristotelian Society*, 33.

Braithwaite, R. B. (1946). 'Belief and Action', *Proceedings of the Aristotelian Society*, suppl. vol. 20.

Brent, J. (1993). *Charles Sanders Peirce: A Life* (Bloomington, Ind.: Indiana University Press).

Burks, A. (1964). 'Peirce's Two Theories of Probability' in E. C. Moore and R. Robin (eds.), *Studies in the Philosophy of Charles Sanders Peirce*, 2nd series (Amherst, Mass.: University of Massachusetts Press).

Carnap, R. (1934). *The Unity of Science*, trans. M. Black (London: Kegan Paul, Trench, Trubner).

—— (1945). 'The Two Concepts of Probability', *Philosophy and Phenomenological Research*, 5/1.

—— (1950). *The Logical Foundations of Probability* (Chicago: University of Chicago Press).

—— (1963). 'Philosophical Problems', in *The Philosophy of Rudolf Carnap*, in P. A. Schilpp (ed.), The Library of Living Philosophers (LaSalle, Ill.: Open Court).

Carus, P. (1892). 'The Founder of Tychism: His Methods, Philosophy and Criticisms', *The Monist*, 3.

Cheng, C. (1966). 'Peirce's Probabilistic Theory of Inductive Validity', *Transactions of the C. S. Peirce Society*, 2.

—— (1969). *Peirce's and Lewis's Theories of Induction* (The Hague: Martinus Nijhoff).

Churchland, P. (1979). *Scientific Realism and the Plasticity of the Mind* (New York: Cambridge University Press).

Comte, A. (1844). *Discourse on the Positive Spirit*, trans. E. S. Beesly, 1903 (London: William Reeves).

Dauben, J. W. (1982). 'Peirce's Place in Mathematics', *Historia Mathematica*, 9.

Davidson, D. (1983). 'A Coherence Theory of Truth and Knowledge', in D. Henrich (ed.), *Kant oder Hegel?* (Germany: Klett-Cotta).

—— (1996). 'The Folly of Trying to Define Truth', *Journal of Philosophy*, 93.

Descartes, R. (1637). *Discourse on Method*, in *Philosophical Works of Descartes*, ed. E. S. Haldane and G. R. Ross (Cambridge: Cambridge University Press).

Dewey, J. (1938). *Logic: The Theory of Inquiry* (New York: Henry Holt).

Dipert, R. (1981). 'Peirce's Propositional Logic', *Review of Metaphysics*, 34.

—— (2004). 'Peirce's Deductive Logic: Its Development, Influence, and Philosophical Significance', in C. J. Misak (ed.), *The Cambridge Companion to Peirce* (Cambridge and New York: Cambridge University Press).

Du Bois-Reymond, E. (1882). *Uber die Grenzen des Naturerkennens: Die Sieben Weltrathsel* (Leipzig: Verlag von Veit and Co.).

Dummett, M. (1978). *Truth and Other Enigmas* (Boston: Harvard University Press).

—— (1982). 'Realism', *Synthèse*, 52.

198 Bibliography

Eisele, C. (1979). *Studies in the Scientific and Mathematical Philosophy of C. S. Peirce*, ed. R. S. Martin (The Hague: Mouton).

Ellis, B. (1985). 'What Science aims to Do' in P. Churchland and C. Hooker (eds.), *Images of Science* (Chicago: University of Chicago Press).

—— (1992), 'Critical Notice of Cheryl Misak's *Truth and the End of Inquiry: A Peircean Account of Truth*', *Canadian Journal of Philosophy*, 22/3.

Fann, K. T. (1970). *Peirce's Theory of Abduction* (The Hague: Martinus Nijhoff).

Feigl, H., and Sellars, W., eds. (1949). *Readings in Philosophical Analysis* (New York: Appleton-Century-Crofts).

Feigl, H., and Broadbeck, M., eds. (1953). *Readings in the Philosophy of Science* (New York: Appleton-Century-Crofts).

Fisch, M. (1954). 'Alexander Bain and the Genealogy of Pragmatism', *Journal of the History of Ideas*, 15.

—— (1967). 'Peirce's Progress from Nominalism to Realism', *The Monist*, 51.

—— (1982). 'Introduction' in C. S. Peirce, *CE* i.

Fitzgerald, J. (1966). *Peirce's Theory of Signs as Foundation of Pragmatism* (The Hague: Mouton).

—— (1968). 'Peirce's Theory of Inquiry', *Transactions of the C. S. Peirce Society*, 4.

Forrest, P. (1985). 'An Indubitability Analysis of Knowledge', *The Monist*, 68/1.

Frankfurt, H. (1958). 'Peirce's Account of Inquiry', *Journal of Philosophy*, 55/14.

Goldman, A. (1979). 'What is Justified Belief?', in G. Pappas (ed.), *Justification and Knowledge* (Dordrecht: Reidel).

Goodman, N. (1955). *Fact, Fiction, and Forecast* (Cambridge, Mass.: Harvard University Press).

Goudge, T. (1950). *The Thought of C. S. Peirce* (Toronto: University of Toronto Press).

—— (1964). 'Peirce's Evolutionism: After Half a Century', in E. C. Moore and R. Robin (eds.), *Studies in the Philosophy of Charles Sanders Peirce*, 2nd series (Amherst, Mass.: University of Massachusetts Press).

Greenlee, D. (1973). *Peirce's Concept of Sign* (The Hague: Mouton).

Haack, S. (1976). 'The Pragmatist Theory of Truth', *British Journal of Philosophy of Science*, 27.

—— (1979). 'Fallibilism and Necessity', *Synthèse*, 41.

—— (1982). 'Peirce, Descartes and the Cognitive Community', *The Monist*, 65/2.

Habermas, J. (1968). *Knowledge and Human Interests*, trans. J. Shapiro (Boston: Beacon).

Hacking, I. (1965). *Logic of Statistical Inference* (Cambridge: Cambridge University Press).

—— (1975). *The Emergence of Probability* (Cambridge: Cambridge University Press).

—— (1980). 'The Theory of Probable Inference: Neyman, Peirce and Braithwaite', in H. Mellor (ed.), *Science, Belief and Behavior: Essays in Honour of R. B. Braithwaite* (Cambridge: Cambridge University Press).

Haeckel, E. (1899). *Die Weltratsel*, trans. J. McCabe, 1929, as *The Riddle of the Universe* (London: Watts).

Hanson, N. R. (1958). *Patterns of Discovery* (Cambridge: Cambridge University Press).

—— (1965). 'Notes Toward a Logic of Discovery', in R. Bernstein (ed.), *Perspective on Peirce: Critical Essays on C. S. Peirce* (New Haven, Conn.: Yale University Press)

Harman, G. (1965). 'The Inference to The Best Explanation', *Philosophical Review*, 74.

Harris, J., and Hoover, K. (1980). 'Abduction and the New Riddle of Induction', *The Monist*, 63/3.

Hempel, K. (1965). 'Empiricist Criteria of Cognitive Significance', in *Aspects of Scientific Explanation* (New York: Free Press).

Herschel, J. (1881). *Preliminary Discourse on the Study of Natural Philosophy*, 2nd edn. (London: Longmans, Brown, Green).

Herzberger, H. (1981). 'Peirce's Remarkable Theorem', in L. Sumner, J. Slater, and F. Wilson (eds.), *Pragmatism and Purpose: Essays in Honour of T. A. Goudge* (Toronto: University of Toronto Press).

Holmes, L. (1966). 'Peirce on Self-Control', *Transactions of the C. S. Peirce Society*, 2/2.

Hooker, M. (1978). 'Peirce's Conception of Truth', in J. C. Pitt (ed.), *The Philosophy of Wilfred Sellars: Queries and Extensions* (Dordrecht: Reidel).

Hookway, C. (1980). 'Inference, Partial Belief and Psychological Laws', in D. H. Mellor (ed.), *Prospects f or Pragmatism: Essays in Memory of F. P. Ramsey* (Cambridge: Cambridge University Press).

—— (1984). 'Naturalism, Fallibilism and Evolutionary

200   Bibliography

Epistemology', in C. Hookway (ed.), *Minds, Machines and Evolution* (Cambridge: Cambridge University Press).
—— (1985). *Peirce* (London: Routledge and Kegan Paul).
—— (2000). *Truth, Rationality, and Pragmatism: Themes from Peirce* (Oxford: Clarendon Press).
Hume, D. (1888). *A Treatise of Human Nature*, ed. L. A. Selby-Bigge (Oxford: Oxford University Press).
James, W. ([1897] 1979). 'The Moral Philosopher and the Moral Life', in *The Will to Believe and Other Essays in Popular Philosophy* (Cambridge, Mass.: Harvard University Press).
—— (1907). *Pragmatism: A New Name for Some Old Ways of Thinking* (New York: Longmans, Green, and Co.).
—— (1909). *The Meaning of Truth* (New York: Longmans, Green, and Co.).
Jardine, N. (1986). *The Fortunes of Inquiry* (Oxford: Clarendon Press).
—— (1995). 'Science, Ethics and Objectivity', in J. E. J. Altham and R. Harrison (eds.), *World, Mind and Ethics: Essay on the Ethical Philosophy of Bernard Williams* (Cambridge, Mass.: Cambridge University Press).
Kant, I. (1781). *Critique of Pure Reason*, trans. N. Kemp-Smith (New York: St Martins).
—— (1785). *Foundations of the Metaphysics of Morals in Critique of Practical Reason and Other Writings in Moral Philosophy*, trans. L. White Beck (Chicago: University of Chicago Press).
Kolenda, K. (1979). 'Truth and Fallibilism', *Transactions of the C. S. Peirce Society*, 15/3.
Kuklick, B. (1977). *The Rise of American Philosophy* (New Haven, Conn.: Yale University Press).
Ladd-Franklin, C. (1916). 'Charles S. Peirce at the Johns Hopkins', *The Journal of Philosophy*, 13.
Laudan, L. (1974). 'Peirce and the Trivialization of the Self-Correcting Thesis', in R. Griere and R. Westfall (eds.), *Foundations of Scientific Method: The Nineteenth Century* (Bloomington, Ind.: Indiana University Press).
Leib, I., ed. (1953). *C. S. Peirce's Letters to Lady Welby* (New Haven, Conn.: Yale University Press).
Lenz, J. (1958). 'Problems for the Practicalist's Justification of Induction', *Philosophical Studies*, 9/1–2.
—— (1964). 'Induction as Self-Corrective', in E. C. Moore and R. Robin (eds.), *Studies in the Philosophy of Charles Sanders Peirce*, 2nd series (Amherst, Mass.: University of Massachusetts Press).

Lenzen, V. (1964), 'Charles Sanders Peirce as Astronomer', in E. C. Moore and R. Robin (eds.), *Studies in the Philosophy of Charles Sanders Peirce*, 2nd series (Amherst, Mass.: University of Massachusetts Press).

Levi, I. (1980). 'Induction as Self-Correcting According to Peirce', in D. H. Mellor (ed.), *Science, Belief and Behavior: Essays in Honour of R. B. Braithwaite* (Cambridge: Cambridge University Press).

—— (1983). *The Enterprise of Knowledge* (Cambridge, Mass.: The MIT Press).

—— (1984a). 'Truth, Fallibility, and the Growth of Knowledge', in *Decisions and Revisions* (Cambridge: Cambridge University Press).

—— (1984b). 'Messianic vs. Myopic Realism', in P. D. Asquith and P. Kitcher (eds.), *Proceedings of the 1984 Biennial Meeting of the Philosophy of Science Association*, ii (East Lansing, Mich.: Philosophy of Science Association).

—— (1991). 'Induction According To Peirce', in K. Ketner (ed.), *Proceedings of the C. S. Peirce Sesquicentennial International Congress* (Lubbock: Texas Technical University Press).

—— and Morgenbesser, S. (1964). 'Belief and Disposition', *American Philosophical Quarterly*, 1.

Luntley, M. (1988). *Language, Logic and Experience: The Case for Anti-Realism* (LaSalle, Ill.: Open Court).

McDowell, J. (1982). 'Criteria, Defeasibility, and Knowledge', *Proceedings of the British Academy*, 68.

Mackie, J. (1977). *Ethics: Inventing Right and Wrong* (Harmondsworth: Penguin).

Madden, E. (1964). 'Peirce on Probability', in E. C. Moore and R. Robin (eds.), *Studies in the Philosophy of Charles Sanders Peirce*, 2nd series (Amherst, Mass.: University of Massachusetts Press).

—— (1981). 'Scientific Inference: Peirce and the Humean Tradition', in L. Sumner, J. Slater, and F. Wilson (eds.), *Pragmatism and Purpose: Essays in Honour of T. A. Goudge* (Toronto: University of Toronto Press).

Merrill, D. (1984). 'The 1870 Logic of Relatives Memoir', in C. S. Peirce, *CE* ii.

Mill, J. S. (1891). *A System of Logic*, 8th edn. (New York: Harper Bros).

Miller, D. (1974). 'Popper's Qualitative Theory of Verisimilitude', *British Journal for the Philosophy of Science*, 25.

Miller, R. (1975). 'Propensity: Popper or Peirce?' *British Journal for the Philosophy of Science*, 26.

Misak, C. (1987). 'Peirce, Levi, and the Aims of Inquiry', *Philosophy of Science*, 54/2.
—— (forthcoming). *Pragmatists, Truth and Morality*.
—— (1995). *Verificationism: Its History and Prospects* (London: Routledge).
—— (2000). *Truth, Politics, Morality: Pragmatism and Deliberation* (London and New York: Routledge).
Murphey, M. (1961). *The Development of Peirce's Philosophy* (Cambridge, Mass.: Harvard University Press).
Murray, D. L. (1912). *Pragmatism* (London: Constable).
Newton-Smith, W. H. (1989). 'The Truth in Realism', *Dialectica*, 43/1–2.
Neyman, J., and Pearson, E. S. (1933). 'On the Problem of the Most Efficient Tests of Statistical Hypotheses', *Philosophical Transactions of the Royal Society of London*, A231.
Olshewsky, T. (1983). 'Peirce's Pragmatic Maxim', *Transactions of the C. S. Peirce Society*, 19/2.
Parker, K. (1998). *The Continuity of Peirce's Thought* (Nashville, Tenn.: Vanderbuilt University Press).
Peacocke, C. (1988). 'The Limits of Intelligibility: A Post-Verificationist Approach', *The Philosophical Review*, 97/4.
Perkins, M. (1952). 'Notes on the Pragmatic Theory of Truth', *Journal of Philosophy*, 49.
Popper, K. (1959). *The Logic of Scientific Discovery* (London: Hutchinson).
—— (1960). 'The Propensity Theory of Probability', *British Journal of the Philosophy of Science*, 10.
—— (1963). *Conjectures and Refutations: The Growth of Scientific Knowledge* (New York: Harper and Row).
—— (1966). 'A Theorem on Truth Content', in P. Feyerabend and G. Maxwell (eds.), *Mind, Matter and Method* (Minneapolis: University of Minnesota Press).
Post, J. (1987). *The Faces of Existence: An Essay in Nonreductive Metaphysics* (Ithaca, NY: Cornell University Press).
Potter, V. (1967). *Charles Peirce on Norms and Ideals* (Amherst, Mass.: University of Massachusetts Press).
Pratt, J. B. (1909). *What is Pragmatism?* (New York: Macmillan).
Price, H. (2003). 'Truth as Convenient Friction', *Journal of Philosophy*, 100.
Prior, A. N. (1967). 'Correspondence Theory of Truth', in P. Edwards (ed.), *Encyclopedia of Philosophy* (New York: Macmillan).
Putnam, H. (1975). 'Language and Reality', in *Mind, Language and Reality* (Cambridge: Cambridge University Press).

—— (1981). *Reason, Truth and History* (Cambridge: Cambridge University Press).

—— (1982). 'Peirce as Logician', *Historia Mathematica*, 9.

—— (1987), 'The Diversity of the Sciences: Global versus Local Methodological Approaches', in P. Petit, R. Sylvan, and J. Norman (eds.), *Metaphysics and Morality: Essays in Honour of J. J. C. Smart* (Oxford: Basil Blackwell).

Quine, W. V. O. (1960). *Word and Object* (Cambridge, Mass.: The MIT Press).

—— (1975). 'The Nature of Natural Knowledge', in S. Guttenplan (ed.), *Mind and Language* (Oxford: Oxford University Press).

—— (1981). 'The Pragmatist's Place in Empiricism', in R. Mulvaney and P. Zeltner (eds.), *Pragmatism: Its Sources and Prospects* (Columbia: University of South Carolina Press).

Ramsey, F. P. (1926). 'Truth and Probability'. repr. in H. Kyburg and H. Smokler (eds.), *Studies in Subjective Probability* (New York: Robert E. Krieger).

—— (1929*a*). 'Knowledge', repr. in D. H. Mellor (ed.), *Foundations: Essays in Philosophy, Mathematics and Economics* (Atlantic Highlands, NJ: Humanities Press).

—— (1929*b*). 'Law and Causality', repr. in D. H. Mellor (ed.), *Foundations: Essays in Philosophy, Mathematics and Economics* (Atlantic Highlands, NJ: Humanities Press).

Reichenbach, H. (1938). *Experience and Prediction* (Chicago: University of Chicago Press).

—— (1939). 'Dewey's Theory of Science', in P A. Schilpp (ed.), *The Philosophy of John Dewey* (Evanston, Ill.: Northwestern University Press).

—— (1949). *The Theory of Probability* (Berkeley, Calif.: University of California Press).

Rescher, N. (1978). *Peirce's Philosophy of Science* (Notre Dame, Ind.: University of Notre Dame Press).

Reynolds, A. (2000). 'Statistical Method and the Peircean Account of Truth', *Canadian Journal of Philosophy*, 30/2.

Roberts, D. (1973). *The Existential Graphs of Charles S. Peirce* (The Hague: Mouton).

Robin, R. (1964). 'Peirce's Doctrine of the Normative Sciences', in E. C. Moore and R. Robin (eds.), *Studies in the Philosophy of Charles Sanders Peirce*, 2nd series (Amherst, Mass.: University of Massachusetts Press).

—— (1967). *Annotated Catalogue of the Papers of Charles S. Peirce* (Amherst, Mass.: University of Massachusetts).

Rorty, R. (1982). *Consequences of Pragmatism* (Minneapolis: University of Minnesota Press).

Royce, J. (1885). *The Religious Aspect of Philosophy* (Boston: Houghton).

—— (1899). *The World and the Individual* (New York: Macmillan).

Russell, B. (1908). 'James' Conception of Truth', repr. in *Philosophical Essays* (London: Longmans Green, 1910).

—— (1939). 'Dewey's New Logic', in P. A. Schilpp (ed.), *The Philosophy of John Dewey* (New York: Tudor).

Ryle, G. (1949). *The Concept of Mind* (London: Hutchinson).

Salmon, W. (1957). 'The Predictive Inference', *Philosophy of Science*, 24.

Savan, D. (1964). 'Peirce's Infallibilism', in E. C. Moore and R. Robin (eds.), *Studies in the Philosophy of Charles Sanders Peirce*, 2nd series (Amherst, Mass.: University of Massachusetts Press).

—— 'Decision and Knowledge in Peirce', *Transactions of the C. S. Peirce Society*, 1/3.

—— (1981). 'The Unity of Peirce's Thought' in L. Sumner, J. Slater, and F. Wilson (eds.), *Pragmatism and Purpose: Essays in Honour of T. A. Goudge* (Toronto: University of Toronto Press).

Scheffler, I. (1974). *Four Pragmatists: A Critical Introduction to Peirce, James, Mead, and Dewey* (New York: Humanities Press).

Schiller, F. C. S. (1907). *Studies in Humanism* (London: Macmillan).

Sellars, W. (1962). 'Truth as Correspondence'. *Journal of Philosophy*, 59.

Shapere, D. (1979). 'The Scope and Limits of Scientific Change', in L. J. Cohen (ed.), *Logic, Methodology and Philosophy of Science VI* (New York: North-Holland).

Shimony, A. (1970). 'Scientific Inference', in R. G. Colondny (ed.), *The Nature and Function of Scientific Theories* (Pittsburgh: University of Pittsburgh Press).

—— (1987). 'Integral Epistemology', in A. Shimony and D. Nails (eds.), *Naturalistic Epistemology* (Dordrecht: Reidel).

Short, T. L. (1982). 'Life among the Legisigns', *Transactions of the C. S. Peirce Society*, 18/4.

—— (2002). 'Robin on Perception and Sentiment in Peirce', *Transactions of the C. S. Peirce Society*, 39/1.

Skagested, P. (1980). 'Pragmatic Realism: The Peircean Argument Reexamined', *The Review of Metaphysics*, 33/3.

—— (1981). *The Road of Inquiry* (New York: Columbia University Press).

—— (1987). 'Peirce's Conception of Truth: A Framework for Naturalistic Epistemology?', in A. Shimony and D. Nails (eds.), *Naturalistic Epistemology* (Dordrecht: Reidel).

Skyrms, B. (1966). *Choice and Chance: An Introduction to Inductive Logic* (Belmont, Calif.: Dickenson).

Smart, J. J. C. (1986). 'Realism v. Idealism', *Philosophy*, 61.

Tarski, A. (1949). 'The Semantic Conception of Truth', in Feigl and Sellars (1949).

—— (1956). *Logic, Semantics, Metamathematics* (Oxford: Oxford University Press).

Thayer, H. S. (1968). *Meaning and Action: A Critical History of Pragmatism* (Indianapolis: Bobbs-Merrill).

—— (1981). 'Peirce on Truth', in L. Sumner, J. Slater, and F. Wilson (eds.), *Pragmatism and Purpose: Essays in Honour of T. A. Goudge* (Toronto: University of Toronto Press).

Thompson, M., 'Peirce's Verificationist Realism', *The Review of Metaphysics*, 32/1.

Tichy, P. (1974). 'On Popper's Definition of Verisimilitude', *British Journal for the Philosophy of Science*, 25.

Trammell, R. (1972). 'Religion, Instinct, and Reason in the Thought of C. S. Peirce', *Transactions of the C. S. Peirce Society*, 8/1.

van Fraassen, B. (1980). *The Scientific Image* (Oxford: Clarendon Press).

von Mises, R. (1928). *Probability, Statistics and Truth* (New York: Macmillan).

Wallace, J. (1972). 'Belief and Satisfaction', *Nous*, 9.

Weiner, P., ed. (1958). *Charles S. Peirce: Selected Writings* (New York: Dover).

Wells, R. (1959). Review of Berry (1952), *The Journal of Symbolic Logic*, 24.

Wiggins, D. (1980). 'What would be a Substantial Theory of Truth?', in Z. van Straaten (ed.), *Philosophical Subjects: Essays in Honour of P. F. Strawson* (Oxford: Oxford University Press).

—— (1987). *Needs, Values, Truth* (Oxford: Basil Blackwell).

—— (1996). 'Reply to Cheryl Misak', in Sabina Lovibond and S. G. Williams (eds.), *Essays for David Wiggins: Identity, Truth and Value* (Oxford: Basil Blackwell).

—— (2002). 'An Indefinibilist cum Normative View of Truth and the Marks of Truth', in R. Schantz and W. de Gruyter (eds.), *What is Truth?* (Berlin and New York [publ.]).

—— (2004). Reflections on Inquiry and Truth Arising from

Peirce's Method for the Fixation of Belief', in C. J. Misak (ed.), *The Cambridge Companion to Peirce* (Cambridge and New York: Cambridge University Press).

Williams, B. (1973). 'Deciding to Believe', in *Problems of the Self* (Cambridge: Cambridge University Press).

—— (1985). *Ethics and the Limits of Philosophy* (Cambridge, Mass.: Harvard University Press).

Wittgenstein, L. (1953). *Philosophical Investigations*, trans. G. E. M. Anscombe (Oxford: Basil Blackwell).

Wright, C. (1986). 'Does "Philosophical Investigations" I.258–60 Suggest a Cogent Argument against Private Language?', in P. Pettit and J. McDowell (eds.), *Subject, Thought, and Content* (Oxford: Clarendon Press).

—— (1987). *Realism, Meaning and Truth* (Oxford: Basil Blackwell).

—— (1992). *Truth and Objectivity* (Cambridge, Mass.: Harvard University Press).

Index